The Feminine and Faulkner

The Feminine
and Faulkner

Reading (Beyond)
Sexual Difference

Minrose C. Gwin

The University of Tennessee Press
KNOXVILLE

The paper in this book meets the minimum requirements
of the American National Standard for Permanence
of Paper for Printed Library Materials.

∞

The binding materials have been chosen
for strength and durability.

Library of Congress Cataloging-in-Publication Data

Gwin, Minrose C.
    The feminine and Faulkner : reading (beyond) sexual difference /
Minrose C. Gwin.—1st ed.
        p.   cm.
    Bibliography: p.
    Includes index.
    ISBN 0–87049–619–0 (cloth: alk. paper)
    1. Faulkner, William, 1897–1962—Knowledge—Psychology.
2. Faulkner, William, 1897–1962—Characters—Women. 3. Sex
differences (Psychology) in literature. 4. Femininity (Psychology)
in literature. 5. Women in literature. I. Title.
PS3511.A86Z78418   1990
813'.52—dc20   89–14729   CIP

*In memory of my mother, Erin Taylor Clayton Pitner,
a musician and poet who found her voice only to lose it.*

*And for those living women who are in the process
of seeking and sustaining the voices
that are theirs, and ours . . .*
  *Linda Jane Barnette, Marleen Barr, Anna Blade,
  Ellen Brown, Terry Brown, Lynn Doughty,
  Carol Gwin, Susan Morehouse, Joan Randall,
  and Ruth Salvaggio.*

Contents

Acknowledgments

For whatever insights this volume may offer, I am especially indebted to Ruth Salvaggio's generous intellectual and personal support. Her readings and rereadings of my "conversations" with Faulkner resulted in conversations of our own which gave birth to the theoretical underpinnings of this book and stimulated and sustained my own voice in ways I am only beginning to realize.

For their thoughtful and challenging readings of the completed manuscript, I thank Judith L. Sensibar and Judith Bryant Wittenberg. Their perspectives on Faulkner's life and work, along with their critical acumen and creative engagement with theoretical issues, have enriched and enlarged this book. I also owe debts to Patricia S. Yaeger and Beth Kowaleski-Wallace, whose readings of parts of the first two chapters led to important clarifications and elaborations. What shortcomings remain I claim as mine alone.

I wish to thank Marleen Barr and Terry Brown for their continuing commitment to our linked lives and work—a commitment which has become more and more sustaining as the years pass. I am grateful as well to Noel Polk and Robert Siegle for their interest and enthusiasm at the most difficult stage of this project, its beginning. The initiation of the book was eased by summer funding from the College of Arts and Sciences at Virginia Polytechnic Institute and State University. In addition, I appreciate the care taken with this manuscript by Becky Cox, whose help was particularly needed in the final stages of preparation.

This book was longer in coming than I had anticipated, and I appreciate Carol Orr's patience and continued support of my work. I also have much to be thankful for in Mavis Bryant's careful and creative editing and Nancy Sheets's assistance with proofreading.

I am grateful as well to Southern Illinois University Press for permission to republish herein in slightly different form portions of the article "(Re)Reading Faulkner as Father and Daughter of His Own Text," which appeared originally in *Refiguring the Father: New Feminist Readings of the Patriarchy,* edited by Patricia S. Yaeger and Beth Kowaleski-

Wallace, Southern Illinois Press, 1989. Extensive excerpts from the following texts are quoted with permission from Random House, Inc., Chatto & Windus Ltd., and Curtis Brown Ltd.: *Absalom, Absalom! The Corrected Text*, by William Faulkner. Copyright 1986 by Jill Faulkner Summers; *The Sound and the Fury*, by William Faulkner. Copyright 1929 and renewed 1957 by William Faulkner; *The Wild Palms*, by William Faulkner. Copyright 1939 and renewed by Mrs. William Faulkner and Mrs. Paul D. Summers; and *Intruder in the Dust*, by William Faulkner. Copyright 1948 by Random House, Inc.

Finally, I can only attempt to thank Louis Gwin for twenty years of good conversation.

Note on Documentation

Because this book is intended as a conversation, I have used internal documentation for all "voices"—narrative, theoretical, and critical. Although such documentation at times may crowd the spaces in my own rhetoric, it allows us to see who is doing the talking while the talking is being done and hence does not privilege one voice over any other in the process of exchange.

Abbreviations for Faulkner's Texts

AA	*Absalom, Absalom!*
AILD	*As I Lay Dying*
ID	*Intruder in the Dust*
LA	*Light in August*
SF	*The Sound and the Fury*
WP	*The Wild Palms*

The Feminine and Faulkner

I Beginnings

That is all I had to say to you about femininity. It is
certainly incomplete and fragmentary and does not always
sound friendly. But do not forget that I have only been
describing women in as far as their nature is determined
by their sexual function. It is true that that influence extends very far; but we do not overlook the fact than an individual woman may be a human being in other respects
as well. If you want to know more about femininity, en-
quire from your own experiences of life, or turn to the
poets, or wait until science can give you deeper and more
coherent information.

Sigmund Freud, "Femininity"

It is impossible to dissociate the questions of art, style and
truth from the question of the woman. Nevertheless the
question "what is woman?" is itself suspended by the simple
formulation of their common problematic. One can no
longer seek her, no more than one could search for woman's femininity or female sexuality. And she is certainly not
to be found in any of the familiar modes of concept or
knowledge. Yet it is impossible to resist looking for her.

Jacques Derrida, *Spurs/Éperons*

. . . for whoever is encumbered with the phallus, what is a
woman?

A woman is a symptom.

Jacques Lacan, "Seminar of
21 January 1975," *Feminine Sexuality*

The question "what is . . . ?" is the question — the metaphysical question — to which the feminine does not allow itself to submit.
　　　　　Luce Irigaray, *This Sex Which Is Not One*

I would be I: I would let him be the shape and echo of his word.
　　　　　Addie Bundren in *As I Lay Dying*

This is a book which I admit does not present itself as a model of co-herence. In its earlier and more self-assured drafts it was accountable to and for itself. It was individuated, unified, and (temporarily) manage-able. It knew itself as a study of the creativity of Faulkner's women characters, a delineation of their intellectual velocity and of the connec-tion of that velocity to Faulkner himself as the male creator of the (creative) female created. It constructed hierarchies of order that sepa-rated male from female consciousness, creativity from procreation, life-giving forces from destructive ones, beginnings from endings, and so on. It knew what a narrative was. It knew what a character was. It knew what a woman was. It knew what *it* was — a critical discourse upon Faulkner's narrative texts, one (to use dust jacket terminology) which possibly might have come to "shed new light" or "turn new ground" in some area relating to Faulkner and feminist studies.

That is what this book was supposed to have become. The reasons it did not are as complex as the issues at stake, some of which I will attempt to move around, hover over, or — a bit more bravely — explore in a tentative theoretical elaboration in this introduction. The chapters which follow will be equally tentative and exploratory, but they will in-volve what I will call conversations, some of them intimate, with Faulk-ner's texts. I will be reading and speaking in a way that is new to me, attempting to create what Luce Irigaray would call a feminine economy — that is, an economy of spending, one which "puts into question all prevailing economies,"[1] which generates more questions than it ever answers, which pushes out boundaries and dissolves margins wherever they are, which grafts and regrafts its own renewal. I am trying to open up Faulkner's texts as that same kind of economy, one (or not one, but multiples of one) of enormous productivity and generative powers; and I would ask that you follow them to the point of "embracing force as movement, as desire, for itself, and not as the accident or epiphany of lines. To the point of embracing it as writing" (Derrida, *Writing and Difference* 28).

If I sound self-conscious, it is because I am. It is disconcerting, if not frightening, to have one's critical runway suddenly fogged in by problematics so intricately interrelated that it is impossible to treat them in any orderly manner. One must either take off in the fog or not take off at all. I am reminded of the beginning of Houston A. Baker, Jr.'s *Blues, Ideology, and Afro-American Literature,* in which he admits he no longer believes in the autonomy and centrality of the speaking subject, a premise at the very foundation of his earlier work (1). I take heart, however, not only in Baker's inventive "blues" playfulness, which allows language to "speak" a decentered and illusory subject, but also in the observation that great works of literature are ahead of their critics: "They are there already. They have anticipated explicitly any deconstruction the critic can achieve" (J. Hillis Miller, "Deconstructing" 31). This is particularly true of Faulkner, whose greatest works are about decentered subjectivity and loss. My first question, then, is that of Julia Kristeva: "How does one speak to literature?" (*Desire in Language* 92). And how does one converse (involving both reading and speaking) in a way that will at once liberate the text's energies (and one's own) and fulfill the critic's more extensive obligations to liberate the energies of other texts as well? (Mehlman 69) In particular, how does one speak to literature about a specific matter—woman? Even more problematically, how does one speak *as* a woman *with* a man *about* woman? Woman of his creation? What is to be discovered here? What is there to gain for the feminist reader who converses with a male text? In Irigaray's words, "Why try to speak with a man?" Irigaray answers her own question by saying, "Because what I want, in fact, is not to create a theory of woman, but to secure a place for the feminine within sexual difference." She sees her efforts as attempts "to go back through the masculine imaginary, to interpret the way it has reduced us to silence, to muteness or mimicry, and I am attempting, from that starting point and at the same time, to (re)discover a possible space for the feminine imaginary" (*This Sex* 159, 164).

This is part of my motivation in speaking with Faulkner, and it relates to culture as well as to art (though how can we separate them?). As one who has evolved out of Faulkner's North Mississippi, I speak to the paradoxical, even subversive relationship between what I will call his "bisexual" artistic consciousness and its cultural milieu. The paradox is that Faulkner himself, although very much *of* his culture, becomes in his greatest works the creator of female subjects who, in powerful and creative ways, disrupt and sometimes even destroy patriarchal structures. This is the mystery which binds Faulkner to the feminine and toward which I speak.[2] Even Hélène Cixous, who believes that male-coded writing (which can be written by both men and women) is for the most part "self-admiring, self-stimulating, self-congratulatory phallocentrism," admits that some male writers are "failures" in their culture's schooling. They are:

> men capable of loving love and hence capable of loving others and of wanting them, of imagining the woman who would hold out against oppression and constitute herself as a superb, equal, hence "impossible" subject, untenable in a real social framework. Such a woman the poet could desire only by breaking the codes that negate her. Her appearance would necessarily bring on, if not revolution — for the bastion was supposed to be immutable — at least harrowing explosions. At times it is in the fissure caused by an earthquake, through that radical mutation of things brought on by a material upheaval when every structure is for a moment thrown off balance and an ephemeral wildness sweeps order away, that the poet slips something by, for a brief span, of woman. ("Laugh of the Medusa" 249)

This sense of woman borders on the catastrophic, the apocalyptic. And although I make no such radical claims for Faulkner's creation of female subjects, I do speak to their (and his) powers of creative disruption, which connect them to him and him to them in a peculiar bisexuality that decenters our notions of the relationship between male creator and female created. My particular interest lies both in actual characters, "personages," as Cixous would call them, and in the idea of the feminine as a disruptive force — though I would by no means suggest that the two are mutually exclusive. I am peering into the dimness of interstices, those in-between spaces where the codes constituting character intersect cultural codes and create the relationship of character to cultural matrix, out of which both character and authorial voice(s) emerge.[3] Whether these spaces are *between* texts, as in the reciprocal discourses of race and gender in such fictions as *Absalom, Absalom!* and *Intruder in the Dust,* or whether they are embedded *within* a text (for example, within the silenced but articulate voice of Caddy Compson), they harbor complex and intricate webs of meaning which entangle even as they allure. I am interested in disruption, in the unexpected in Faulkner, in the unconscious rather than the conscious voices of author and character. In several of Faulkner's most compelling and, I would suggest, most problematic texts, woman is force—not force which derives simply from procreation, as many of Faulkner's critics have maintained, but one which extends procreativity beyond its obvious boundaries toward an intellectual velocity relating to subversion and modernity. I am speaking to that force, yet in so doing I am resisting (impossibly) the concomitant structuring or organizing of it. I am remembering Derrida's admonition: *"To comprehend* the structure of a becoming, the form of a force, is to lose meaning by finding it" (*Writing and Difference* 26).

As Irigaray shrewdly observes, methodology is never as simple as it might appear (*This Sex* 135). In the relationship between reader and text, the question of methodology is compounded by gender. If American and French feminists agree on anything, it is that reading and writing are sex-coded: that to assume that a writer and a reader are not sexually differentiated (either biologically or ideologically) is to run the risk of creating an androcentric model of interconnection between the two. Elizabeth Abel notes, "sexuality and textuality both depend on difference" (*Writing* 1). Barbara Johnson goes further to say, "If human beings were not divided into two biological sexes, there would probably be no need for literature" (*The Critical Difference* 13). Other feminist critics have pointed to the difficulties (and thus the necessity) of reading as women in a culture in which women are trained to identify with male experience.[4] " . . . [W]hether we speak of poets and critics 'reading' (and thereby recording for us) the world," Annette Kolodny writes, "we are calling attention to interpretive strategies that are learned, historically determined, and thereby necessarily gender-inflected" ("A Map for Rereading" 243). Writing in her journal, a frustrated women's studies student put it more bluntly: "I have been taught by men to read like a man, to write like a man, to think like a man. *I do not know how to do otherwise.*" Alterity is one lesson that feminist criticism tries to teach as it "undertakes, through the postulate of a woman reader, to bring about a new experience of reading and to make readers — men and women — question the literary and political assumptions on which their reading has been based" (Culler 51). This is Judith Fetterley's project in her book about the woman reader's conversations with an American literature that often renders her powerless, invisible, or both. Fetterley calls for the female reader to resist and read differently those fictions in which she "is co-opted into participation in an experience from which she is explicitly excluded" or, even worse, in which she is required "to identify with a selfhood that defines itself in opposition to her; she is required to identify against herself" (vii). This is also Simone de Beauvoir's contention in the groundbreaking *The Second Sex:* that woman is required by culture to define *herself* as males have defined her, as other — even as other to herself.

Reading thus becomes a political act, and the hypothesis of a female reader confronts the contention that male reading is not sex-coded.[5] Not insignificantly, such a hypothesis implies the autonomy of woman as speaking subject, as one who has something to say *to* the text, as a *woman who speaks,* who is not (as in the Nietzschean model) *truth,* but who speaks it, or at least who speaks herself. To read as a woman (as well as to write as one) is thus to speak oneself rather than to be spoken. It is the essential process of desire, production, and renewal of desire which, as Jacques Lacan has shown us, reproduces the self. This may be at least part of what Adrienne Rich means when she says, "Revision — the act of looking back, of seeing with fresh eyes, of entering an old text from a new critical direction — is for us more than a chapter in cultural history: it is an act of survival" ("When We Dead Awaken" 18). In such a mode I may declare myself to be speaking to, as well as reading, Faulkner's books. This is not to say, however, that the woman reader must speak to the text from a position of certainty and authority. This, in fact, may defeat her before she starts and place her in the camp of what Derrida calls "phallogocentrism," a mode of thought based upon three types of rigidity: "patriarchal authority, unity of meaning, and certainty of origin" (Culler 61). Feminist theory investigates the way rationality (and, concomitantly, the will to power) has been tied to male interests (Culler 58); such investigations should open conversations between texts in alternate modes which do not rely on certainty and unity, but instead on a willingness to accept uncertainty and decentering. This is, of course, where American and French feminists collide, and where the French, with their connections to deconstruction and psychoanalysis, may be more pertinent to my project.

It is with trepidation that I attempt to dance in the minefields[6] of argument over how the woman reader *should* read the male text. In the context of my project, I wish to avoid thinking of the woman reader-male writer relationship in terms of control and power, though I certainly would not go to the opposite extreme "by not asking questions of the text that it does not ask itself" (Jehlen, "Archimedes" 73). To the contrary, it seems to me that I would like to ask Faulkner questions he does not *openly* ask himself, just as I would have his texts ask me similar questions, questions which startle and disconcert, questions which my answers don't fit. Yet asking these questions necessarily involves me in a project that some feminists might view with suspicion. Patrocinio P. Schweickart, for instance, would prefer not to allow the male text its own autonomy. In her essay "Reading Ourselves: Toward a Feminist Theory of Reading" Schweickart argues that the woman reader must struggle against the text for mastery:

> Taking control of the reading experience means reading the text as it was *not* meant to be read, in fact, reading it against itself. Specifically, one must identify the nature of the choices proffered by the text and, equally important, what the text precludes—namely, the possibility of reading as a woman *without* putting one's self in the position of the other, of reading so as to affirm womanhood as another, equally valid, paradigm of human existence. (50)

Schweickart ends her essay by warning feminists against deconstruction and suggesting that the "validity" of an interpretation "is contingent on the agreement of others" in the feminist literary community (56).

Although I am sympathetic to the ends she seeks, the strengthening of that community and the affirmation of female experience, I find such an approach to reading male (or female) texts restrictive and problematic.[7] While I believe with Fetterley that many male texts and their attendant myths must be resisted (and some female ones as well), surely we must allow for Cixous's observation that culture fails to mold *all* male texts into phallocentric clones. In such cases, that which the feminist reader must resist may be not so much the male text as its androcentric interpretations.

I would not valorize all of Faulkner's texts in this way, but I would suggest that such characters as Caddy Compson, Rosa Coldfield, Charlotte Rittenmeyer, and others are indeed active disruptive subjects in their narratives; theirs are voices which denounce and subvert male power. If we are able to converse with their *force,* if we acknowledge it as *subject* (perhaps split, incoherent, hysterical subject, but subject nonetheless), then we may find "a new consciousness in the text" which has hitherto eluded Faulkner scholars and which thus "may be new only in the sense that we, as readers, are seeing it for the first time" (Heilbrun and Stimpson 64). Instead of beginning in an adversarial relationship with the male text, I set forth uncertainly; I admit to flying uncharted courses under foggy conditions. Such an approach is consonant with Carol Gilligan's observations about women in general: that they are more involved in relational than power discourses and are more likely to employ a mode of thinking that is "contextual and narrative rather than formal and abstract" (19).

Generative though I hope this approach will be, I nonetheless anticipate a path fraught with slippery spots. As Alice Jardine says, it is difficult to find a place from which to speak (31). Nor do I necessarily wish to place myself: movement, even slippage, is desirable here. Neither would I minimize the difficulties in finding male texts with which one would *wish* to speak. Instead of further elaboration, I would take as theoretical texts for my observations on Faulkner and the feminine the thoughts of two French women theorists, Julia Kristeva and Hélène Cixous, about the nature of women's intellectual processes. In *Desire in Language* Kristeva suggests that women not renounce theoretical reason but "compel it to increase its power by giving it an object beyond its limits" and thus force it to become open to the "heterogeneous

economy" of literature (146). She believes that women readers are peculiarly capable of the inexhaustible generation which allows an *"instinctual drive,* across and through the constitutive and insurmountable frontier of *meaning"* (146). Whether only women are capable of this kind
of reading is, of course, a matter of debate; yet many feminists, French
and American, would agree that the woman reader brings to the text
an ability to embody and embrace its otherness which allows the text
to be experienced more productively than formally. Cixous sees her own
reading, thinking, and speaking as endlessly generative and enigmatic:
"I cannot even imagine that I will get to the end of the questions asked
of me in such overabundance. I do not cease not to understand. Simply,
the things I do not understand renew themselves incessantly" (Conley
161). In an interview she distinguishes her own conceptual processes
from those of Derrida, the male philosopher. Out of his concepts, he
builds a ford of a river, Cixous says; yet the problem is that "he must
jump from concept to concept, or from rock to rock, whereas I allow
myself to say, since I do not have any obligation toward philosophy, I
really do prefer swimming. I prefer being in the water and openly in
the water . . . " (Conley 151).

Being in the water (or flying through the fog) implies a willingness
to defer, to let go of safety, to encounter loss and disunity, to involve
oneself in the play of possibility rather than expecting certain (or even
possible) arrival *somewhere.* Schweickart warns feminist scholars against
the danger of being overly enthralled with "the theme of impossibility"
(56). I find instead that it is the theme of unlimited *possibility* that
is implied here. To be "openly in the water"—to allow ourselves to let
go of certainty about male writing—is from a feminist perspective both
risky and exhilarating. Yet, in doing so we may find that, in the case
of Faulkner, "a male writer may have imagined more than we were able
to see . . . " (Heilbrun and Stimpson 65). For centuries men have made
reductive, dismissive judgments about female texts, based upon an an-
tipathy toward the otherness of those texts. I would suggest a more productive and, I would argue, more *active* reading strategy with regard
to certain male texts, a strategy that derives from Cixous's theory of artistic bisexuality. As stated, her definition of bisexuality applies to writers.
I would expand it to suggest that women readers think of bisexuality
as a tropological space for conversing with *some* male texts which are

(and must be, for the interchange to evolve) themselves "bisexual" by Cixous's definition. Baker suggests that, to approach Afro-American literature, one should take up the mantle of a "blues critic," one who is agile and interdisciplinary enough to "play" with Afro-American literature, to allow for and even celebrate its creative ability to "negotiate slavery's tight spaces" and, by expansion, to "challenge investigative *understanding* to an unlimited play" (11). I would proffer Cixous's concept of bisexuality as a similar deconstructive process, one that I will put into play in my conversations with Faulkner's texts, as well as in my thoughts about the relationship of the male creator to the female created.

In Cixous's schema the term *bisexuality* does not mean *neuter*.[8] To the contrary, it denotes an *exacerbation* of both male and female elements in the self and in writing. Bisexual writing is in a permanent state of tension; it is generated and regenerated by an interaction between the feminine and masculine, between self and other. It does not "annul differences but stirs them up, pursues them, increases their number" ("Laugh" 254). Such writing, according to Cixous's definition in "Laugh of the Medusa," exists "(in) the in-between" and from that (non)place is "infinitely dynamized by an incessant process of exchange from one subject to another" (254). In a similar passage in *The Newly Born Woman,* Cixous elaborates upon this bisexual practice of writing:

> Writing is working: being worked; questioning (in) the between (letting oneself be questioned) of same *and of* other without which nothing lives; undoing death's work by willing the togetherness of one-another, infinitely charged with a ceaseless exchange of one with another — not knowing one another and beginning again only from what is most distant, from self, from other, from the other within. A course that multiplies transformations by the thousands. (86)

This creates what Cixous calls "an economy without reserve," one (or multiples thereof) which constitutes its own terrors: "And that is not done without danger, without pain, without loss — of moments of self, of consciousness, of persons one has been, goes beyond, leaves. It doesn't happen without expense — of sense, time, direction" (86). Cixous is valorizing the splitness of the subject and showing the generative power of the interaction of self and other, other and self. This is a dynamic which must work both ways, however. Self and other, other and self must desire interaction, to the point of grave risk.

I believe that Faulkner himself, as speaking subject, interacts in just such a way with some women characters of his own creation, whose disruptive *female* voices articulate his male artistic consciousness *even as they differ from it.* We may recognize elements of that consciousness in Cixous's definition of the bisexual self as

each one's location in self [*répérage en soi*] of the presence—variously manifest and insistent according to each person, male or female—of both sexes, non-exclusion either of difference or of one sex, and, from this "self-permission," multiplication of the effects of the inscription of desire, over all parts of my body and the other body. ("Laugh" 254)

The transformation of bisexuality into literary text, according to Kristeva, results in a "traversal" of the "process of [sexual] differentiation." This "bisexuality" is "precisely the possibility to explore all the sources of signification, that which posits a meaning as well as that which multiplies, pulverizes, and finally revives it" ("Oscillation" 165).

Although Cixous believes that women are more open to bisexuality, she acknowledges that some male writers "(all too few) aren't afraid of femininity" ("Laugh" 256). Faulkner is not always in this company, but I would suggest that, in his creation of creative female subjects and in his ability to allow the feminine the role of subject, sometimes he is. It is those times and those texts with which I would converse. Evolving from the creativity and force of some of these women and Faulkner's participation in their femaleness, this area of "in-between" affirms rather than denies difference but *at the same time* dissolves binary constructions of gender. It is an "in-between" that seems to lend itself to neither of Elaine Showalter's two categories of feminist critical methodology delineated in her essay "Feminist Criticism in the Wilderness"; elucidating it becomes more than a feminist reading of a male writer's works; nor (obviously) is it a "gynocritical" pursuit (women reading women in a relational mode). It is, I would hope, a bridge between the two. What it says about Faulkner is that he accorded some of his women characters an intellectual and creative velocity that we have not yet reckoned with and that may be seen as powerfully connected to his own creative impulse. Just as Faulkner's bisexuality connects him to these female subjects and to the disruptive power of the feminine in his own texts, so the woman reader may adopt the mantle of bisexuality to traverse the "in-between" spaces of these texts.

These are, of course, (they must be) the troublesome, the problematic areas. These are the questions that lead us back into the fog.

> To give a new language to these other spaces is a project filled with both promise and fear. . . .
>
> Alice Jardine, *Gynesis: Configurations of Woman and Modernity*

The first of these questions (surely you are expecting it) is: What is woman? This is, of course, an unanswerable question, nor would we wish it otherwise. Here I am thinking of the inscription *woman,* rather than of women as sexual beings. In Faulkner's texts we shall be exploring both the *idea* of the feminine and those subjects in narrative who are called female characters. My theoretical explorations at this point concern the former, although, I must repeat, ultimately the two are inseparable. If we think, with Jean-François Lyotard, of all of Western culture as having "master narratives" (i.e., Marxism, capitalism, etc.) and, with Thomas Kuhn, of scientific progress as having occurred in a linear manner through a series of changing paradigms, we realize that the structuring of cultural reality is largely a matter of power. Since Western culture and philosophy are thus constructed from the dominant male perspective, it is no surprise to think of the feminine as "other" to such a world, and therefore as a subversive and disruptive threat to it. Eve eats the forbidden fruit, Pandora opens her box, and male structures confront the other space of woman—the space which is unstructured, chaotic, bottomless, terrifying . . . seductive.

Alice Jardine's *Gynesis* is an elaboration of what she calls the "process" of woman: the rethinking of the master narratives of Western culture and philosophy, the creation and exploration of new space designated as feminine. Jardine defines modernity in terms of its exploration of "these new female spaces: the perhaps historically unprecedented exploration of the female, differently maternal body." In contemporary French thought, she notes that this exploration has settled on the concept of "woman" or "the feminine" as "both a metaphor of reading and topography of writing for confronting the breakdown of the paternal metaphor . . ." (33). As a way of thinking about the configurations of the feminine in Western culture, she offers the neologism *gynesis,* which she calls "the putting into discourse of 'woman' as that process diagnosed in France as intrinsic to the condition of modernity; indeed, the valorization of the feminine, woman, and her obligatory, that is, historical connotations, as somehow intrinsic to new and necessary modes of thinking, writing, speaking" (25). In Jardine's explorations woman becomes trope; she is "new presentation of the irrepresentable" (39); she has come to signify "those *processes* that disrupt symbolic structures in the West" (42). Jardine's proffer of *gynesis* as a "radical strategy of reading and writing" (47) has provocative implications for our conversations with Faulkner's texts.

Such a strategy cannot be anything but deconstructive. There are certain "unknowables," Anne McLeod maintains, that are excluded from stable systems which are based upon age-old dichotomies (same and different, presence and absence, subject and object, etc.). These "unknowables" are excluded because they are not definable: they show such systems what is beyond their understanding and control. One name given to such indefinable elements is woman; she "dislocate[s] the hinge on which alternativism swings." As McLeod summarizes, "Woman offers feminism (as) deconstructive diacritics" (59). McLeod's concern is with getting outside the confining frame of dichotomous thinking (as is Cixous's in "Sorties," which translates as "Ways Out"). Similarly, in a discussion about the place of woman in Derrida's discourse, Gayatri Chakravorty Spivak elaborates the implications of the feminine for Derrida's deconstructive project of undoing oppositions. Woman, Spivak says, "is perhaps the most tenacious name for the limit that situates and undermines the vanguard of every theory seeking to be adequate to its theme" ("Love me, Love my Ombre, Elle" 23). Derrida offers woman as a "counter-narrative" to "undo the abstract-concrete ranking in judgments and, secondly, to change the shifting grounds of judgments and decisions. . . . It is the implications of this counter-narrative that provoke the moral outrage against Derrida, which ranges from the conservative to the radical in literary criticism" (Spivak, "Love Me" 21). Deconstructing those dichotomies that Cixous points to as being ideological bulwarks of Western culture is, of course, Derrida's project; and, as Jardine, Spivak, and McLeod suggest, woman herself becomes the process of this deconstruction. This is, Spivak suggests, *because* she "possesses this special quality: she can occupy both positions in the subject-object oscillation" ("Love Me" 24). Like Caddy Compson, woman traverses the space between presence and absence, between her own subjectivity and her bounded status in male discourse.

This obviously problematic position is one with which women are all too familiar. We think of Nietzsche's *woman-in-distans,* woman portrayed in frozen, deathlike postures. This oscillation between subject and object, as Jardine points out in discussing Roland Barthes' description of being turned into an image, "sounds remarkably similar to how *women* have described the process they undergo in patriarchal systems of representation" (75). We are reminded not only of the predicaments of Caddy and Temple Drake, but of such diverse female characters as Drusilla Hawk, Minnie Cooper, Emily Grierson, and Rosa Coldfield. As Myriam Díaz-Diocaretz suggests, the patriarchal world creates its own images of woman (images which, she says, Faulkner both reproduces and challenges): "Systematically confined by individual and collective assumptions expressing a glimpse of presupposed 'truth,' woman is named by a male-oriented ideology that speaks to itself, and in the process the image in which she is to be seen is created. *What she is named she becomes*" (260).[9] Culler points us in another discomfiting direction when he reminds us that

> . . . various discourses — psychoanalytical, philosophical, literary, historical — have constituted the notion of man by characterizing the feminine in terms that permit it to be set aside. . . . Cele-

brations of woman or the identification of woman with some powerful force or idea—truth as a woman, liberty as a woman, the muses as women—identify actual women as marginal. Woman can be a symbol of truth only if she is denied an effective [and, I would add, affective] relation to truth, only if one presumes that those seeking truth are men. (166–67)

The issue here is the difference between woman as symbol of truth or some kind of certainty, and woman as the process of disruption. Can the feminist accept the latter while decrying the former? I would argue in the affirmative. In the first place, the symbolization of woman renders her immobile, just as belief in the systems of truth, order, knowledge, hierarchy disallows the free play of what Derrida has termed *différance*, "which prevents any word, any concept, any major enunciation from coming to summarize and to govern from the theological presence of a center the movement and textual spacing of differences" ("Implications" 13). This is to deny risk, to strive toward certainty and closure. Woman as process is an altogether different trope: this is woman in motion, the cauldron boiling, constant play and disruption of order, Irigaray's "expanding universe" of the feminine.[10]

We may approach this woman-in-motion through male as well as female texts. Of particular interest may be any text, male or female, which emerges out of a patriarchal culture (certainly an apt description of the Deep South of Faulkner's experience).[11] What sort of disruption do such narratives create, and how is that disruption assimilated into the cultural mesh of the text? Paul de Man suggests that we look for the "blind spot of the text as the organizer of the space of the vision contained in the text, and the vision's concomitant blindness" (xxix). In Faulkner's texts I shall explore what I would term the "other spot"— that space which is woman, and out of which women speak. I believe this space exists. It is the space of the unconscious, of the disruption and subversion of fixity, of *something else*. The problem, as Kristeva and Jardine point out, is not the *idea* of the space (thinkers from Plato to Derrida have questioned and probed this space, whether they call it a cave or a text). The problem is that the woman-subject becomes a kind of "filter" for thinking about this space (Jardine 89). This leads us back to the consideration of the female character's (the woman-subject's) connection to the *process* of woman (the space itself).

If we think of the process of woman as the space of disruption in Faulkner's texts, then we may begin to rethink the whole notion of "character" and approach the female subject, the *woman character,* as the discursiveness of that space, as the rebellious unconsciousness of patriarchy. As we emerge from thinking of woman as the process of cultural critique to woman as both process and character in Faulkner, we must explore theoretical implications of psychoanalysis upon the notions of the subject, hence upon character—and hence the interrelationship of female character and male consciousness. Dorin Schumacher writes that "the feminist critic assumes a self in woman and interprets the data of the text as though a self exists" (33). I go beyond (or between) such a premise to question the nature of that self and to suggest that, in Faulkner's narrative, the female self may be experienced as a self-in-motion, a group of superimposed codes, which serves as a matrix of semiotic, psychoanalytic, and cultural interaction.

As Baker points out in reference to his project, a matrix is "a point of ceaseless input and output, a web of intersecting, crisscrossing impulses always in productive transit" (3). The blues constitute such a network, Baker maintains: "They are the multiplex, enabling *script* in which Afro-American cultural discourse is inscribed" (4). Our conversations with Faulkner's texts may lead us to think similarly of *their* feminine space, as a fluctuating location whose inscription, in Cixous's words, "unthinks" history and disrupts structures ("Laugh" 252). This is a more complex and problematical relationship between a matrix of disruption and its creator than that posited by Baker. Faulkner is man writing woman; he is presumed to be in a relationship of otherness to the feminine matrix. Its presence and power in his work may have more to do with its fragmentation, contradiction, and ruptures—the stuff of the unconscious—than its coherence and autonomy. This is particularly true when we think of the feminine matrix of Faulkner's texts as being a network of woman-as-process and characters coded as *subjects.*

The "subject" as subject of the unconscious is always born from the other and is always about to disappear. It never constitutes itself as a subject that can be identified.

Verena Conley,
Hélène Cixous: Writing the Feminine

As we begin to think about Faulkner's female characters and their connection to the feminine matrix of these texts, we must allow ourselves to become entangled in a problem which has been said to pose "an ontological difficulty of the highest order"—namely the revolution of thought surrounding the status of the subject and its impact on the way we understand narrative (Davis, *Lacan and Narration*, 858). The humanistic tradition, with its Cartesian splitting of subject and object, taught us to think of the subject in terms of presence and consciousness—as Culler puts it, "the 'I' . . . which thinks, perceives, and feels" (161). Freud shattered this concept of the autonomous, unified self by privileging the unconscious as "the true psychical reality" from which the consciousness derives (*The Interpretation of Dreams* 5:613). In the psychoanalytic schema the subject is other to itself; it is split, fragmented, disordered. It becomes a network of desires and productions rather than a unified, coherent force. In this position, as Baker points out, the subject is no longer capable of "speaking" out of wholeness and autonomy, but is instead a code which is always in the process of deconstructing and producing itself (1).[12]

As we move toward Faulkner's texts, then, we may carry with us the recognition that the postmodern rethinking of subjectivity has had significant reverberations in the rethinking of narrative. Of enormous significance in linking ideas about the subject to ideas about the nature of language itself has been the work of Jacques Lacan, which above all "challenges the notion of the subject in control" (Mitchell 4). Lacan's basic premise is that "identity is constructed in language, but only at a cost. Identity shifts, and language speaks the loss which lay behind the first moment of symbolisation" (Mitchell 31–32). Loss becomes language in such texts as *The Sound and the Fury, Absalom, Absalom!*, and *Light in August*: not only do they emerge from loss but they are produced, fueled by it; they speak the discourse of loss and desire. They bespeak a subjectivity which is, according to Lacan, itself a fiction embodying only the "illusion of autonomy" (*Écrits* 7). This subjectivity of loss and desire replays itself in processes which take shape as character—for example, as a Rosa Coldfield whose narrative desire both plucks out and reweaves the pattern of a culture which has at once denied her subjectivity and propelled her to produce it through imagination. In this sense she is caught between the real and the symbolic and can be read only out of that in-between space.

More generally, this whole notion of the subject's fluidity may enable us to read character in new ways, in those spaces between presence and absence, emergence and disappearance, which have eluded us.[13] In the concentric spaces of psychoanalysis and semiotics, Kristeva's notion of the subject-in-process enables us to see the dynamics of character as a function of language, and language itself as an unsettling process. Poetic language embodies a "questionable subject-in-process," one that makes and remakes itself as utterance and desire (*Desire in Language* 120). This thought progression implies not just the presence of absence, but the necessity of that absence. The subject must desire part of its lost self in order to speak that desire. Rosa Coldfield must have lost her *"world of living marriage"* before she can speak its loss. John T. Matthews, in fact, points out that many of Faulkner's texts begin with loss, and that these narratives seem to *need* to inscribe absence before beginning to speak the desire for what has been lost (59–60).[14] The subject must not be whole, for to be whole is to be silent. It is only by negotiating the economy of loss and desire that the subject learns to speak what is not. This is what Matthews seems to mean when he says, "I want to suggest that one thing Faulkner's novels tell us is that our life is our language, and that language means more than it can say" (62).

If we find it difficult to converse about subjects whom we cannot (and may not wish to) place in the arena of presence and consciousness, then we may despair at our next foray into the problematics of "character" and the female Faulknerian subject. As Cixous points out in her persuasive essay "The Character of 'Character,'" the traditional concept of character as something to be "figured out," i.e., a discoverable truth, implies a *whole* subject, conscious and knowable. Yet when we consider the subject as an effect of the unconscious, we are faced with the problem of analyzing the unanalyzable. Conceptualizing "character" as more than a convention requires acknowledgment that "the 'subject' is an effect of the unconscious and that it never stops producing the unconscious—which is unanalyzable, uncharacterizable . . ." (387). What is desirable in narrative, then, is "not to make the subject disappear, but to bring it back to its divisibility," to have the effect of showing "the fragility of the center and the partitions of the ego" (Cixous, "Character" 389–90). Such a text "refers us back to its effects of multiplying incertitude. There will always be extra meaning, space enough for everyone, for each more-than-one, and for each one of me" (402). As Cixous implies in this, the final sentence of her essay, such a reading of "character" actually reduces the distance between the personage(s) of the text and the reader. The conventionalizing of "character"— the freezing of identity— distances reader and text simply because identity is, as Cixous says, always in process, not frozen: "It is precisely this open, unpredictable, piercing part of the subject, this *infinite* potential to rise up, that the 'concept' of 'character' excludes in advance" (384).

Although Cixous does not discuss gender in this essay, her description of narrative personage as process and multiplicity leads us to think of woman coded as "character." Woman is, Irigaray maintains, "this sex which is not one," which is by its very biological nature multiplicitous. "'She' is indefinitely other in herself" (*This Sex* 28). Likewise, Nancy Chodorow has shown that women's ego boundaries are less rigidly fixed than those of men because they do not have to differentiate themselves from the mother; thus "the feminine sense of self remains connected to others in the world" (169), much like Cixous's (non)character. Gilligan's research, as I have said, shows women to be more concerned about relationships than about rules and regulations which would structure and separate egos. Indeed, as Judith Kegan Gardiner suggests, "today's women too may feel that the old unified subject was never a female subject, and women may therefore find little advantage in the current project of dismantling it" (115). I offer an alternative suggestion: that one thing we are after in our conversations with these texts is a sense of a play of differences, which in turn allows us insight into the process that is the human subject. And I would suggest further that Faulkner's texts converse with us with enormous energy and openness about the nature of this process and its complex encounters with the feminine.

Mitchell's comments may be helpful here as they point out that both Freud's emphasis on the castration complex and Lacan's insistence upon the significance of the phallus place the female in a permanent position of loss and desire (and, I would add, thus impel her to speak). Within such a schema, *female* sexuality always leads directly to the question of the decentered, split human subject and thereby to the "difficulty at the heart of being human to which psychoanalysis and the objects of its enquiry—the unconscious and sexuality—bear witness" (25). Yet, Lacanian psychoanalysis in particular *accepts* the "fragmented subject of shifting and uncertain sexual identity" (26). Like Cixous's "personage" of narrative and Irigaray's woman, the Lacanian human subject "is not one"; nor does it wish to be. For,

> To be human is to be subjected to a law which decentres and
> divides; sexuality is created in a division, the subject is split; but
> an ideological world conceals this from the conscious subject
> who is supposed to feel whole and certain of a sexual identity.
> Psychoanalysis should aim at a destruction of this concealment
> and at a reconstruction of the subject's construction in all its
> splits. (Mitchell 26)

Are we then positing narrative worlds of female loss and female lack, as Elaine Showalter describes the androcentric assumptions of Freudian and Lacanian psychoanalysis? ("Feminist Criticism in the Wilderness" 194) Is a narrative voice like Rosa Coldfield's "displaced, disinherited, and excluded" (194) and nothing more? The answer is, of course, no and indeed much more than no. Perhaps we may take Irigaray's and Jane Gallop's lead in "reading" psychoanalytic theory in deconstructive ways: what is at stake in our reading of Faulkner is not man's creating of woman in terms of her desire for what he has, the phallus. The more interesting and problematic question concerns man's creating of "character" coded as woman, who in turn becomes creative *in response to* loss, who is herself deconstruction and production—who becomes all that "disturbs the Subject, Dialectic, and Truth" (Jardine 183). The relationship between Faulkner and certain female characters—in these conversations, Caddy Compson, Rosa Coldfield, and Charlotte Ritten-meyer—constitutes that area of "in-between" in which male creator and female created are present in an ever-heightening tension which generates the bisexual space of the fiction and which may be approached (not measured) only as a constant process of deconstruction and production.

I believe that we may write our own texts of Faulkner's world as one which explodes with female creativity and feminine force. There is, in Faulkner's creation of that creativity and in the creativity itself, Kristeva's "heterogeneousness" which is peculiar to the "semiotic activity" of poetic language and which requires a "questionable subject-in-process" (*Desire in Language* 133–36). Through their own creative processes, some of the female characters in these texts become "subject[s]-in-process," not as images created by the author but as the *processes* of desire, imagination, and signification. In response to desire, and indirectly in response to cultural loss (rigidity, repression, violence, etc.), Caddy Compson, Rosa Coldfield, Charlotte Rittenmeyer, Temple Drake, Drusilla Hawk, Joanna Burden, and Addie Bundren become makers themselves, and thereby precipitators of what Cixous sees as the initial act of female creativity, the process of "unthink[ing] the unifying, regulating history that homogenizes and channels forces" ("Laugh" 252). Such creativity, again, does not imply a whole subject, but rather one which is in *process*.

How then do we approach the connection between the male creator and the creative process and desire of these female voices? Jardine describes the relationship between male author and female subject in terms of statements made by Michel Leiris. She translates his comments as follows:

> Always writing at the very edges of traditional narrative, he addresses himself to a woman, but "only because she is absent"; "she" is not in any way "an object," but rather the "melancholic substance" of that which is missing for "him": that which forces him to desire, that is, to write. The function of writing is, for him, to "fill a void or at least to situate, with respect to the most lucid part of ourselves, the place where gapes this incommensurable abyss." And that place, the emptiness of that abyss in his self, is female. (115)

To peer through the fog into the spaces between Faulkner and, for example, Caddy (certainly the passage reminds us of her) is a murky enterprise, but one that should eventually dissolve into new ways of conversing with Faulkner and his texts. Our conversations will probe the relationship between male author and the feminine in himself, and open into the bisexual space Cixous speaks of as constituting the multiple and regenerative process of infinite creativity.

> Rare are the men able to venture into the brink where writing, freed from law, unencumbered by moderation, exceeds phallic authority, and where the subjectivity inscribing its effects becomes feminine.
>
> Hélène Cixous, "Sorties"

Philosophical discourse traditionally has relied upon dialectic modes of thought to relegate woman to the sphere of passivity—to lock her into the Father's House. Similarly, the oppositional thinking behind sustained critical approaches to Faulkner's female characters may close and control, rather than converse with, the texts and characters. And however insistently and perceptively revisionists have begun to reject thinking which labels these characters who are coded as women as all one thing or all another, still we are haunted by those linguistic dichotomies which constrict our observations and questions, our give and take with the narrative, into reductive categories. "Faulkner's women," we have been told, are either "creative" or "destructive" (Page xxiv); "earth-mothers" or "ghosts" (David Miller 3–17); "sexual" or "asexual" (Malin 31); "feminine" or "defeminized" (Parks 3–6); "mindless daughters of peasants" who resemble "beasts in heat" or "sexually insatiable daughters of the aristocracy" (Fiedler 310); "the earth mother," "the foster mother," or "the grandmother" (Kenneth Richardson 91). These female subjects have been viewed as stereotypes, archetypes, and projections of their creator's own gender-based conflicts,[15] while Faulkner himself has been seen as both misogynist and gyneolatrist, and his "women" as reflections of whichever side of the dialectic one chooses to accept as truth.[16] Most recently, we have been warned, convincingly, that generalizations about Faulkner's female characters are clearly problematical and may lead to "transtextual exercises" that inevitably distort and oversimplify single texts (Wittenberg, "William Faulkner," 327–35).[17] Yet we persist. As the length of Patricia Sweeney's bibliography suggests, these female voices of Yoknapatawpha continue to fascinate and, I believe, elude us.

My purpose here is to converse with what is feminine and therefore bisexual in Faulkner's texts rather than to critique other kinds of conversations with "characters" coded as women in those texts. Briefly, my view is that the two most extensive treatments of female characters in Faulkner's writing speak in androcentric tones about woman who is in most senses invisible, in Cixous's words, "because she isn't there where she is"; that is, because she isn't where the image projected of her is. In this paradigm, she is like Joyce's woman who, as Cixous says, "inscribes herself from bed to bed"; she moves from "bridebed" to "childbed" to "deathbed"; she "wanders but lying down." She journeys on "woman's voyage: as a *body*. As if she were destined — in the distribution established by men . . . — to be the nonsocial, nonpolitical, nonhuman half of the living structure. On nature's side of this structure, of course, tirelessly listening to what goes on inside — inside her belly, inside her 'house.' In direct contact with her appetites, her affects" ("Sorties" 66). I would not be so rash as to say that this description does not apply to such a fictional image as the young Eula Varner. I would argue, though, that in writing a critical text binding "Faulkner's women" so unalterably to the "natural roles" of reproduction and nurturance, Sally Page participates in what Susan Gubar has called "a long tradition identifying the author as a male who is primary and the female as his passive creation — a secondary object lacking autonomy, endowed with often contradictory meaning but denied intentionality" (77). Page, in fact, goes a step farther. In Faulkner's world, she writes, "woman's intense physical attractiveness, her wisdom, and her tranquility indicate that she is a creature of another order not burdened by the *limitations* of a total humanity"(16).

As Cixous points out, if one is not burdened with the limitations of being human, neither is one allowed the pleasures, desires, and pain of that status, those which make us both powerful and vulnerable. Those which make us *subjects* — disjointed, disconnected, dislocated though we be. (I would add too that even Eula grows up to become such a human subject.) In David Williams' paradigm, Faulkner's women characters become part of an archetypal symbology that likewise renders them "the passive victims of male authorial desire . . . rather [than] powerful figures that elicit texts crafted to appropriate or mute their difference" (Abel 2). What we have here is Nietzsche's woman-at-a-distance, the figure on the urn, stationary and transfixing but powerless within the margins of the male gaze. We are reminded of what Derrida says about Nietzsche's writing of woman: "There is no such thing as a woman, as a truth in itself of woman in itself. That much, at least, Nietzsche has said. Not to mention the manifold typology of women in his work, its horde of mothers, daughters, sisters, old maids, wives, governesses, prostitutes, virgins, grandmothers, big and little girls" (*Spurs* 101–103). Here woman is placed in the position of object rather than subject; concomitantly, the voice within the threatening and disruptive feminine space, that voice which questions logocentric modes of thought and practice, is silenced.

Although, as I have said, I would not approach these female characters in Faulkner as autonomous subjects, neither would I suggest that they are not subjects at all. What they seem to be, above all, are creative soundings of the feminine, which echo through Faulkner's narrative voice(s). Those voices are, in themselves, polyphonic. They speak in what Mikhail Bakhtin has called "dialogical" modes of discourse, created by synthesizing "the seeds of social heteroglossia embedded in words" as well as "those language characterizations and speech mannerisms (potential narrator-personalities) glimmering behind the words and forms . . ." (298). They are semiotic, cultural, and psychological strands of meaning that must be considered in all their multiplicity and creativity.

I need to define what I mean by "creativity." Sally Page, as I have said, and Cleanth Brooks view the "creativity" of Faulkner's female characters in terms of their reproductive and nurturing functions. "Because woman can participate directly in the natural process," Page writes, "she has an identity and creative role which tie her inextricably to the natural world in which she lives. When she is true to her nature, she can experience the serenity of that past ideal" (16). This type of woman has, according to Brooks, "natural force of tremendous power" ("Faulkner's Vision of Good and Evil" 697); but it is not, I would argue, a force from within the feminine space but rather one that is postulated from without. It requires, Brooks and Page agree, adherence to what has been seen as natural procreativeness embodied in the "female principle," a "creativity" which privileges physical productivity but does not connect sexual difference to intellectual and artistic generativity. Indeed, according to the Page-Brooks paradigm, Faulkner's female characters *must be* either creative or destructive, for their "creativity" must reproduce and nurture the validity of the patriarchal universe in which they live, or it becomes destructive to that milieu. In this paradigm, "woman" becomes the created, the *image* of creation — but not the creator, the doer, the maker, the *agent* of creation.[18] The creativity I will converse with is a different thing altogether. It is in fact not a thing at all, but a process engendered by desire which always seeks more than it has. This process resides within the female character who remakes herself and the world through imagination. Such creativity may or may not be linked to physical fertility; it is both physical and metaphysical. Born out of sexual difference, it is enormously powerful as it emerges out of the tension between Faulkner's male creative consciousness and his subversive deconstructive feminine voice which undercuts its own discourse as it expands into new and unknown spaces. It is the bisexual space of Faulkner's texts.

What happens to these female subjects, then, is the same thing that seems to have happened to Faulkner as he created them and their responses to the world. Their creative impulse (and his, as irrevocably linked to theirs) transforms the artistic consciousness by temporarily extending its creative boundaries into a narrative process that both derives from and intensifies sexual difference at the same time that it questions its binary construction. Faulkner thus writes difference by allowing the female subject's capacity for creation to remain open and productive. Some of these subjects, because of loss and desire engendered by loss, enter what Derrida calls "the play of *différance.*"[19] They create new meaning through the disruption of presence, by taking the risk of "meaning nothing" (*Positions* 14). This ability to "play" without seeking center or boundary we find in such diverse characters as Rosa Coldfield, Temple Drake, and Charlotte Rittenmeyer; Joanna Burden, Caddy Compson, and Addie Bundren. Tensions between denial and desire, the father and the mother, rigidity and flexibility, repression and sexuality give birth to the disrupted and disrupting female subject's narrative desire and by extension to Faulkner's insistence upon play, upon the plasticity of experience, upon the power of the human mind to break down rigidity and boundary.

A disclaimer: we are accustomed to treating Faulkner's world in terms of moral oppositions, to seeing characters in negative and positive terms; Faulkner himself encouraged such judgments. Yet this creative process of mind that we observe in some of these female personages, while evolving out of situations involving questions of morality, seems in itself to be morally ambiguous. For example, the imaginative capacities of Emily Grierson, Minnie Cooper, Joanna Burden—their abilities to rearrange reality and "play" creatively—have morally negative results, at least in conventional terms. Yet their creativity is nonetheless a powerful freeing force for their own psyches, which have been squeezed, compartmentalized, and devalued bcause of gender. If we consider what it means to "play" in language—that is, to free oneself from the necessity of closure or center, to defer meaning indefinitely—we may expand our notion of "character" still further to conceptualize female characters as feminine texts which defer themselves and differ from themselves *ad infinitum*. Emily Grierson "plays" creatively by breaking down paternal and societal restraint. She subverts the Law of the Father. Within her own physical space, the bedroom, she subverts the culturally defined signifiers of marital love—the rose-shaded lights, the tarnished hairbrush, the discarded clothing. She thereby creates a play of signifiers which undermine their own referentiality, even within the repressive margins of patriarchal order—inside the Father's House. Joanna Burden insists, above all, upon the *process* of her subjectivity, the narrative desire to invent and reinvent herself. It is the very multiplicity of her creativity, her insistence upon "playing it out like a play" (LA 244–45), which both frightens and excites Joe Christmas.[20] She must dismantle her austere past, "the frustrate and irrevocable years" of the Father's Law and re-create herself insistently, compulsively, unilaterally. If we continue to think of the female character as a text, we may see that Joanna Burden actually *becomes* the movable texts of desire: sexuality, jealousy, religiosity. Her narrative desire propels her to reinvent herself variously, yet that same desire deconstructs those texts as part of the ongoing process of invention. In this sense she is not so different from Lena Grove, who is herself the disruptive feminine process *outside* cultural codes, who, like Joanna, is a female subject propelled by loss and desire. Between these two female "texts," which are each both disruptive and productive, we feel the force of Faulkner's narrative desire in constant process and motion.

How to read process and motion? Caddy Compson has been thought of as a silent text constructed by her brothers, "a blank screen" imprinted by male fear and desire (Bleikasten, *The Most Splendid Failure*, 65). I would suggest that we try to "hear" Caddy Compson as the feminine voice of difference within male discourse, as the counter-narrative that speaks the possibility of play. If we "listen" for Caddy's voice as what Irigaray would call a *"disruptive excess"* that "jams" phallocentric economies, then we may begin to hear some of the ways in which *The Sound and the Fury* comes to speak against its own binary "story" of nihilism *versus* endurance. To hear Caddy's voice in this way, however, we may need to rethink her position and envision her as more than "a signifier referring always to the opposing signifier that annihilates its particular energy, puts down or stifles its very different sounds" (Cixous, "Sorties" 95). We may need to ask, with Irigaray, "what if the object began to speak?" We may indeed need to free the "character" of Caddy Compson, free her to follow Cixous's urging "to displace this 'within,' explode it, overturn it, grab it, make it hers, take it in, take it into her women's mouth, bite its tongue with her women's teeth, make up her own tongue to get inside of it. And you will see how easily she will well up, from this 'within' where she was hidden and dormant, to the lips where her foams will overflow" ("Sorties" 95–96).

We may then begin to hear Caddy's articulation of how ego boundaries may come to evaporate in a maternal space in which self and other are indistinguishable.[21] We may then come to see her as she moves through Benjy's world as its creator, the maker of stars, the creator of color and motion and natural beauty. Her willingness to play imaginatively, to become herself a subject-in-process, extends to participation in Quentin's text of incest and death. From within Quentin's tortured psyche, she speaks to him of the feminine within himself— that part of himself he must deny in order to become a man in a patriarchal order. Her creativity plays, differs from itself, never settles; and it does so within a "bounded text."[22] Like Benjy, she is enclosed. She is like the "stars" in the box she gives Benjy, "the infinite space . . . bounded in a nutshell," as Hamlet would have it, with no room for escape or expansion. She is trapped within male discourse ("Once a bitch always a bitch . . ."), but her creative play within its folds and layers whispers an alternative ordering of experience.

Capable of play and joy in play, her *jouissance*[23] becomes that indefinable element of this book that we are always in the process of finding and losing. It is what language cannot say. Caddy is the space in the text that Faulkner the author dissolves into and that we may retrieve his narrative desire from. It is her force which deploys the book's velocity, its motion. As Faulkner himself said, Caddy is "the only one that was brave enough to climb that tree to look in the forbidden window to see what was going on. And that's what the book—and it took the rest of the four hundred pages to explain why she was brave enough to climb the tree to look in the window" (*Faulkner in the University* 31). As the disruptive, incoherent, unindividuated, but infinitely creative female process of subjectivity, Caddy is the feminine voice within the bisexual space of Faulkner's text, its willingness to subvert its own meaning and thus to produce itself out of its own difference.

We may converse similarly with Addie Bundren, Rosa Coldfield, and Charlotte Rittenmeyer as processes of female subjectivity that create bisexual spaces in Faulkner's texts. These are spaces of alterity and mystery. They are that indefinable *something more,* that excess which generates narrative production and makes stories flood over their own boundaries. Addie Bundren insists upon her own subjectivity: "I would be I," she says, and she inscribes her self upon the text in an inescapable way. She knows that one never gets to the end of words, that the search for a center is fruitless, that language is not representative but constitutive. What she speaks and thus what she creates is her own sexuality.[24] In response to the deadening force of the Father's Law, Addie redesigns her desire into the images of beautiful "garments which we would remove in order to shape and coerce the terrible blood to the forlorn echo of the dead word high in the air" (*AILD* 167). Addie becomes woman writing her own body, and, as Cixous says, "her flesh speaks true. She *inscribes* what she is saying because she does not deny unconscious drives the unmanageable part they play in speech" (Sorties" 92).[25]

This is true of Rosa Coldfield's narrative voice as well. Her story becomes in the cultural progression of desire, repression, and discourse what Foucault would call "something akin to a secret whose discovery is imperative, a thing abusively reduced to silence, and at the same time difficult and necessary, dangerous and precious to divulge" (*History* 35). This is the sense of things we have from Rosa, that what she thinks she knows, or desires to know, is indeed both dangerous and precious. She is the hysterical woman who "reads" the inexplicable repressiveness of masculinist ideology articulated in the shared texts of Thomas Sutpen, Mr. Compson, Quentin, and Shreve. Together these patriarchal texts, with their culminative authority, devalue woman and silence women who, like Rosa, speak difference from the position of subject. The men of *Absalom, Absalom!*—even Quentin himself—eventually shut Rosa Coldfield up because they cannot stand the sound of her voice which so shrilly, insistently tells the story of their own "madness." Even silenced, she becomes the uncanny feminine sign of what must be repressed by such a culture in order for it to function. Yet, at the same time, Rosa's creativity, her hysterical narrative and its writing of female desire, can be read as the deconstructive process constituting *Absalom, Absalom!*—its refusal to end, its gaps and ruptures, its own hysteria.

If we converse with Rosa, we must converse with the ambiguity and anguish of her creativity. She creates, for example, the disturbing memory of herself and Clytie on the stairs of Sutpen's Hundred; yet she destroys the human recognition she receives in that encounter with her denial of female connection (*"Take your hand off me, nigger!"*). She knows the power of the flesh, but she must repress her own desire and render it into discourse, for her desire to enter the sexual world of "living marriage" is always prohibited in a culture that denies white female sexuality. Her only recourse is what Cixous describes as the initial act of female creativity: Rosa "unthinks the unifying, regulating history that homogenizes and channels forces" ("Laugh" 252). Matthews points out that Rosa must continually defer her desires and thus speaks the loss she feels (124). I would suggest that she speaks that loss from a feminine space which disrupts cultural texts, yet she cannot help but speak her culture as well, with its complex and pain-filled polyphonies of racial and sexual repressiveness.

Rosa Coldfield thus speaks difference in two senses. She herself is the feminine text of difference within patriarchal culture—that which it must deny in order to construct and maintain its systems—*at the same time* that her actions cement patriarchy's fixity and rigidity. The voice conveys her difference from the Father, but it also reveals that she is still his daughter. She is trapped in history. Her feminine voice is that of the hysteric, described by Catherine Clément as one "whose body is transformed into a theater for forgotten scenes, [and who] relives the past, bearing witness to a lost childhood that survives in suffering" (Cixous and Clément 5). For Rosa, as for the hysteric, "This is history that is not over" (Clément, in Cixous and Clément 6), nor, as Faulkner tells us through the text that is Rosa, will it ever be. "Was" can never be "was," and cultural texts continue to imprint even their own deconstruction. Faulkner creates Rosa, and himself, as makers of differences, but also as those who are ever in the process of being bound by their culture even as they are eluding it.[26]

Charlotte Rittenmeyer extends the discourse of love beyond cultural codes, creating it as a living thing which is itself the ongoing process of deconstruction and regeneration. Love does not fail, she tells Harry; it is people who fail. In a study of Faulkner's treatment of race, James A. Snead has written that Faulkner's novels show the "futility of applying strictly binary categories to human affairs" and dramatize the problem of cultural division (ix). In its very excessiveness, in its tendency to "flood" over cultural boundaries in the same way the Mississippi River floods the landscape in "Old Man," Charlotte's desire problematizes the binary structure of *The Wild Palms* by mediating the very motion of difference in this watery bloody book. Her feminine "flooding" leads us into the bisexual spaces, the fluid fluctuations in Faulkner's writing which allow us a way of reading and thinking outside binary opposition, a means of dissolving either/or, male/female, active/passive systems. Charlotte's desire speaks the difference within this binary narrative, the possibility of *something else*. Such a possibility implies a connection between woman as a desiring subject and the ways in which Faulkner's art floods beyond its own self-constructed levees.

As Faulkner creates female creativity, then, and compels female subjects to "unthink" the world, we feel his participation in their creative processes. Faulkner's style and meaning, his narrative desire, become immersed in these female subjects, whom he himself has made yet also *is.* Spivak's tracing of the position of woman in Derrida's schema seems to articulate the meaning of this immersion: as the image of "originary undecidability," woman can "occupy both positions in the subject/object oscillation" ("Love Me" 24).[27] Female characters in Faulkner's texts may be both subject and object in the sense that he creates them yet in a mysterious way also permits his own subjectivity to become entangled with theirs, thus blurring the boundaries of what is male and what is female, who writes and who is written.

I would emphasize at this point that I am writing/speaking *toward* Faulkner and his texts; I seek conversations with that which is bisexual in his narrative. This is a space of in-between that is explorable only in a highly speculative way. In choosing the medium of conversation, I am all too aware of the risks, the uncertainties, the uncomfortable pauses of such a discourse. Yet I have no desire to avoid it. Barbara Johnson has suggested that literature is the discourse most preoccupied with what we do not know, in the sense that it "often seems to tell us . . . the consequences of the way in which what is not known is not seen as unknown" (xii). One way to know what it is that we don't know is to approach the spaces of literature, those intratextual spaces which, as Johnson says, subvert "the very idea of identity, infinitely deferring the possibility of adding up the sum of a text's parts or meanings and reaching a totalized, integrated whole" (*The Critical Difference* 4)—which thus allow the text to differ from itself. Conversations with such spaces are likely to be disjunctive and unpolished. Such conversations require the critic to adopt a relativistic posture and an open inventiveness which eschews empiricism and moves toward "processes, objects, and events that he or she half-creates (and privileges as 'art') through his or her own speculative, inventive energies and interests" (Baker 10). In other words, such a conversation requires of the critic an active tropological imagination and a willingness to play creatively with the difference of the text—that which disturbs and disrupts meaning, that which is always moving beyond language's appropriative gesture.

If we wish to converse with Faulkner's narrative at the points where it differs from itself, which in my observations are those spaces where it becomes bisexual, then we may find it helpful to approach those differing spaces from differing angles. Besides conversing with the creative and powerful female voices in *The Sound and the Fury, Absalom, Ab-*

salom!, and *The Wild Palms*, I will be exploring those openings and differences both within and between Faulkner's texts which present the feminine as cultural disruption. At the same time I will attend to the mutual conversations Faulkner's narrative initiates between itself and the narratives of psychoanalysis, semiotics, deconstruction, feminism, and history. In the same way that Shoshana Felman points to literature as the unconscious of psychoanalysis (*Literature and Psychoanalysis* 9), we may find that Faulkner's conversations with these theoretical texts offer an intertextual space in which we ourselves may play creatively with the shared imaginary realm of the literary and the hermeneutic, seeing one reflected in the other.[28]

Faulkner's texts lend themselves to what Roland Barthes would call these "rereadings," to a dis-ease with interpretive closure. As Barthes warns us, "those who fail to reread are obliged to read the same story everywhere" (*S/Z* 15–16). John T. Irwin begins his influential psychoanalytic study of Faulkner's texts in this way, by writing about his own critical text as "a continuing act of deferment and accumulated tension" (6), one which would refuse to "come to intermediate conclusions" but instead would create "a kind of multidimensional imaginative space in which there existed the possibility of simultaneously placing every element side by side with every other element" (7). This same disinclination to be too sure about anything to do with Faulkner's texts, and an accompanying fascination with what is hidden, surprising, decentered, and dark, marks some of the most persuasive recent readings of Faulkner.[29] That some of these may be constituted as feminine spaces and that we may approach Faulkner through and between these spaces, are, I feel, possibilities worth pursuing.

It has been observed, accurately and perceptively, that Faulkner wrote out of his own experience as a white southern male in a patriarchal culture. Yet we know also that, paradoxically, Faulkner's texts both explore and explode the boundaries of culture through creative probings of their limits and nuances. It is this disruptive freedom of mind, this willingness to disallow the *idea* of center and to differ from itself in infinitely various ways that we find reverberating through Faulkner's narrative. Out of this expansiveness of mind and its deconstruction of the forces that would arrest and restrict free play of multiple meanings we see the freeing motion of Faulkner's own artistic consciousness—and its bisexual shape. This is what Derrida calls "the form of a force," and one we cannot (and must not attempt to) arrest in the process of attempting to comprehend; for in doing so, we will only lose meaning through the finding of it.

What we would wish for in our conversations with Faulkner, and what will be the measure of them, is a willingness to remain, as readers, "subjects-in-process"—readers who are willing to remain in the feminine economy of excessiveness, who are willing *to spend*. Our reward may be that we will see Faulkner's texts in the same way, a new way, as processes of *jouissance* which continually spend and replenish themselves, which never are and never can be "one." But before we can converse with such expansiveness, before we can follow the process of the feminine in Faulkner, we must turn away from the search for a center and must be willing to enter the process of desire, production, and renewal of desire; we must be able to spend, to play creatively without regret. We must be able to say with Cixous, "I do not care not to understand."

Then we may begin.

2 *Hearing Caddy's Voice*

Caddy, as we have already seen, is first and foremost an image; she exists only in the minds and memories of her brothers. . . . She is in fact what woman has always been in man's imagination: the figure par excellence of the Other, a blank screen onto which he projects both his desires and his fears, his love and his hate. And insofar as this Other is a myth and a mirage, a mere fantasy of the Self, it is bound to be a perpetual deceit and an endless source of disappointment.

André Bleikasten,
*The Most Splendid Failure: Faulkner's
"The Sound and the Fury"*

But what if the object began to speak?

Luce Irigaray,
Speculum of the Other Woman

I must begin by saying that I do not believe in Caddy Compson's silence. For if I believed in it, there would be no point in beginning at all. I will admit also that, although I do not believe that Caddy is silent, I do not understand fully what she is saying. And so I am seeking Caddy Compson. I am like young Rosa Coldfield, lurking behind closed doors in shadowy corridors, straining to hear untranslatable snatches of sounds, the kind of "silence out of which language speaks" (Felman, "Rereading Femininity" 44) and the kind of language out of which alterity is spoken—one's own. Rosa's kind of listening places her outside the markers of mastery and safety and leads her (and us) into a labyrinth of the greater and darker spaces of unconscious discourse. She (and we) listen for that of which we can hear the sense but not the substance, that which is always escaping language's appropriative gesture. Certainly this tentativeness is not an accustomed posture for those of us trained in the staid uprightness of the "objective" stance. Yet, as Jane

Gallop points out in her reading of Lacan, such a (non)position as ours, vulnerable and unsettling as it is, not only allows a different relationship to the many contradictory voices of a text, but calls into question "the phallic illusions of authority" and therefore is, and must be, "profoundly feminist" (19–20). Our willingness to relinquish mastery, to admit that we do not know, frees us to seek out what it *is* we do not know, to become as Barthes would have us — rereaders rather than consumers of texts.

And so when I say I am listening for Caddy's voice as it will, I believe, float up to us muted but articulate out of the feminine space of *The Sound and the Fury,* I am saying that we are listening for what we know not and for much more than we know. Just as the inscription of woman decenters and challenges the phallocentrism of Western culture and metaphysics and its "structuring of man as the central reference point of thought, and of the phallus as the symbol of sociocultural authority," Caddy as female subject becomes, as Jardine and Kristeva would suggest, the "filter" for thinking about this liquid space of the disruptive and seductive play of presence and absence, that space which speaks women's libidinal energies (Ann R. Jones, "Inscribing Femininity" 80). She becomes the discursiveness of that space which she *is* but which she also speaks out of. This is a space which expands and contracts with the force of its own motion. I do not see it as a "blank counter" or an "empty center" (Bleikasten, *Most Splendid Failure* 58, 51), a "cold weight of negativity" (Brooks, *Faulkner and Yoknapatawpha* 334), or a "still point" (Sundquist 10). Indeed, by relinquishing our (imagined) mastery over it, our attempts to *fix* it, we may find ourselves being engulfed by it (much, I think, as Faulkner allowed himself to be) and losing ourselves in it and to it. We may believe ourselves in danger.

But it is then, I believe, that we may begin to hear the whisper of Caddy's voice from within the folds of Faulkner's text and from within our own willingness to be absorbed into the concentric and bisexual spaces *between* the "manifest text" of Faulkner's male creative consciousness and the "unconscious discourse" of its own feminine subjectivity.[1] This is a space which Faulkner both makes and is subsumed by as a function and result of writing, which, as Foucault says, is itself an interplay of signs, regulated less by the content it signifies than by the very nature of the limits of its regularity, transgressing and reversing an order that it accepts and manipulates. Writing unfolds like a game that inevitably moves beyond its own rules and finally leaves them behind. Thus, the essential basis of this writing is not the exalted subject into language. Rather it is primarily concerned with creating an opening where the writing subject endlessly disappears. ("What Is an Author?" 116)

Foucault enlists us in the examination of "the empty space left by the author's disappearance" (121). In *The Sound and the Fury* this "opening" of the text is, I would suggest, Caddy herself; and the interface between Faulkner and this space of authorial self-effacement evolves within that bisexual space Cixous defines as "writing working (in) the in-between . . . infinitely dynamized by an incessant process of exchange from one subject to another" ("Laugh" 254). As Faulkner disappears into the rhetoric of the text, Caddy emerges with her own language of desires, loss, subversion, and, of course, creativity.

At this point our dilemma becomes linguistic: how to converse with space, motion, force—"the nontext of the text" (Conley 7). And how to listen to the language Caddy speaks, to that voice we hear between and beyond the contours of narrative—to the space which speaks both from and toward the half-light of the unconscious. In our yearning to hear that voice as it *is* (and not as we would render it through the alembic of consciousness and Being) and in our frustration at being able to catch only snatches and whispers of it, we are tempted to become like Melissa Meek, the frantic librarian, who seizes the frozen photographic image that will *place* Caddy somewhere and who cries, "It's Caddy! We must save her!" (SF 416). Burdened by the weight of consciousness and afraid we will not catch what it is we are meant to hear, we might hasten to fix Caddy in history and culture, in myth, as Other, as anima, as double, as nothing, as everything—and hence to erect some safe, recognizable boundaries around the feminine space of the text. Yet most of us would agree, I think, that Caddy *as character* flows beyond our ability to read her. She is *something more* than we can say, yet her presence is crucial to the deployment of language.[2]

We are like Benjy "trying to say" Caddy, but we, like Faulkner himself, always fail. Faulkner's feeling of failure (as well as his sense of the splendor of it), I believe, derives from his frustrations at "trying to say" Caddy, trying to write the female subject through a male consciousness and always failing—but *in the failure* creating the enormous bisexual tensions which play themselves out so powerfully within *The Sound and the Fury*, which in fact are essential to its subversion of the whole idea of a unified subject. We know Faulkner's passion (Bleikasten uses the term "tenderness") for Caddy, his "beautiful one," his "heart's darling."[3] Yet we also are aware that Eric Sundquist is right in saying, "There is probably no major character in literature about whom we know so little in proportion to the amount of attention she receives" (10). I would suggest another way of seeking the mystery that is Caddy, but one which I admit will not allow us to "find" her. The inevitability of our failure, though, does not mean we should not look and listen; for in seeking Caddy as feminine space and female subject-in-process we will be tracing the elusive shape of Faulkner's bisexual artistic (un)consciousness and, in terms of feminist criticism, employing Jardine's *gynesis* as a radical strategy of reading.

What we seek in seeking Caddy Compson is not only the language and force and mystery of woman within Faulkner's text and consciousness. This is also an inquiry into the nature of female subjectivity within a male text and the relationship of that subjectivity to what language can and cannot say. *The Sound and the Fury* itself asks the questions posed by Maurice Merleau-Ponty: "But what if language speaks as much by what is between words as by the words themselves? As much by what it does not 'say' as by what it 'says'?" (Lanser 42). Caddy's ability to speak to us as she traverses the spaces between presence and absence, text and nontext, the conscious and the unconscious, stretches our sense of the urgency of these questions. Simultaneously, her ability to play creatively within the bounded text of male discourse expands our sense of female energy and power, of its pressure upon the productivity of that text. Often we feel that Caddy isn't where we think she is, that her space is *somewhere else*.[4] She is continually arising from and fading into her brothers' discourse, always in the process of emerging and disappearing in the male text. Her subjectivity, as the "punctuation" of the male discourse which bounds it, is always on the brink of *aphanisis*, fading and being lost. It thus speaks out of the play of presence and absence, moving up and down the pear tree, in and out of that hazy area between the conscious and the unconscious. As Régis Durand points out, Lacan has shown us that texts may be seen as existing around "the living moment" of the fading of the subject (868).[5] Benjy's final musings are indeed so strangely moving, I suggest, because they allow us to feel almost simultaneously *both* the epiphany within the maternal space created between himself and Caddy *and* its *aphanisis:*

> Father went to the door and looked at us again. Then the dark came back, and he stood black in the door, and then the door turned black again. Caddy held me and I could hear us all, and the darkness, and something I could smell. And then I could see the windows, where the trees were buzzing. Then the dark began to go in smooth, bright shapes, like it always does, even when Caddy says that I have been asleep. (*SF* 92)

And yet the paradox is that Caddy *won't* fade completely; her voice and her presence emerge and reemerge throughout the narrative. She will not leave us; she rushes out of the mirror of male discourse, smelling like rain, offering Benjy's box of stars, speaking to us the language of creative play, of *différance,* of endless deconstruction and generation. Or grieving in a black raincoat, she appears suddenly out of nowhere on the periphery of the text, saying . . . what?

How do we listen to her? It is, as Derrida says of woman, "impossible to resist looking for her," yet she "will not be pinned down. . . . That which will not be pinned down by truth is, in truth—*feminine*" (*Spurs* 71, 55). And how do we converse with Faulkner about Caddy? In creating her as she is, he becomes one of "those writing modernity as a crisis-in-narrative, and thus in legitimation [who] are exploring newly contoured fictional spaces, hypothetical and unmeasurable, spaces freely coded as *feminine*" (Jardine 69). Caddy becomes Faulkner's "Other Text"—the one which hides itself, remains "beyond representation" (Jardine 127), and at the same time speaks itself and thereby constitutes its own force, a force which, as Derrida tells us, "is the other of language without which language would not be what it is" (*Writing and Difference* 27). Quoting Nietzsche, Derrida mourns the current tendency of criticism to disallow "the privilege given to vision, the Appollonian ecstasy which 'acts above all as a force stimulating the eye, so that it acquires the power of vision.'" The problem he poses is pertinent to our seeking of Caddy. With such rational and structural limits as it imposes upon itself, Derrida says, critical discourse loses its ability to "exceed itself to the point of embracing both force and the movement which displaces lines, nor to the point of embracing force as movement, as desire, for itself, and not as the accident or epiphany of lines. To the point of embracing it as writing" (*Writing and Difference* 28).

This is precisely our difficulty in approaching Caddy. For, as I have said, what we are moving toward in our conversations with Faulkner's text, is an inquiry into the unseating of structure, the relinquishing of the still point around which revolve certainty, presence, truth. In reading Caddy as this force, this *fluctuation* of meaning, we acknowledge the complementary textuality of *The Sound and the Fury* to the major "narratives" of modernity, those of psychoanalysis, philosophy, history, and literature. We may go on to remark upon *The Sound and the Fury*'s homology between textuality and subjectivity, and the gaps in both. To question Faulkner about those gaps in language, those ruptures in his text, is simply to follow where he leads; for he has taught us to listen as much to what language does not say as to what it does. Yet we may go a step beyond thinking of Faulkner's obvious "influence."[6] We may, in fact, think of him as authoring—and conversing with other texts of modernity *through*—this narrative's mysterious process of motion, from its own location in history and culture as *text,* into the crevasses and interstices of modernity and its manifold fictions, narrative and theoretical.[7] The fact that the feminine is, as we have seen, a space of disruption in those fictions should suggest what is at stake and also the referential weight our inquiries must bear.

We may initiate those inquiries by continuing to imagine Caddy as the feminine space which covers and enfolds the novel, and, at the same time, as the female subject who both speaks out of that space and plays creatively within it. In her essay, "Women's Time," Kristeva points to the fact that woman has been more associated with space "generating and forming the human species" than with time, "becoming, or history" (15). Women's lives and maternal experiences challenge "a certain conception of time: time as project, teleology, linear and prospective unfolding; time as departure, progression, and arrival—in other words, the time of history" (17). Is it then possible to conceptualize the feminine as *space* in a book which is, as Jean-Paul Sartre and Douglas Messerli have shown, about *time?*[8] Can Caddy tell us another story? As a theoretical base, Kristeva goes on to posit *maternal space* as the ordering principle for one of two modalities she designates as being within the signifying system of language—the "semiotic," which "introduces wandering or fuzziness into language," as opposed to the "symbolic," "language as nomination, sign, and syntax." The "semiotic" is the language of poetry. It utters "the workings of drives." As symbolic function, language "constitutes itself at the cost of repressing instinctual drive and continuous relation to the mother. On the contrary, the unsettled and questionable subject of poetic language (for whom the word is never uniquely sign) maintains itself at the cost of reactivating this repressed instinctual, maternal element" (*Desire* 136).

These two signifying processes imply, of course, a subject split between conscious and unconscious drives and motives. As Ann Rosalind Jones points out, Kristeva derives the semiotic from "infants' pre-oedipal fusion with their mothers, from the polymorphous bodily pleasures and rhythmic play of mother-infant communication, censored [as incest] or harshly redirected by paternal (social) discourse" ("Inscribing Femininity" 86). Kristeva theorizes maternal space in terms of Plato's concept of the *chora* which she appropriates as "an essentially mobile and extremely provisional articulation constituted by movements and their ephemeral stases." The semiotic *chora* is an "uncertain and indeterminate articulation" which constitutes a "nonexpressive totality" (*Revolution* 25). As "rhythmic space," the *chora* can never be defined or placed. It is the process through which language is born and nourished.

The semiotic modality of language—its constitutive, playful, creative, expressive side—is thus connected to those fluctuations of subject and object allowed and desired within the space of the maternal. This connection between the maternal and the creative seems crucial to our hearing of Caddy in Benjy's section and to our understanding of how narrative may break down oppositions between self and other, subject and object. Also, as Kristeva herself points out, the semiotic is inseparable from the unconscious workings of the human subject. We may take these connections a step further in our conversations with the

Caddy of Benjy's fuzzy longings to think of the feminine space of this first section of *The Sound and the Fury* as its semiotic *chora*, its place of motherhood which by its very nature must deconstruct rational and linear thought by privileging desire. In a like manner, Spivak points to the space of woman in Derrida's texts as the site of "affirmative deconstruction," particularly in relation to childbearing and the maternal sphere which breaks down the oppositions between self and other ("Love Me" 25). As Kristeva points out in "Motherhood According to Giovanni Bellini," some visual artists have displayed mothers as "graspable, masterable *objects*" who are always within reach. Bellini instead presented maternal space as "fascinating, attracting and puzzling" and depicted motherhood as the site of an unrepresentable *jouissance* (*Desire* 243–47). Such is the maternal space of Caddy within Benjy's discourse. Out of it Caddy speaks what Kristeva has called "the *unsettling process* of meaning and subject" rather than "the coherence or identity of either *one* or a *multiplicity* of structures" (Desire 125).

A subject who so speaks the heterogeneity of meaning and signification (all that disrupts opposition and hierarchy) must be, in Kristeva's theorizing, "a questionable *subject-in-process*" (*Desire* 135), one whose identity is always in motion to support the signifying economy of its semiotic text. This is the Caddy that Benjy gives us, and that he and we find and lose again and again and again. Matthews says that Caddy "is the figure the novel is written to *lose*" (23). But now, let us try (unsuccessfully, of course) to find her, remembering always that we are "in pursuit of what is in the act of escaping" and that to find Caddy would be to lose her.

I

> "Why, Benjy." she said. She looked at me and I went
> and she put her arms around me. "Did you find Caddy
> again." she said. "Did you think Caddy had run away."

Caddy's voice speaks in rhythms most of us understand, for she speaks what Kristeva has called "maternal language" out of the maternal space created in Benjy's discourse.[9] The flatness and homogeneity of her speech

evoked by punctuation and syntax have the paradoxical effect of inten-
sifying the rhythms of mediation between self and other, of nurturance, of that "cleaved space" Kristeva describes as part of the maternal
"process" she finds in Bellini's paintings (*Desire* 264). Hearing Caddy
through the flatness of Benjy's mind, we may be reminded of the peculiar effect of hearing poetry read with a purposeful lack of expression
designed to permit the language of the text to speak itself *as language.*
Matthews has pointed to the fact that Benjy in his "fallen world of loss,
memory, time, and grief" converts time into space (65). I would take
this idea further by suggesting that feminine space *overlays* time in the
novel. We may think of this privileged space, created in Benjy's mind
and in Caddy's maternal voice within his mind, as the semiotic *chora*
of this section of the narrative and as the section's rhythmic receptacle,
"the process by which signifiance is constituted." As Kristeva says, "Plato
himself leads us to such a process when he calls this receptacle or *chora*
nourishing and maternal, not yet unified in an ordered whole because
deity is absent from it" (*Revolution* 26). The space created between
Benjy and Caddy, then, defies the hierarchies of time and structure;
its language is the mother tongue.

Within such a space Caddy the child becomes Caddy the mother.
Benjy the man is Benjy the child. Linear time is decentered and displaced by maternal space. Language is constitutive: Caddy's "saying"
makes it so. Within one conversation, she makes words into exchange
commodities traded for a jar of lightning bugs for Benjy and remakes
grief into pleasure:

> "If I say you and T.P. can come too, will you let him hold it."
> Caddy said.
> "Aint nobody said me and T.P. got to mind you." Frony said.
> "If I say you dont have to, will you let him hold it." Caddy said.
> "All right." Frony said. "Let him hold it, T.P. We going to
> watch them moaning."
> "They aint moaning." Caddy said. "I tell you it's a party. Are
> they moaning, Versh." (*SF* 44)

Linda W. Wagner writes persuasively of Caddy's attempts to "bring
[Benjy] to speech" and of Caddy's roles as "creator and conveyor of

language," a language of love and interconnection which is inevitably replaced by meaningless sound and fury (50–51, 61). Matthews thinks of these initial attempts at definition and articulation as prefiguring an infinite play of meanings which suggest the inability of language to "reappropriate presence and the recognition that such a limitation opens the possibility of the endless pleasures of writing" (76–77). Although Caddy's generative maternal language is eventually replaced, it is not lost. As she creates language for Benjy, she inscribes herself upon it, becoming what Jardine has called "new rhetorical space" (38). Benjy has lost Caddy but he remains within her maternal discourse, for her voice has imprinted both itself and *himself* upon the receptacle of his memory. We can envision him at the state mental hospital, still hearing her speak his name and still recognizing the sound of her name within language — a maternal language which traverses the chasm between her subjectivity and his. We may look at the movement of Benjy's reality within this section as illustration. At the beginning he has lost Caddy and is bellowing at the sound "caddie" and yet by the end, the maternal space of Caddy, as we have seen, has enclosed his mind with the "smooth, bright shapes" of that hazy entry to the womb-like darkness of maternal interconnection through which the boundaries between self and other are blurred. By its ability to name what is not, or what seems to be absent (Benjy's subjectivity), Caddy's maternal voice dissolves the boundary between presence and absence and thereby creates the semiotic matrix of the novel, the unconscious discourse that will go on to speak the reciprocal rhythms between the conscious and the unconscious in Quentin's tortured thoughts.

Athough she is a girl and although she speaks as a girl, her voice carries this referential weight because she speaks from the *position* of the mother, whose very acts of giving birth, of gestation and nurturance, dissolve the otherness of the other. In many of the scenes created in Benjy's memory, Caddy encloses him within this maternal space which transcends the teleologies of time and distance, and thus becomes their counter-narrative. In this sense, Caddy's voice subverts some of the very meanings of Faulkner's narrative, which, as we have been shown, is indeed about the effects of time and loss. What Caddy's voice says out of the maternal space created for it in Benjy's mind is precisely *opposite* to what Benjy's narrative as a whole seems to be saying, i.e., that originary plenitude can never be regained, that creativity and play have given way to despair, rigidity, meaningless order—sound and fury signifying nothing.[10]

The maternal Caddy deconstructs such a message. Her voice tells another story—the creative play of *différance* within the bounded text of Benjy's mind. With her words and touch she dissolves the boundaries between herself and Benjy. His snatches of memories often end with Caddy reaffirming the maternal space that connects them. For example, Benjy remembers her persuading their mother to let her take him out in the cold, instructing the relieved Versh not to come, and then embracing him:

> He went on and we stopped in the hall and Caddy knelt and put her arms around me and her cold bright face against mine. She smelled like trees.
> "You're not a poor baby. Are you. You've got your Caddy. Haven't you got your Caddy." (*SF* 8)

Caddy plays creatively within the bounds of coldness and rigidity. She speaks warmth to Benjy, even as they are being used by Maury to deliver his letter: "Keep your hands in your pockets, Caddy said. Or they'll get froze. You don't want your hands froze on Christmas, do you" (3). She connects her self to Benjy's other, even to the point of becoming other to herself, speaking of herself in the third person, connecting her desires to Benjy's, pretending, "We dont like perfume ourselves" (51). She is like the bowl of food she feeds Benjy; she empties herself into him and then fills herself back up again for his consumption. Much like the female subjects of Carol Gilligan's research, she makes her decisions on the basis of her responsibilities to Benjy, and she has difficulty separating her own needs from his.

Yet just as she herself fades into the doomed space of Mrs. Patterson's eyes, the maternal space she creates for Benjy gives way to other more disturbing spaces, and what empowerment she receives as female subject from taking the place of the mother is punctuated by depletion and darkness. As her space constricts, we begin to see her frantic response to the necessity of remaining creative within the narrow margins allowed her own desires as a subject-in-process propelled by the motion of their force. She continues to play, but her text becomes more and more bounded. She is encircled in the concentric spaces of her own maternity created within male discourse, but also of the sexuality which transgresses that maternal space, and finally and inevitably of the patriarchal world she finds herself living within as a female subject-object. She is a subject always in the process of becoming; yet movement becomes less free and eventually, in Jason's economy, impossible.

One of the scenes most often repeated in the novel and certainly among its most central is the one in which a silenced Caddy, no longer a virgin, stands in the door, first in Benjy's and then in Quentin's memories, her eyes speaking terror and despair. Cornered by Benjy's bellowing, she is completely entrapped by male discourse, by both Benjy's inarticulate and Quentin's articulate texts of woman as other. This is a scene which Benjy recalls and then immediately repeats, and it is one which erupts again and again in Quentin's tortured thoughts. Caddy has broken the Law of the Father, that which "requires that woman maintain in her own body the material substratum of the object of desire, but that she herself never have access to desire" (Irigaray, *This Sex* 188). Here she is voiceless; she becomes merely a function of the discourse of others—frozen as image, as silence. Benjy recalls the same scene in two flashes. First he recalls:

> Caddy came to the door and stood there, looking at Father and Mother. Her eyes flew at me, and away. I began to cry. It went loud and I got up. Caddy came in and stood with her back to the wall, looking at me. I went toward her, crying, and she shrank against the wall and I saw her eyes and I cried louder and pulled at her dress. She put her hands out but I pulled at her dress. Her eyes ran. (*SF* 84)

And then again:

> We were in the hall. Caddy was still looking at me. Her hand was against her mouth and I saw her eyes and I cried. We went up the stairs. She stopped again, against the wall, looking at me and I cried and she went on and I came on, crying, and she shrank against the wall, looking at me. She opened the door to

her room, but I pulled at her dress and we went to the bathroom and she stood against the door, looking at me. Then she
put her arm across her face and I pushed at her, crying. (*SF* 85)

This is the image of Caddy silenced. She cannot remake herself in
language for Benjy. She cannot wash off or throw away her desire. This
is the moment of her entrapment, a crucial moment of the novel and
one which Quentin re-creates obsessively. If Caddy in the pear tree is
an image of her creativity and courage, of her ability to negotiate the
economies of death (that which is in the window) and life (that which
is below her, those whom she loves), then Caddy's standing in the door
with eyes, "like cornered rats" as Quentin will say of a similar scene,
is surely the opposite image. Caddy speaks out of the pear tree: she
speaks life to death and death to life. She becomes, as Bleikasten shows
us, a mediator between the two (*The Most Splendid Failure* 54). Yet
she is completely entrapped before Benjy's bellowing; more devastating, she is rendered voiceless. It is significant and strangely disturbing
that these two images of Caddy, weeping after she has entered into her
first sexual relationship, are connected in Benjy's mind by Versh's eerie
tale of maternity's disastrous effects, that of the woman's "bluegum
chillen" who eat a man: "*Possum hunters found him in the woods, et
clean*" (SF 85). Versh's story is about a woman who has, it is implied,
"*about a dozen them bluegum chillen running round the place*" (84–
85). This is the maternal space expanded to monstrous proportions,
becoming enormously threatening and destructive to the male, just as
Caddy's maternal space now threatens Benjy because it has become also
the space of female sexuality, that desire which, as Irigaray tells us, "is
not one," and which, we are told by Spivak, is "a scandal" because of
its delight in excess ("French Feminism" 154–84).

Yet I have said that I do not believe in Caddy Compson's silence.
As female subject, she is indeed silenced at this point. But as woman-
in-effect in male discourse, as the feminine space in Faulkner's narrative, she becomes what Irigaray calls the "*disruptive excess*" that is guilty
of "jamming the theoretical machinery itself, of suspending its preten-
sion to the production of a truth and of a meaning that are excessively
univocal" (*This Sex* 78). She is the text which speaks multiplicity, maternity, sexuality, and as such she retains not just one voice but many. They

make Benjy bellow and Quentin despair. They drive Jason to hatred. Their power is mammoth because they are "not one." Within the constricted space of Quentin's tortured psyche, we will hear them, like the Caddy of Benjy's maternal *chora,* fading in and out. To hear Caddy within the margins of Quentin's text will require listening to a language which transgresses the bounds of consciousness, a language which must be listened to in much the same way that Caddy listened to Benjy—beyond sound and syntax, between the lines.

II

> If woman has always functioned "within" man's discourse, a signifier referring always to the opposing signifier that annihilates its particular energy, puts down or stifles its very different sounds, now it is time for her to displace this "within," explode it, overturn it, grab it, make it hers, take it in, take it into her women's mouth, bite its tongue with her women's teeth, make up her own tongue to get inside of it. And you will see how easily she will well up, from this "within" where she was hidden and dormant, to the lips where her foams will overflow.
>
> Hélène Cixous, "Sorties"

> let me go Ive got to catch him and ask his let me go Quentin please let me go let me go
>
> Caddy Compson

Caddy Compson seeks a way out of male discourse. Resonating from within the dark folds of Quentin's despair, her voice and presence speak the feminine desire that inscribes her woman's body across his male text. Subversively she rises from Quentin's mind to speak her desire for Dalton Ames, for entry into a libidinal economy which allows her to give, to spend herself excessively, to play creatively and productively within that half-light between self and other, much as she did within the maternal space she created within Benjy's discourse. Cixous writes of such a libidinal economy in which female desire, the "desire-that-gives," becomes extraordinarily productive ("Laugh" 263). Caddy's discourse of desire leads us into the productivity of Faulkner's poetics, into the opening in language left by the disappearance of the author as part of the process of creation, that opening which points to the author as "a variety of egos" and "a series of subjective positions" whose name remains only "at the contours of the text" (Foucault, "What Is An Author?" 115, 131). If we think of Faulkner's rhetoric of female desire as one of several such positions of the varied authorial egos within a text, the creative expansiveness of that rhetoric, its progressive subjectivity, seems even more astonishing under the pressure of Quentin's bounded male text. It is a second subjective position (female) which implodes upon a first (male). Caddy becomes even more powerful—her strength reproducing itself endlessly—as she presses upon the vise which squeezes her. And so we may hear Caddy as the space of the feminine, rumbling volcano-like, from deep within all the levels and layers and geographical faults of Quentin's section. She speaks *from* Quentin *to* Quentin of the feminine within himself—that which he, entangled in a cultural narrative already written for him, can but desire and grieve for. The space that Faulkner leaves as he dissolves into this text is the space of Caddy. To examine its shape we may walk around it. To know what it is, or to know that we do not know and perhaps cannot know what it is, we must enter it.

But where do we enter Quentin's seamless narrative as it sweeps him through the shadows of grief and despair toward death? And how do we hear Caddy's voice emerging from those shadows? Perhaps we must seek entry where the text becomes darkest and most fearful, and where the gaps and ruptures in language seem most jarring. When Quentin makes his final preparations to commit suicide, Caddy's voice emerges at its most powerful velocity out of the darkness of her brother's mind. In this passage, described by Noel Polk as "heartbreaking" ("The Dungeon Was Mother Herself" 61), Quentin is remembering the picture of a dungeon in a childhood book or, as well may be the case, is constructing an image of such a book:[11]

> When I was little there was a picture in one of our books, a
> dark place into which a single weak ray of light came slanting
> upon two faces lifted out of shadow. *You know what I'd do if I*

were King? she never was a queen or a fairy she was always a king or a giant or a general *I'd break that place open and drag them out and I'd whip them good* It was torn out, jagged out. I was glad. I'd have to turn back to it until the dungeon was Mother herself she and Father upward into weak light holding hands and us lost somewhere below even them without even a ray of light. Then the honeysuckle got into it. (*SF* 215)

This passage, perhaps more than any other, pulls us down into the darkness of Quentin's fears. As he continues to think of darkness, he remembers having to feel his way through the dark house down the long corridor and stairs "*where a misstep in the darkness filled with sleeping Mother Father Caddy Jason Maury door I am not afraid only Mother Father Caddy Jason Maury getting so far ahead . . .*" (215). As his rhetoric feels its dark way toward death in this passage, Caddy's voice erupts as a powerful challenge to despair. She would be "*King*" and she would "*break that place open and drag them out.*" She would "*whip them good.*" The effect here is one best described by Cixous when she explicates "femininity in writing" as being privileged by *voice*: "*writing and voice* are entwined and interwoven and writing's continuity/ voice's rhythm take each other's breath away through interchanging, make the text gasp or form it out of suspenses and silences, make it lose its voice or rend it with cries" ("Sorties" 92). This is the rhetorical effect; this is what we *hear* in the interchange between Quentin's ponderous cadences of despair and Caddy's jarring, disruptive flashes of speeches which indeed do seem to "make the text gasp." If we converse momentarily with this passage as an entity unto itself, we may find ourselves within a bisexual space which is both paradoxical and darkly intriguing.

"The dungeon," as Polk has emphasized, is indeed "Mother herself":[12] her lack of love has created the dark place from which Quentin cannot free himself. It is a dungeon *built by the mother,* and it cannot be escaped, for it is the place of the unconscious, where fear lives. The feminine is thus not only threatening; it is terribly and tragically destructive. Still, from within this male discourse rises the voice of Caddy, who would become a man in order to "*whip them good*" and thus restore the maternal space, the counter-narrative to despair and entrapment. Within the male mind, then, we see maternal space both as dungeon, the place of castration and anxiety, and as the avenue of escape from it. This is surely the "in-between" which comprises the bisexual space of Cixous's theoretical imagination, and only one among multiple levels and voices. Within Faulkner's male creative consciousness and its multiple subjectivities, we find another male creative consciousness and *its* multiple subjectivities, who are *female* and *both* inhibiting (Mother) and freeing (Caddy) and who moreover are in conflict over the status of the male unconscious—certainly Quentin's and, I believe, Faulkner's as well. We should remember, too, Quentin's connection of his own sense of loss and entrapment to female sexuality in the sentence which follows the image of the dungeon: "Then the honeysuckle got into it." What Faulkner has created here is an opening through which he disappears into the text of a nightmare of male fear. Who or what can save the male? The male seems in Quentin's mind to have only one chance, and that is through the force of the female and her bisexual power, her willingness to traverse the space of sexual difference and to *speak* "(in) the in-between." Of course, it is a chance long lost, one which can only punctuate with a brief spark the twilight of Quentin's fading.[13]

But to embrace the force which is Caddy, "the force and movement which displaces lines" (Derrida, *Writing and Difference* 28), we must conceive of her space as a layer which pervades this section organically, enfolding, burrowing into, and playing within Quentin's thoughts. Paradoxically she both exceeds and is confined inside his text. She is like one of the items Quentin keeps packing in his bag; he tries to squeeze her into the objective position required to "pack it away." Of course he fails. The constricted space cannot contain her or her voice. She may remain inside for a while, but even then she plays creatively within the texts created for her. She speaks out of Quentin's narrative despite his attempts to silence her, always the subject-in-process *becoming,* always disruptive, always rising up from the feminine liquidity of mud and water to speak herself and her bodily energies.

Quentin's dilemma seems at least partly related to his acceptance of his father's discourse of phallic authority. As we have seen, Lacanian theory is based upon the notion of the phallus as signifier. As Gallop points out, women have always been castrated by psychoanalytic thinking, and yet, for Lacan, castration "is not only sexual; more important, it is also linguistic: we are inevitably bereft of any masterful understanding of language, and can only signify ourselves in a symbolic system that we do not command, that, rather, commands us." The message that everyone is castrated is a freeing one for both men and women, Gallop argues, because it releases us from the phallocentric notion "that one must constantly cover one's inevitable inadequacy in order to have a right to speak" (*Reading Lacan* 20). This is, of course, a realization that Quentin cannot accept. He preserves the phallic illusions of authority in all sorts of ways: his obsession with time, his silencing of Caddy's voice within, his machismo activities in fighting Bland, his racism. He literally carries the empowering signifier around in the obviously phallic loaf which slowly emerges from its wrapper as he walks with the "sister" who has no voice in his text. One feels, in fact, the need to struggle with Quentin's text in order to hear the feminine. This is not because it is not there. It is the decibel level of Quentin's need to silence it that drowns it out. Fetterley's advice here would be to read against the text, ask it questions it does not have the answers for. This is, of course, what we must do. I would emphasize, though, that this is *Quentin's* text we are struggling with, one that Faulkner has created but one toward which he seems to have adopted an equivocal ideological stance.

Quentin's most frequent images of Caddy render her voiceless. Yet, despite Quentin's efforts to stifle it, her voice still emerges, still wars with and plays inside the male text she finds herself within. The most obsessively replayed image of Caddy in this section is that same devastating scene in which she stands in the door crying, trapped by Benjy's wailing and groping. She has had sexual relations; this time she cannot wash herself off, restore her virginity to Benjy. This was/is Caddy's moment of inertia, of helplessness, of silence. Quentin retrieves it obsessively in his own memory. It is in fact closely related to the scene which in his mind precedes the terrifying vision of the picture-book dungeon, the scene of his mother and father sitting and listening to Benjy's bellowing, in the dungeon of their own inability and unwillingness to intervene. Within Quentin's memory sequence of picture book, dungeon, darkness, the repetition of the word "door" connects Caddy's terror and helplessness to Quentin's own. At least a dozen times Quentin places a silent Caddy within the margins of that door. Such placements range from momentary ones, in which the word "door" appears in the text, to short sequences such as *"One minute she was standing in the door"* (98), to extended description similar to those in Benjy's mind:

> one minute she was standing there the next he was yelling and pulling at her dress they went into the hall and up the stairs yelling and shoving at her up the stairs to the bathroom door and stopped her back against the door and her arm across her face yelling and trying to shove her into the bathroom when she came in to supper T.P. was feeding him he started again just whimpering at first until she touched him then he yelled she stood there her eyes like cornered rats then I was running in the grey darkness. . . . (*SF* 185)

The image is of Caddy trapped by *both* of her brothers' voices—voices accusing and condemning her sexuality, naming it as a betrayal of their incestuous desires. Quentin's memory of the scene reads like a rape scene: Benjy is trying to shove Caddy through the door into the bathroom. There is, in fact, a strange gap in Quentin's account. What happens in Quentin's mind between Benjy's trying to shove Caddy into the bathroom and her coming in to supper? Something unspeakable?

Yet Caddy will not remain long in the door of Quentin's memory. She runs out of the house and throws herself into the water. When she speaks, she speaks of giving and of desire, of a *jouissance* which is as multiple as female orgasm. She says, "Poor Benjy" and "Poor Quentin." She speaks the rich paradox of her desire for Dalton Ames, her unending pleasure in her own sexuality: "yes I hate him I would die for him I've already died for him I die for him over and over again everytime this goes" (SF 186–88). Such female desire, as Irigaray says, "undermines the goal-object of a desire, diffuses the polarization toward a single pleasure, disconcerts fidelity to a single discourse . . ." (*This Sex* 30–31). Caddy is woman daring to speak about "the possibility of a giving that doesn't take away, but *gives*." Such a discourse of desire subverts the patriarchal codes of what Cixous has called "the realm of the proper." Quentin lives in such a realm, one "in which man's reign is held to be proper" and language is connected to the authority of the father, specifically Quentin's own father. The realm of the proper, Cixous says, functions because of "man's classic fear of seeing himself expropriated, seeing himself deprived [paradoxically] . . . by his refusal to be deprived, in a state of separation, by his fear of losing the prerogative, fear whose response is all of History" ("Castration or Decapitation?" 50). This passage seems to describe Quentin's fears in regard to Caddy, and his inability to hear her as she speaks the endlessness of desire and spending. For such endlessness gazes out over the infinity of bisexual space, and over its possibilities for entanglement and interaction, in a way that Quentin cannot risk from inside the masculine realm of the proper.

Caddy plays so creatively within that space of the text which is between self and other that she can in fact participate in creating the signifiers of her own imagined rape and death. Speaking out of Quentin's text, she urges him to "push it are you doing it," and what we hear from within is the deeper articulation of female subjectivity as she holds Quentin's head against her breast and her voice becomes "her heart going firm and slow now not hammering and the water gurgling among the willows in the dark and waves of honeysuckle coming up the air . . ." (*SF* 189). This is, of course, the text of the unconscious rising to speak, in the process called "character," the splitness of the subject, the inevitability of human divisibility. Cixous might be describing this moment when she says:

> The unconscious is always cultural and when it talks it tells you your old stories, it tells you the old stories you've heard before because it consists of the repressed of culture. But it's also always shaped by the forceful return of a libido that doesn't give up that easily, and also by what is strange, what is outside culture, by a language which is a savage tongue that can make itself understood quite well. ("Castration or Decapitation?" 52)

Although Quentin can hear the "savage tongue" of Caddy's pulse, he cannot respond to it.[14] As his section progresses, her voice becomes hazier and hazier. Often we hear her at a third remove; for example, we hear of her love for Quentin through Quentin's re-creation of Herbert Head's recounting of Caddy's words. That Quentin's text is so sad-

dening and so provocative has something to do with the gradual squeez-
ing out of Caddy's language of the hammering heart, the fading of her
female subjectivity. This is felt so profoundly because of the way Faulkner allows us to hear Caddy speak her passion and creativity out of the
entrapping vise of Quentin's despair and rigidity. We feel Caddy's force
and motion as subject-in-process most powerfully as she runs out of the
mirror of Quentin's mind. As Sundquist points out, this is a central
scene of the book. Caddy is in motion; she is not an image but a *force*
upon the whirl of progressive verbs:

> *Only she was running already when I heard it. In the mirror she
> was running before I knew what it was. That quick, her train
> caught up over her arm she ran out of the mirror like a cloud,
> her veil swirling in long glints her heels brittle and fast clutch-
> ing her dress onto her shoulder with the other hand, running
> out of the mirror the smells roses roses the voice that breathed
> o'er Eden. Then she was across the porch I couldn't hear her
> heels then in the moonlight like a cloud, the floating shadow of
> the veil running across the grass, into bellowing. She ran out of
> her dress, clutching her bridal, running into the bellowing. . . .*
> (*SF* 100)

This passage is crucial because it embodies the complexity of what
Cixous has called "the feminine textual body" ("Castration" 52). Here
is Caddy, doomed, pregnant and forced to marry, running, as Sundquist says, into "the wrenching, mindless vacuum of Benjy's bellowing,"
into the loss and grief which is more her own than her brothers' (11).
And yet . . . we pause. And the reason we pause is to gasp at the force
and energy and movement of Caddy as she comes running out of Quentin's distorted mirror. "A feminine textual body," Cixous writes,

> is recognized by the fact that it is always endless, without ending;
> there's no closure, it doesn't stop, and it's this that very often makes
> the feminine text difficult to read . . . a feminine text goes on and
> on and at a certain moment the volume comes to an end but the
> writing continues and for the reader this means being thrust into
> the void" ("Castration" 53).

Cixous's comments not only describe Caddy in the mirror and in Quentin's text but that "feminine textual body" which is *The Sound and the Fury,* the book which itself goes on and on and spins us out into the void. Caddy's motion is her voice in that she speaks, *even out of the mirrors of male consciousness and female doom,* of the creative power of the split human subject to play bravely and unceasingly in an economy of spending, in an opening of the self which allows the embracing of the other.

The tragedy of *The Sound and the Fury* is the pervasiveness of an economy which diminishes and destroys the desire to spend one's self in negotiating the spaces between self and other, the conscious and the unconscious, male and female. The "something terrible" in Caddy looks out of male faces. Quentin, so burdened by the phallus as signifier, cannot hear her speak to him out of the space his unconscious creates for her. He thus renders her mute ("Nothing but a girl. Poor Sister.") and proceeds to pack her up. Yet she remains the difference within his text, the difference that deconstructs phallic authority. And as he closes his bag for the last time, we hear her feminine voice calling to us "the unflagging, intoxicating, unappeasable search for love" (Cixous, "Laugh" 264).

III

"Wait," she says, catching my arm. "I've stopped. I wont again. You promise, Jason?" she says, and me feeling her eyes almost like they were touching my face, "You promise? Mother — that money — if sometimes she needs things — if I send checks for her to you, other ones besides those, you'll give them to her? You wont tell? You'll see that she has things like other girls?"

Of all the scenes that Quentin re-creates between himself and Caddy, the most wrenching may be a repeated conversation in which Caddy, torn between conflicting responsibilities to her unborn child and to her idiot brother and alcoholic father, tries to make Quentin promise to take care of Benjy and their father. In one such scene he refuses to promise and answers her frantic pleas with scathing sarcasm:

> *Are you going to look after Benjy and Father*
> *The less you say about Benjy and Father the better*
> *when have you ever considered them Caddy*
> *Promise*
> *You needn't worry about them you're getting out in good*
> *shape*
> *Promise I'm sick you'll have to promise. (SF 131)*

In Jason's section Caddy again asks a brother to promise to take care of someone she loves, this time her daughter. Jason's response is more direct: "'Sure,' I says, 'As long as you behave and do like I tell you'" (*SF* 261). Again Caddy is cheated out of her promise, but this time more aggressively, for Jason operates within an economy which takes more than it gives. Caddy is its ideal victim because of her willingness to give excessively. She is woman operating "on the side of loss and spending, associated with life and force" (Conley 61). Hers is "an 'economy' that can no longer be put in economic terms"; it operates out of "a love that has no commerce with the apprehensive desire that provides against the lack . . ." (Cixous, "Laugh" 264).

We may recall Jardine's distinction between woman as process and woman as sexual identity, and we have thought about Caddy as the process of "woman" that disrupts symbolic structures (41) and the point of connection, the opening, of Faulkner's text to the feminine, to those processes which speak the libidinal economy of "woman-in-effect." The Caddy of Jason's discourse still speaks the language of disruption; but, not surprisingly (Jason is above all a realist), her voice speaks a more specific and "realistic" female subjectivity than we have heard before. Filtered through the alembic of Jason's obsessive ("Once a bitch always a bitch") phallic authority, her voice speaks the tragic results of the cultural objectification of real people and the disastrous effects of a system of barter which makes women commodities. And so her tone is becoming pleading and weak; and her ability to overpower, or even to negotiate, the male consciousness she finds herself entrapped by is sadly diminished. The iron claws of Jason's mind and talk clamp down upon her creativity and vocality so that, although she is depicted more realistically as a "real" human subject, she is at the same time stripped of her essence as a *female* subject—that desire to *give,* to spend herself. She is thrust (we seem now to be "saying" her in the passive voice) into Jason's economy, in which she herself as woman is a commodity. Because she is both a sign (a commodity) and a speaker of signs (an exchanger) she cannot negotiate in Jason's phallocentric economy. She cannot get what she wants, nor can she become the valuable commodity, a virgin, that she once was. She is therefore doubly trapped in male systems. Her voice speaks panic and sorrow. To listen is painful and terrible, for what we are hearing is the female voice of patriarchal culture speaking loss, speaking what it means to be denied subjectivity and access to one's own desire.

To understand what is happening to Caddy, and so to be able to hear her voice, we may reconsider the dual process of libidinal economy. Caddy, as I have said, is both a commodity and a dealer in commodities — a sign and a speaker of signs. Cixous defines a feminine libidinal economy as "a regime, energies, a system of spending not necessarily carved out by [phallocentric] culture" ("Castration" 53). Conversing with Lyotard's *économie libidinal,* she finds an economy said to be masculine as "centralized, short, reappropriating, cutting, an alternation of attraction-repulsion" and an economy said to be feminine as "continuous, over-abundant, overflowing" (Conley 98). These economies are, Conley tells us, "found in varying degrees in *both* men and women." Yet, as Quentin can surely attest, an economy said to be feminine may more often be found in women because of cultural narratives written for both men and women. Therefore, when women give excessively, they both fulfill cultural expectation and subvert the phallocentric codes of give and take. This describes the Caddy of Jason's text. Her voice speaks into the void of his economy, spending itself excessively and thus doing exactly what he hopes she will — yet at the same time speaking an ideological stance which questions and subverts Jason's economy and the cultural text it supports.

To further complicate matters, Caddy herself is a commodity in Jason's economy, albeit one without much value. What he remembers, though, and what he cannot forgive her for spending is her *past* value as a virgin, that which was negotiated to Herbert Head but was found worthless. For, as Irigaray reminds us, "woman is traditionally a use-value for man, an exchange value among men; in other words, a commodity" (*This Sex* 31). In her essay "Women on the Market," a feminist reading of Marx, Irigaray suggests that "women-as-commodities" are valuable because of either their usefulness or their exchange value. A patriarchal order is made possible, she says, through the exchange of women. In such a society (certainly in Caddy's) the mother commands use value (she is valuable for her ability to reproduce), the prostitute is good for usage and exchange, and the virgin constitutes *"pure exchange value"* (she is valuable for what she signifies) (*This Sex* 184–86). This is what Jason cannot forgive Caddy—the squandering of the pure exchange value assigned her; for, as Irigaray points out, "once deflowered, woman is relegated to the status of use value, to her entrapment in private property; she is removed from the exchange among men" (*This Sex* 186). Quentin's father acknowledges the phallic authority of this economy when he tells Quentin that virginity is in reality not important except for what it signifies to men. So if we think of Caddy as operating in a phallic economy in which her exchange value is low and her use value next to nothing (she may still retain a bit of both if she is indeed a prostitute, though we do not know that she is), we can understand Jason's power over her—particularly since she is also still operating in what Cixous calls "an economy said to be feminine," one which does not observe checks and balances but spends excessively as desire drawing upon itself for its own production.

Within Jason's inscriptions of economic power we hear Caddy asking questions about money. Where is it going? Is Quentin allowed to use it? What would he do for Quentin if she sent more? Can she buy a glimpse of her daughter? Here we have Caddy's only letter, her inscription of maternal anxiety: Did her letter arrive? Is Quentin sick? Let her know at once (*SF* 236). It is as if she is writing into a void. Jason, as he tells us, "never [keeps] a scrap of paper bearing a woman's hand" (*SF* 240). He destroys women and women's writing. In her bargaining with Jason, she gives too much too soon. She is careless, displaying a handful of money as she bargains for the chance to see her child; and he immediately asks that she double her first offer. Even less wisely, she gives him the one hundred dollars *before* seeing the baby, certainly a serious mistake in the economy in which she is negotiating.

Even while we think that all is lost, still we can hear Caddy's voice in Benjy's bellowing, the positive signal that she has again played creatively within the phallocentric text and overwritten it with a text of her own. She has managed to see her daughter. Jason does not give Caddy's voice much quarter, though. She speaks either to curse him ("'Damn you,' she says, 'Damn you.'") or to bargain with him to elicit a promise that he will take care of Quentin: "Be kind to her. Little things that I cant, they wont let . . . But you wont" (*SF* 256, 258). The helplessness of her position descends upon her when she offers him a thousand dollars for Quentin and then realizes that she cannot care for her in the (undetermined) circumstances she is in. He speaks to her out of an economy which places only use value upon motherhood when he says, "I run more risk than you do, because you haven't got anything at stake" (*SF* 260). At this point we should listen carefully, for this Caddy trapped within Jason's repressive text becomes the hysteric who, as Clément shows us, is herself "symbolic disorder" ("The Guilty One," in Cixous and Clément 8). Her upper lip is jerking. She shakes, laughs wildly, and stutters, causing even the cool Jason some alarm:

> "No," she says, then she begun to laugh and to try to hold it back all at the same time. "No. I have nothing at stake," she says, making that noise, putting her hands to her mouth, "Nuh-nuh-nothing," she says.
> "Here," I says, "Stop that!"
> "I'm tr-trying to," she says, holding her hands over her mouth. "Oh God, oh God." (*SF* 260–61)

He has entrapped her. When she asks him to see that her daughter "has things like other girls" if she will send money for them, he displays that power by saying, "As long as you behave and do like I tell you" (261).

Yet, like the hysteric who, as feminist scholars are beginning to make us see, "is the nuclear example of women's power to protest," Caddy still speaks "a force capable of demolishing" the phallic economy (Cixous, "Exchange," in Cixous and Clément 154). This is why Jason is still so fearful of her, resents her so profoundly, and pays such close attention to her lack of control, her twitching and stammers. For this is Caddy's voice, and it speaks the same message Cixous says Freud's Dora spoke, the disruption of male structures which seek to silence and control it:

> Yes, the hysteric, with her way of questioning others (because if she succeeds in bringing down the men who surround her, it is by questioning them, by ceaselessly reflecting to them the image that truly castrates them, to the extent that the power they have wished to impose is an illegitimate power of rape and violence). —The hysteric is, to my eyes, the typical woman in all her force. (Cixous, "Exchange," in Cixous and Clément 154)

The female hysteric, however, as Cixous reminds us, may become a "complete victim" if her hysteria becomes so intense that "she herself is the place where everything is turned back against her; she is paralyzed by it, physically or otherwise, and thus loses her impact" (155). Caddy does not lose her negotiations with Jason because of hysterical symptoms, but she does in the end become "the place where everything is turned back against her." Jason has created for himself a bulwark of economic power which simply absorbs her spending. She is, as Faulkner tells us, lost and doomed.

Still her voice speaks disruption within the greater (feminine) economy of Faulkner's text. It is a voice to which feminist readers are particularly attuned, for it is the voice of the female subject struggling within a cultural text which seeks her silencing. It has been said that Caddy fades into oblivion at this point in the text. I believe that she does not, that her voice is that of woman squeezed by an economy which denies her subjectivity: she speaks out of a tight place and therefore stammers and pleads and cries — but she is never truly silent within the bisexual space of *The Sound and the Fury,* that place of difference which undermines the cultural text of its origins.

IV

"Caddy! Beller now. Caddy! Caddy! Caddy!"

Like Benjy, we are taunted by the sound of Caddy's name and the apparent absence of her voice. How do we hear Caddy as she fades from our vision in "the moving wall of grey light," into such a yawning chasm of lostness that she seems actually to "disintegrate into minute and venomous particles, like dust . . ."? (*SF* 330) Neither Dilsey who endures, nor Quentin who does not, can "say" the Caddy whose own multiple voice is the difference that female subjectivity and the inscription of woman create within Faulkner's text. Yet, as Matthews so persuasively reminds us, *The Sound and the Fury* is about the intimate and mysterious relation between loss and articulation (65). If we extended this relation into the realm of the constitutive to say that loss articulates itself, that it speaks its own difference, might we then "hear" Caddy *through* that "grey light" of our own loss of her? Might her voice have moved from the space within her brothers' minds and words to another more nebulous space *between* literary text and feminist reader? Might her language be the discursiveness of that bisexual space? For I can still hear Caddy Compson. She is the voice of alterity to the long list of failed men of Faulkner's Appendix. I hear her in the courage of Melissa Meek, "the mousesized mousecolored spinster" who disrupts Jason's thriving phallic economy by bursting into his jail-like domain—"a railed enclosure cluttered with shelves and pigeonholes bearing spiked dust-and-lint-gathering gin receipts and ledgers and cottonsamples" (*SF* 414)—and who, "trembling and aghast at her own temerity," decenters that economy by forcing him to remember the woman whose life he negotiated as loss to attain it. In this space *between* text and reader that we may see the Appendix as perhaps constituting, Caddy still may be heard as the disruptive feminine voice which seeks to give and save and love, and which thus shatters the sound barrier of the male text. Like those who write and speak the rhythms of the feminine, "She is not able to return to herself, never settling down, pouring out, going everywhere to the other. She does not flee extremes; she is not the being-of-the-end (the goal), but she is how-far-being-reaches" (Cixous, "Sorties" 87).

Cixous points to the rarity of men who are "able to venture onto the brink where writing, freed from law, unencumbered by moderation, exceeds phallic authority, and where the subjectivity inscribing its effects becomes feminine." She speaks of the feminine in connection with a willingness to keep alive "the other" ("Sorties" 86) and goes on to say, "Other-Love is writing's first name" (99). When we think of Faulkner and Caddy and the complexity of their relationship, we may find it helpful to think past his often-quoted statements about her to his emphasis upon the expansiveness of his text: how it "seemed to explode on the paper" ("Introduction to *The Sound and the Fury*," in

Bleikasten, *William Faulkner's "The Sound and the Fury"* 12), how it was never "enough" (Faulkner, *Lion in the Garden* 222), how he could not control it in the way he controlled and made other books, how he wanted and made more and more of it. We are then of course reminded of Irigaray's description of the feminine libidinal economy, which is never "*simply one*," which becomes "a sort of expanding universe to which no limits could be fixed" (*This Sex* 31). Or Cixous's definition of "a feminine textual body" as "always endless, without ending: there's no closure, it doesn't stop. . . . a feminine text goes on and on and at a certain moment the volume comes to an end but the writing continues and for the reader this means being thrust into the void." Such a text, Cixous says, "isn't knowable and is therefore very disturbing" ("Castration or Decapitation?" 53). Whatever else *The Sound and the Fury* may be and do, surely it leaves us in the space of difference, leaves us in motion, with the force of our own attempts to read revolving with the pull of its force. As a feminist reader, I am left in the bisexual space created both by the relationship between Caddy Compson's voice and Faulkner's text and by that between his text and my reading of it. Within the (non)position such a space allows, I speak with Caddy and I hear her voice.

What does this textual synergy say about Faulkner and narrative? What we are seeking in our conversations with Faulkner's books is, as I have said, a new sense of them as processes of spending, of an unending productivity that we experience in motion—as *writing*. When we permit ourselves to hear Caddy's voice—*woman's* voice—as it creates the bisexual space within this text, we allow ourselves to enter that opening in the text that Faulkner disappears into, but leaves the female character to guide us toward. What we experience inside that opening is an "in-between" which allows the creative play of meaning and the velocity that derives from the tension created by such play, a velocity felt even at the contours of the text. *The Sound and the Fury* differs from itself within this bisexual space. It subverts its own story, and it transports us into the space where stories come from.

3 *The Silencing of Rosa Coldfield*

... the question underlying madness *writes,* and writes itself. And if we are unable to locate it, read it, except where it already has escaped, where it has moved — moved *us — away —* it is not because the question relative to madness does not question, but because it questions *somewhere else*: somewhere at that point of silence where it is no longer we who speak, but where, in our absence, we are *spoken.*

Shoshana Felman, *Writing and Madness*

You see, I was that sun, or thought I was who did believe there was that spark, that crumb in madness which is divine, though madness know no word itself for terror or for pity.

Rosa Coldfield, *Absalom, Absalom!*

We cannot say madness: madness instead says us. For to interrogate madness — to ask it what it is — is to affirm reason, and thereby to defer "the question underlying madness" in the very process of articulating it (Felman, *Writing and Madness* 55). Rosa Coldfield shows us just how slippery that very question is — and how dangerous — particularly for the woman whose narrative desire to speak the madness of patriarchy — to say what it *is* — may lead her to *become the spoken,* "the place where everything is turned back against her" (Cixous, "Exchange," in Cixous and Clément 154). In short, to become mad. On the other hand, as Shoshana Felman points out, "madness," in its very inexplicability, makes literature what it is, "by virtue of the dynamic *resistance to interpretation* in the literary thing" (*Writing and Madness* 254). In our conversations with *Absalom, Absalom!* it may be helpful to keep the inexplicable nature of madness alive, to let it go in all directions at once.

For whether the "mad" text is literary or cultural, we converse with its madness, it seems to me, by trying to read and write its questions, its erratic oscillations, its gaps and spaces which deploy those workings of narrative which resist interpretation. In this regard, what we may find most mysterious and provocative about *Absalom, Absalom!* is the way it produces itself out of "the question underlying madness"—how it allows, even insists upon, the free flow of its own text's madness and so generates its poetics out of madness's resistance to interpretation. This is a tricky trick, what Derrida would call a "meaning-to-say-nothing" ("Implications" 13); for such a text must be always already deconstructing itself every inch of the way through. Its meaning depends on its not meaning. For its madness is a silence which floats away whenever language moves to say it.

And so, although we may breathe a sign of relief at hearing Rosa Coldfield's voice in a way we cannot hear Caddy Compson's (It rises, breathing its italic breath. Up off page after page it comes at us. It won't shut up.), we also may find that voice disappearing in strange ways when we least expect it to fade. For that moment when we begin to hear it most distinctly may also be that moment when we, like Quentin, move to silence it ourselves—when we cease to listen without even being aware that we are doing so. And, like Quentin, we have our reasons, albeit quite different ones. Feminist readers may have much to fear from Rosa Coldfield's narrative desire to say the madness of her culture, for what happens in *Absalom* is that Rosa disappears into the text of madness which she herself creates and which generates the force of the narrative. The bisexual space of the narrative is thus shaped by the struggle between the male desire (Quentin's, Mr. Compson's, Shreve's) to make Rosa disappear (or at least to make her shut up) and *her* narrative desire to speak madness, to say the feminine difference within a masculinist culture, to tell a story of her own.

Rosa thus places us (and Quentin) at the brink of the unrepresentable—a "madness" which is both terrifying and seductive—and always unknowable. What may be frightening to feminist readers, though, is that in the end, our Rosa is constituted, objectified, by Quentin's male imagination. She is finally constructed as an object of man's desire to silence the feminine. Held struggling between two men, still trying to enter the Father's House,[1] this is the Rosa who silently foams at the mouth, the Rosa whom cultural madness inscribes itself upon, a living text which is at once everywhere and nowhere. What we must take into account, then, in reading Rosa's mad text is that we are reading *both* woman's subversive power to speak the madness of patriarchal culture (we remember Caddy in this regard) and the *direst consequence* of female power and female desire, what we all fear: the annihilation of the female subject. In this sense, as Rosa's woman's text creates madness, its desire to speak what cannot be spoken leads it to *become* what cannot be spoken, and so to become the site of its own erasure.

If this is true, then *Absalom, Absalom!* is both a greater and darker book than we have thought. Teresa de Lauretis writes that the specificity of a feminist theory must be sought in the articulation of female subjectivity, "in that political, theoretical, self-analyzing practice by which the relations of the subject in social reality can be rearticulated from the historical experience of women" (*Alice Doesn't* 186). Yet Rosa tells us the price of such articulation. What she says is that "trying to say" can make us language's site — that we, as female subjects in history, may be not only inscribed but also objectified by our own narrative desire to speak a cultural text of sexist and racist repression. Female creativity thus may serve ironically to dismantle female subjectivity.

This is the theoretical problem which faces those readers who listen to Addie Bundren as she rethinks subjectivity in terms of female space. Through her own creative deconstruction of the Father's Word, of a language which cannot speak to her or for her, she herself becomes an alternate space that cuts across the teleologies of time and measurable space. Yet, she articulates her "I" from inside a coffin as her dead body is being grotesquely inscribed by "real" time. Similarly, part of Temple Drake's tragedy in *Sanctuary* may be that in trying to say her sexuality as a female adolescent (and so as a commodity) in a masculine sexual economy, she becomes *the said* — the bloody inscription on the phallic corn cob, the whore in the bed, the Father's daughter. For these female characters, the articulation of feminine desire inside patriarchal order entraps them in a dark bisexual space in which the feminine becomes inscribed by what it is in the process of creating. Women's own creativity, their beautiful shattering force which generates Faulkner's texts by pointing toward the unrepresentable (surely this is the function of Rosa, Addie, Temple, Caddy), finally entombs them in a vault of silence.

Their insistence upon subjectivity kills them off as subjects. Our questions of *Absalom* — again I request permission to ask questions I am not sure I can answer — must be obvious, then: is Faulkner struggling against the feminine of his own creative consciousness? Is he seeking to "master" his own text by silencing the woman in it? Or may we see the bisexuality of the text as intimately related to what is resistant to interpretation in its textuality? to its madness?

Felman writes that certain texts actually *enact* madness; that is, they "enact the *encounter* between 'speaking about madness' and the 'madness that speaks.'" If these texts are not conscious of their own madness, it is because they have themselves become mad (*Writing and Madness* 252). I would take this point further in thinking about Rosa Coldfield: the madness of her text, the text of her madness. What we have here is woman trying to speak, and coming to constitute, the text of masculinist madness. (Need I argue that the Old South was a masculinist culture, and hence Sutpen its natural outcome?) Rosa's mad text is not unique — think of the sisterhood of Medea, Ophelia, Blanche DuBois — all male-created female subjects whose desire to say masculinist culture's mad resistance to interpretation leads them to become "mad." And so Rosa's narrative desire, her need to speak not only her own sexuality in a culture which denies it but also the madness of that denial, fuels *Absalom* even as it devours her. Whatever else Rosa says, then, she tells us the same thing that Dora and her sister hysterics said with the texts their bodies enacted: "the impossibility of the position of the woman within a discourse that would prefer to suppress the question of desire . . ." (Rose, "Dora" 146).

At the same time, though, Rosa's desire to play creatively with the question of madness allows her to oscillate freely between the positions of subject and object — the movement Spivak has pointed out as the peculiar (non)position of woman ("Love Me" 24). Rosa enacts, then, what Gallop shows us in her reading of Lacan — an alternative to seeking mastery over a text (in this case the cultural text of madness), a way of signifying "in a symbolic system that we do not command, that, rather, commands us" (20). And this is, as we know, not only the terror of *Absalom*, but its pleasure, its *différance*, its very life. In this oscillation lies the freedom which allows us to discard the position of the reader presumed to know, which permits us to improvise and mediate — to play.

And yet . . . even Derrida recognizes the fearsomeness of relinquishing the dream of "full presence: the reassuring foundation, the origin and the end of play." Play, he reminds us, must always disrupt presence. Interestingly, in thinking of the relationship between play and history, Derrida ends his pivotal essay "Structure, Sign, and Play in the Discourse of the Human Sciences" with what can only be described as a terrifying but fascinating image—a woman (invisible) giving birth to a monstrous child. The "common ground" between the insistence upon presence and the necessity of play is

> a kind of question, let us still call it historical, whose *conception, formation, gestation,* and *labor* we are only catching a glimpse of today. I employ these words, I admit, with a glance toward the operations of childbearing—but also with a glance toward those who, in a society from which I do not exclude myself, turn their eyes away when faced by the as yet unnamable which is proclaiming itself and which can do so, as is necessary whenever a birth is in the offing, only under the species of the nonspecies, in the formless, mute, infant, and terrifying form of monstrosity. (*Writing and Difference* 292–93)

The story which Rosa gives birth to is much like this formless form of monstrosity; for although Rosa insists upon presence, her story differs from itself and defers itself so that it (and she) cannot reach full presence: by her very culpability in and enactment of the cultural madness she attempts to speak, she becomes what Johnson calls "the difference within" the text, and hence its generator. Like Caddy, she is both the sign and its producer. She *cannot not* both be and convey its arbitrariness. In this sense she, like Caddy, plays within the spaces, the gaps and ruptures, of language by becoming their site.

Because she both constructs and becomes the text's difference—that which, as Johnson shows us, makes it "speak against itself" (in speaking its text of madness and the madness of its text)—Rosa, like her sisters the hysterics and like Caddy, reflects back to the males around her (to their terror and fascination) the very image of their loss of control, *their* decentered subjectivity, *their* castration. She becomes the feminine space over which the narrative, or rather *their* narrative, their "master narrative," has lost control. As Jardine and Kristeva would say, she becomes the new space that objectifies man through language — the uncanny presence of his lack of mastery. Much of the narrative's force, in fact, derives from Mr. Compson's, Shreve's, even Quentin's efforts to master Rosa's text by distancing and diminishing her as a subject. These efforts culminate in Quentin's final creation of the speechless mad old woman "struggling with silent and bitter fury, clawing and scratching and biting" at the deputy sheriff and driver as they drag her out of the burning house (*AA* 300).

As feminist psychoanalytic theorists have pointed out, the hysteric has likewise been distanced and objectified throughout the history of psychoanalysis, although her "madness" wrote much of its theoretical text. For example, André Brouillet's well-known 1887 painting, *A Clinical Lecture at the Salpetriere,* depicts Jean-Martin Charcot and Blanche Wittman demonstrating hysteria to the intense gaze of an all-male audience. The top of Wittman's dress has fallen to her waist, she has fallen backward into the arms of attendants, and her eyes are closed.[2] The most striking aspect of the painting is the space which separates the audience from Wittman, the embodiment of the hysterical object. The floor space is enhanced by a broad wall panel between two windows, one serving as a backdrop for the male audience and the other for Charcot, Wittman, and attendants. How can we "read" this space?

It is the same space Nietzsche constructs, and Derrida affirms, to keep woman at a distance because her silence is tantalizing and her speech dangerous, powerful. Woman who speaks may generate the narrative of her own sexuality, her difference, her ability to engage difference, and through that engagement to raise the question of where madness lies. In constructing such a space between himself and woman speaking, Quentin attempts to silence difference. He shuts Rosa Coldfield up by placing her *somewhere else,* somewhere outside the Father's House. The question thus becomes: (how) can difference still speak?

As we think about Rosa as a female subject attempting to speak cultural madness which denies the feminine *and simultaneously* as a construction of male imagination (Quentin's, Mr. Compson's, Shreve's, Faulkner's), we find ourselves drawn back to the problem of the unanalyzability of "character." "Character" is, as Cixous says, "an effect of the unconscious" and so functions in narrative to show the divisibility of the subject, its multiplicity and fluidity rather than its wholeness ("The Character of 'Character'" 387). As we have seen in the previous chapter, when writing about Dora's (the hysteric's) power to reflect to men the image of castration (their own), Cixous writes also about the power of female desire embodied in the hysteric: "A desire that is also, often, love—for love. The source of Dora's strength is, in spite of everything, her desire" ("Exchange," in Cixous and Clément 154). We may go further to think of the hysteric (Rosa) as the embodiment of the human subject's divisibility. Her body, as we shall see, becomes the site of divisibility. Rosa both speaks and is spoken. She is both presence and absence, subject and object. She creates the fluctuation between oppositions that seems powerfully connected to the rhythm of narrative itself. Felman has said that madness, like literature, constitutes a rhythm— "unpredictable, incalculable, unsayable"—between "excessive fullness and excessive emptiness of meaning" (*Writing and Madness* 254). I wish to read *Absalom, Absalom!*, and Rosa, in fluctuation with this rhythm, for what we are after here is a feeling for the madness of this text, a madness that *is* Rosa's to say and to be, and ours as well perhaps. We are proceeding to nudge at those very thin, very delicate membranes at the interstices of deconstruction, psychoanalysis, and feminism. And we are asking the questions which make such divisions dissolve before our eyes. The space we create is unrepresentable. And so, in a discomfiting and tantalizing way, *Absalom* turns back upon us. It reads us.

Barbara Johnson has spoken to the interesting results accrued when theory doesn't fit its target—when literature asks theory questions it cannot answer: "For literature stages the modes of its own misreading, making visible the literarity of the heart of theory and rendering the effects of its project of understanding unpredictable" (*Critical Difference* xii). Faulkner, and Rosa—the Rosa who is the textual process of narrative fluidity and play, hence the feminine force of the text, as well as the female character Rosa whose desire to speak madness generates that process—do exactly that. The space between them constitutes what Jardine sees as the interstice between "*woman as process* and *woman as sexual identity*" (41). As we have seen, Jardine finds the inscription of woman in philosophical discourse to be that which is unrepresentable, unstructured, hidden, outside systemization—that which challenges Western systems of thought. Yet, as she herself points out, the need is for a feminist interrogation to operate both rhetorically and ideologically, "first, metonymically in discourse *about* women; and second, metaphorically in discourse *by, through, as* woman" (36). What feminist theory must grapple with, then, is the recognition that "the status of women is determined not only at social and political levels, but *by the very logical processes through which meaning is produced*" (44) (my emphasis). This is, it seems to me, where we enter the generativity of the bisexual space between male text and feminist reader and where we may discover new loci for conversations among various discourses of modernity and hear what they say about, and to, and through, woman.

If we turn back to Rosa's text of madness for illustration, we may find it to be a feminist discourse which questions and challenges patriarchy. At the same time, however, it deconstructs the very structures of its own feminist discourse; its creative madness avoids the strictures of ideology altogether as Rosa, in telling her story, makes (herself) the madness of the text—its jars and ruptures, its improvisations, its difference and deferral, its *différance*—as her language creates and erases the "central I-am" over and over and over again as it plays within the space between subject and object. *At the same time,* or at least at certain points, Rosa also erects her own phallocentric boundaries and so participates in the cultural madness she speaks. As she sits "bolt upright," legs dangling from the too-tall chair, "talking in that grim haggard amazed voice" (*AA* 3), Miss Rosa's message is both terrifying and tantalizing. For what she says, querulously, insistently, provocatively, is that madness is contagious. For the feminist reader, then, the question becomes if, as McLeod says, woman "unhinges" culture's texts, how, in the process, does she prevent herself from becoming "unhinged"? How can she interpret herself as a subject? Is it necessary to rethink our notions of subjectivity in order to even approach the question?

In her essay "Arachnologies: The Woman, the Text, and the Critic," Nancy K. Miller asks questions of women's writing which may be applied to Rosa's text of madness. The theoretical question is, as Miller sees it, how do we approach the "text maker" as subject when "the productive agency of the subject is self-consciously erased by a model of text production which acts to foreclose the question of identity itself"? (271) This question operates on various levels in *Absalom.* Foucault and Barthes have shown us how the author dissolves into the text. We have spoken of how Caddy in *The Sound and the Fury* becomes the feminine space which marks Faulkner's place of disappearance. In *Absalom*, though, the situation is more complex. Faulkner creates the text which is Rosa and so, Barthes would say, "unmakes himself, like a spider dissolving in the constructive secretions of [her] web" (*Pleasure of the Text* 64). Rosa, then, is the textuality of Faulkner's text even as she weaves her own narrative web and even as the narrative she generates unmakes her. Yet, in Quentin's narrative imagination, she finally becomes the text of madness she insisted upon trying to speak. It says her. Held in patriarchal arms, conceived in patriarchal imagination, foaming silently in front of the Father's House, she becomes the feminine space that male narrative writes itself upon.

Where does this leave the feminist reader who is thinking of women as social, political subjects? Indeed, where does this leave the feminine libidinal economy? In Rosa's twitchings we see only a horrible parody of *jouissance*. At this point our questions must be: can we continue to trust Faulkner in these conversations? Does Faulkner want Rosa silenced, or is he writing her silence as the hysterical symptom of the Old South's patriarchal narrative of mastery? Like Rosa herself, we cannot know until it is perhaps too late. Yet we also may not wish to stop ourselves; for, as Rosa-Faulkner's mad text writes itself for us and upon us, we may find that, like Quentin, we have been both seduced and terrorized by it. We may turn away to the controlling mechanism of the objective stance only if we deny madness—and so deny what is most fully our own as feminist readers of cultural madness. To experience the madness of Rosa's text we must allow ourselves to be inscribed by it. We must acknowledge our complicity in its otherness.

Psychoanalysis may help us feel our way through these dark spaces, but not in a way we might expect. For we must force ourselves to continue seeing from the vulnerable perspective of the analysand if we are to get anywhere. If we take the position of the Father, the subject presumed to know, we will find ourselves constructing a phallocentric discourse which tells only one story, hence denying madness of any sort—Rosa's or our own. We then deny the productivity of the text by denying the textuality of madness as a deconstructive discourse which must go all ways at once, which must, as Felman says, fluctuate between fullness and emptiness and realize itself as fluctuation. I would begin by continuing to trust Faulkner, and so to read Rosa and *Absalom, Absalom!* (and Faulkner and myself) as mad texts whose "active incompletion of a meaning . . . ceaselessly transforms itself, offers itself but to be misunderstood, misapprehended." The question now becomes how to read when "the question underlying madness *writes*, and writes itself." Upon Rosa? Upon us?

II   *Reading Hysterically*

> In the end, the woman pushed to hysteria is the woman who disturbs and is nothing but disturbance.
>
> Hélène Cixous, "Castration or Decapitation?"

> As hysteria produces symptoms, so symptoms produce stories.
>
> Mary Jacobus, *Reading Woman*

Rosa Coldfield is more disturbing than her story because she ends up becoming her story. This is not surprising if we converse with Rosa's story as the repressed hysterical (to say both is redundant) narrative of patriarchy, as the feminine *symptom* of what patriarchy has silenced in order to construct its systems. In rereading Freud's analysis of Dora, Lacan observes in hysteria a lower threshold and a more transparent screen between the unconscious and the conscious (*Feminine Sexuality* 73). This lowering of the threshold between the conscious and the unconscious, and its association with woman, links Rosa's text to what we may call the hysterical text, the narrative of repressed desire which converses in the space between the conscious and the unconscious and thus, as we have seen with *The Sound and the Fury,* exists between and beyond the symbolic order of language.[3] The hysterical text is thereby the figuration of all that the symbolic order must repress in order to speak. Rosa Coldfield's female desire, her "summer of wistaria," and her mad text which engages the space between consciousness and unconsciousness are precisely what Thomas Sutpen must deny in order to maintain the "innocence" that privileges rationality by repressing desire. Like the hysteric, who always has been associated primarily with woman,[4] Rosa marks the uncanny return of repressed desire. And this desire, figured as feminine, fuels the madness of this narrative, and becomes that about it which is resistant to interpretation, which goes in all directions at once, which makes everything more, and less, than it seems.

As both its mad author and author of its madness, Rosa must dissolve into her woman's text to produce that text. This is both a terrifying and exhilarating process. We may view it as both repressive and generative. We do not know what to think about it. Within a psychoanalytic schema, Mitchell associates the castration complex with the phenomenon of "splitting," which she says evokes in the patient a feeling of intense horror, "a horror that is about absence but which can become filled with phantasmagoria." This description of "splitting" seems to describe the silencing of Rosa Coldfield by the male discourse of this book: "In splitting, the subjectivity of the subject disappears. The horror is about the loss of oneself into one's own unconscious—into the gap" (*Women* 307). We are reminded of the narrator of Charlotte Perkins Gilman's "The Yellow Wallpaper," who becomes the woman in the wallpaper, who moves into the mad text and inscribes herself *as* it. In our last glimpse of Rosa through Quentin's eyes, we see this speechless "becoming" of the text of all that Sutpen's Hundred has repressed: its madness, its grotesqueness, its uncanniness, its castration. We see Rosa Coldfield silenced.

As we know, the hysterics of psychoanalytic literature (I am thinking especially of the famous "Dora") wrote madness on their own bodies. Their symptoms (for example, Dora's cough) became their discourse; hence they themselves became resistant to interpretation. *They* became the hysterical text. Freud theorized the hysteric, as Flieger points out, as a "blocked" speaker who either misused or refused to use language, whose hysterical symptom was the obstruction of her own discourse (961), and who, I would add, thereby rendered herself unanalyzable. Until she is finally shut up at the end of the book, Rosa is anything but silent. Certainly, to the males who have to listen, Rosa talks too much.[5] But here is the rub. What Rosa's talking does is to write the hysterical symptom upon us. And by "us" I mean those feminist readers who enter the bisexual space of this narrative, and enter it as gendered subjects who figure *upon themselves* Rosa's hysterical text and allow her to write *her body as symptom* upon us *without* retreating to the position of interpreter, without marking off that space in the painting between analyst self and hysterical other. As Mitchell says, "If femininity is by definition hysterical, feminism is the demand *for* the right to be hysterical" (*Women* 117). For those of us who are this brave, Rosa leaves us holding the bag, and we are in it.

To read Rosa, then, is to read our own predicament as feminist readers of the tricky male text which is *Absalom, Absalom!*, which *itself* is in the predicament of reading the tricky male text of patriarchy. We may have little choice but to read Rosa's hysterical text . . . hysterically: in Mary Jacobus's words, "to reenact the hysterical processes" we are describing and so become "hysterical tellers" of the texts we read rather than "analytic listeners" (198). Such reading allows that which has been repressed in patriarchal discourse, that which bears the name of woman (Dora, Rosa), to move us from here to there and there to here, to jar and displace us from where we think we are and what we think we know. Johnson says that literature's preoccupation is with "what is not known," which itself is "often the unseen motivating force behind the very deployment of meaning" (*Critical Difference* xii). What Rosa tells us is that we do not know. And if that is an easy thing to say, it is not an easy thing to know.

Neither Freud nor Lacan knew what they did not know: that is, Dora herself. Dora's problem, according to Lacan, was basically that of accepting herself as an object of male desire. But reading Dora hysterically as gendered subjects allows us to experience her desire to say the madness of *her* culture, which denied her sexuality by making her a commodity of exchange in an economy generated by male desire and divided (uniquely in Dora's case, perhaps) into what Irigaray calls "categories of usefulness and exchange value" (*This Sex* 176). Dora's father, we will remember, allowed Herr K. access to his daughter in return for acquiescence in his affair with Herr K.'s wife. I am not interested in reading correspondences between Dora's case of hysteria and Rosa Coldfield's "madness."[6] Yet the resemblance in situations is striking. Mr. Coldfield buys Sutpen's silence with a daughter. At first Rosa watches as Ellen becomes the object of exchange; then she herself steps in to fill that role — only to discover, in Sutpen's outrageous proposal of marriage as reward for son-bearing, that she herself has become a commodity of exchange as surely as her sister had been (and, incidentally, as Judith

Sutpen was in the negotiations between father and sons). Rosa's shock—her outrage, her desire to speak the madness of a culture which makes commodities of white women as well as slaves and which encourages white fathers to sell their white daughters as easily as selling livestock—ties the southern patriarchy to sexual commerce in white females as well as black human beings, and so blurs the boundaries between racial and sexual arenas in the Sutpen saga.

As we open our own doors leading into that "dim hot airless room" where Rosa begins her hysterical narrative, we may do well to remember Felman's instruction that madness is an irreducible resistance to interpretation. We need also to keep in mind that the hysteric, Dora in particular, occupies a central place in the contemporary questioning of "the relation between interpretation and sexual difference" (Kahane 20). When Dora flees what Madelon Sprengnether calls "Freud's bias in favor of Herr K. as an unconventional though perfectly acceptable lover," Freud interprets her resistance and rejection as vengeful (66). His "Fragment of an Analysis of a Case of Hysteria" is an attempt to "read" Dora by constructing "an intelligible, consistent, and unbroken case history" (Freud 7:18). His interpretation of Dora's hysterical narrative is therefore "structured around a central irony—the attempt to complete a story and to achieve a narrative closure rendered forever impossible by Dora's deliberate rupture" (Sprengnether 67). In the end, then, Freud writes his own desires rather than Dora's, and in this sense Dora reads *him*. What she (and we) may read in the Freudian text, then, is, as Bernheimer suggests, not only Freud's resistance to Dora's feminine text, but his rejection of the feminine side of himself which he had accepted in other countertransferential situations (17). As we gather at the interface of psychoanalysis, feminism, and deconstruction to converse with Rosa's hysterical narrative, we must caution ourselves, I believe, to allow *Absalom, Absalom!* to be Dora's text rather than Freud's. And by this, I mean that if we disallow its hysteria, its resistance to interpretation—if we attempt to complete it—then we will end up like Freud, reading the wrong story: "finding" Faulkner's book only to have lost it.

To read hysterically, then, is to follow Rosa's lead in putting the feminine into discourse at the same time that we, as Jacobus would say, put "the reader [ourselves] in question" (286). Jacobus uses the process of hysteria as a trope for reading women writers. I would take her approach in another direction by suggesting that if we continue to inquire about the bisexual spaces within Faulkner's writing, spaces in which the feminine and/or the female character create their own discourses, *then* we may be able to read the "woman-in-effect" in Faulkner (in this case in Rosa Coldfield), in ways similar to those Jacobus uses with the texts of women writers. Through this tropological approach, we may come to see hysteria as linking the feminine, its writing of the body, to the deconstructive process constituting *Absalom*—its refusal to end, its gaps and ruptures, its rhythm between fullness and emptiness. At the same time hysteria may show us how woman may both speak madness and become it, and what happens when she does.

In *Reading Woman* Jacobus points to the close connections among women, hysteria, and repression—connections which are figured not only in literature but in the reading process itself. "'Femininity' and 'hysteria' name the otherness or strangeness which inhabits psychoanalytic theory (and literature) and which psychoanalysis has marginalized in order to found itself as a theoretical body of knowledge" (200). As Jacobus points out, the return of the repressed, in Freud's schema, figures itself as woman, "the castrated female body" (248). Yet hysteria, figured as woman (as it has been since its beginnings), also reflects the feminine creative freedom which comes from acknowledging one's castration and renaming castration as pleasure. If we think of Rosa as weaving her own text of madness and then disappearing into it, we may examine its uncanniness as the feminine sign of what must be repressed in a masculinist culture. Similarly, hysterical narrative (and I see *Absalom, Absalom!* as the hysterical narrative *par excellence*) exposes "the repressive assumptions" of all narrative and all theory which fails to hear its own unconscious voices.

What are the theoretical implications of the hysterical narrative's ability to subvert coherence, meaning, presence? In arguing for a Lacanian theory of narrative, Robert Con Davis valorizes "the 'symbolic father,' the agency of law"—whose power of the phallus defines the power of language and whose presence narrative yearns after ("Discourse of the Father," in *Fictional Father* 2–3). In the same volume, André Bleikasten calls *Absalom* "Faulkner's most sustained invocation of the father" ("Fathers in Faulkner" 143). Similarly, John Irwin's psychoanalytic study of *The Sound and the Fury* and *Absalom, Absalom!* focuses much of its energy upon the son's desire for phallic power as embodied in the father, the competitiveness between father and son, and the cycle of paternal reincarnation which prohibits "authority through originality" (113–55). Reading hysterically, I find *Absalom, Absalom!* to be Faulkner's most sustained *re*vocation of the Father and his mastery. In this regard, my focus is more closely allied to Matthews' assessment that "*Absalom* challenges more traditional views of what we might call the paternal phallic authority of a text's meaning" (152). Rosa's hysterical narrative reveals, above all else, that the Father controls discourse only by denying its *différance,* and so is himself antithetical to the plurality that Faulkner insists upon in most of his writing, and especially in *Absalom.*[7]

Before listening to Rosa Coldfield's mad story of madness, I need to show what elements of Jacobus's theory of "hysterical reading" I am most heavily indebted to and where I perceive my reading of Rosa (and Rosa's of the cultural text) to diverge from Jacobus. Feminist readings, Jacobus argues, must not, in their efforts to prove that women are not mad or that madness is not their fault, fall into the rationalist trap of reading toward the knowable (the relations of the text to social constructs) rather than toward the unknowable (the text's strangeness), and thus fall into the dualistic trap of "translating the text . . . into a cryptograph (or pictograph) representing either women in patriarchal society or the woman as writer and reader" (233–34). By repressing what is strange, such readings, Jacobus writes, deny the unconscious, hence language itself. As Jacobus points out, the "strangeness of hysterical desire is inseparable from femininity" (199). To read the feminine in Faulkner, we must acknowledge its strangeness—what is not known about it, what it does not know—the mystery of its textuality. Our reading must become, in Jacobus's words, "the shadow-image of hysteria" (199); Rosa must become our sister, just as Dora is hers.

Like Jacobus, I will be attempting to read strangeness in several directions at once; hence my sudden forays into the text at points where I perceive the strongest disruptions, the most *trouble,* playing themselves out. In reading strangeness, I am striving to preserve it *as strangeness* rather than tame it, whip it into shapes that are congruent and harmonious. This will be a jarring exchange. There will be hysterical symptoms, uncomfortable silences, unanswered questions. There will be intertextual as well as textual conversations, racial as well as sexual questions. Similar to the hysteric who disrupts temporal order, whose "narrative exists in the time of its telling rather than the order of its events" (Jacobus 218)—certainly an apt description of *Absalom* itself—I may seem at times to have little regard for the chronology of the book, to take great liberties with its structure. For I am reading hysterically as a way of approaching the strangeness of the feminine text of madness in *Absalom* as the difference within that generates its textuality.

I diverge from Jacobus by trying to preserve that sense of strangeness *at the same time* I am reading the madness—the insanity and its "irreducible resistance to interpretation"—of a culture which devalues *woman,* and silences *women* who, like Rosa, speak as gendered subjects. I am trying to engage strangeness and madness, in all their multiple meanings, with each other without weighting one over the other. I am trying to hear them speak to each other. For I believe that Alice Jardine is right in insisting that feminist theory must open the dialogue between "woman" as configuration in Western culture and "women" as female subjects in history.

I am, at the same time, wondering what my hysterical reading will reveal about the creator of this hysterical narrative and his relationship to what I perceive to be the mad (thus the uninterpretable) feminine within himself, his own generative difference which textualizes *her* self in strange and unorganizable ways. Irwin sees Faulkner's relation to his material, the act of writing, as "a self-castration," an "act of progressive self-destruction" which results in loss—i.e., the feminine artifact (171–72). Yet, as we have seen in *The Sound and the Fury,* the feminine talks back. She speaks *both* loss *and* desire across that space in the painting which so comfortably separates spectator from hysterical action; she insists upon her own female self as the *subject* of madness. Rosa Coldfield is a woman, a hysterical woman; and the space that separates her from us, the hysteric from her readers, is dissolving even as we converse. As it does, we may begin to realize the implications of Jacobus's reminder that "reading itself can be 'read' as a diacritical rather than specular process—one that puts the reader, as well as reading itself, in question" (286).

III   *Rosa in the Father's House*

You do it, you do it, and you do it; then you become it.
> Linda Lovelace, *Ordeal*

It should be clear by now that I am conversing with Rosa Coldfield not only as the decentered character split between conscious and unconscious drives, and so as a prototype of us all, female and male, but as a *gendered* subject who speaks that split doubly—from a cultural as well as an individual perspective. I am searching for *that* Rosa inside a dark bisexual space between the madness of the phallic order, and its transference to the woman who must speak it and who, in the process of speaking ("doing it"), finds herself constituted as the otherness it imposes upon her. It may seem less outrageous than one might think to compare Rosa Coldfield to Linda Lovelace, for both enact cultural madness. Rosa says it, and says it, and says it; then she, like Linda, becomes it—"it" being, in both cases, a symbolic system of cultural thought which places women in discomfiting poses within its structures and then freezes them with the gazing eye. Within these male constructions, women remain frozen in a system of exchange which values them either for their sexual functions (in Linda Lovelace's case) or their procreative possibilities (in Rosa's). (We may remember that Caddy was originally valued and then devalued in both categories.) Woman thus, as Lea Melandri says, "enters history having already lost concreteness and singularity: she is the economic machine that reproduces the human species, and she is the Mother, an equivalent more universal than money, the most abstract measure ever invented by patriarchal ideology" (de Lauretis, *Alice Doesn't* 30).[8] And so, whether within the real world of hardcore porn or the historical world of the Old South, women, as Teresa de Lauretis points out in her discussion of Claude Lévi-Strauss,

are doubly negated as subjects: first, because they are defined as vehicles of men's communication—signs of their language, carriers of their children; second, because women's sexuality is reduced to the 'natural' function of childbearing, somewhere in between the fertility of nature and the productivity of a machine. *Desire, like symbolization, is a property of men.* . . . (my emphasis) (*Alice Doesn't* 20)

Like Caddy, though with a different "woman's tongue," Rosa insists upon the possibility of female desire and female symbolization within what Cixous has called "the realm of the proper"; that is, within a patriarchal culture which turns upon the male fear of deprivation of power ("Castration or Decapitation?" 50). Sutpen's actions throughout the book are obviously motivated by such a fear, set in motion by his rejection at the front door of the plantation. Sutpen's "innocence" is indeed based upon the economy of "the realm of the proper," which is founded on a system of returns through which power is given away only upon the condition that it be returned (Cixous 50). Sutpen's is a precise system of measures, much, as we are told through three levels of male Compson discourse, like the ingredients of a cake or pie: what you put in, you get out. This is an economy ruled by "the movement of reappropriation," contradictory, as we have seen in our conversations with Caddy Compson, to "the possibility of a giving that doesn't take away, but *gives.*" *At the same time,* though, Rosa tells of her own complicity in "the realm of the proper." Even though her outpourings may be perceived, as they are by Mr. Compson, as a "breathing indictment . . . of the entire male principle" (*AA* 46), she nonetheless speaks the seductive power of that principle. In this way, Rosa, like Cixous's hysteric, "is given images that don't belong to her, and she forces herself, as we've all done, to resemble them" ("Castration or Decapitation?" 47).

And so, in beginning to converse with Rosa, I envision her as being, as she is literally, *inside* (later I will envision her *outside*) what Mr. Compson calls the "dim grim tight little house" of the Father, in the sense that she is implicated in "the realm of the proper," whether by entrapment or seduction, or something other than either or both. Yet she is also the strangeness within "the house"—the patriarchal structuration of man's systems. In this sense, she, like Cixous's prototypical hysteric, "plays the father . . . turns herself into him, [and] unmakes him at the same time" ("Castration or Decapitation?" 47). This is, of course, woman's deconstructive play both producing and, at the same time, dismantling man. It is woman's *becoming* man in order to "unmake" him—a tricky business indeed. Moreover, this is woman *within the male text* producing its hysterical narrative, with its contradictions, gaps, ruptures, discontinuities, centerlessness, *within* the structure (stricture?) of the Father's House — the madwoman in the . . . office.[9]

. . . they sat in what Miss Coldfield still called the office because her father had called it that. . . .

Decades after his death Goodhue Coldfield retains the power of the Word. It is he who has named the "dim hot airless room" which still encases his daughter as an old woman, within which she speaks the madness of the Father's House.[10] There is indeed "something" (uncanny) in this tomblike house, and it is Rosa herself. Like a corpse in the "black which did not even rustle," she is what it has repressed in order to erect its symbolic order. In his essay on the uncanny, Freud shows just how interrelated *heimlich* and *unheimlich* are: *Heimlich* means both *familiar* (*homelike*) and *concealed,* while *unheimlich,* seemingly its opposite, actually means *concealed* also. Freud's point is that the uncanny resides very close to home; it is, in fact, "nothing new or alien, but something which is familiar and old-established in the mind and which has become alienated from it only through the process of repression" (17:241). We may think, then, of the relationship of the uncanny to the conscious mind in the same way we would think of woman's relationship to masculinist culture: she is both familiar and hidden to it. She is what is repressed in order for it to become what it is. She is its vision of its own castration. More radically, sometimes she renames castration as pleasure.

Contained within her own father's house, her old woman's body hysterically rigid, Miss Rosa, as Quentin first sees her, is the image of castration and impotence. To the male gaze, which attempts to' objectify and distance her in various ways throughout the book, Rosa's "female old flesh long embattled in virginity" configures lack. From "the too tall chair in which she resembled a crucified child," she embodies the frontal view of phallic absence, "the faint triangle of lace at wrists and throat" forming a repetitive pattern of blankness, of female genitalia—those uncanny sites (sights) of male fear, what Freud calls the *"unheimlich* place" which is ironically familiar in that it "is the entrance to the former *Heim* [home] of all human beings, to the place where each one of us lived once upon a time and in the beginning. . . . In this case . . . the *unheimlich* is what was once *heimisch*, familiar; the prefix *'un'* ['un-'] is the token of repression" (17:245). As the male gaze is confronted with Rosa's white triangle, which, at once, speaks man's castration and woman's infantilization, her voice gushes forth as the pouring flood of blood which we may recall from Joe Christmas's castration, "not ceasing but vanishing into and then out of the long intervals like a stream, a trickle running from patch to patch of dried sand . . ." (*AA* 4). An uncanny bisexual text of impotence is thus written across Rosa's (old) woman's body. She becomes the site of discourse between man's fear of expropriation, of castration, and woman's loss of access to her own desire. Yet Rosa's body seems also to tell how woman's loss of her sexuality actually results from man's fear, from patriarchy's movement to cover its own lack (or the possibility of lack) by appropriating that which it constructs as other: woman and woman's body. Through a cycle of anxiety and appropriation, then, patriarchy encodes and empowers itself. And so, as Rosa's "unmoving triangle of dim lace" speaks her own loss, it also conveys to Quentin the threat of male castration as that fear which fuels the economy of the "realm of the proper." In this regard, at least, Mr. Compson is more accurate than he knows when he constructs Rosa (her younger self) as "not only a living and walking reproach to her father, but a breathing indictment ubiquitous and even transferable of the entire male principle" (*AA* 46).

And yet, in this initial encounter with Rosa, which seems crowded with male presences (Quentin, the ever-present watcher and listener Mr. Compson, even Sutpen himself are all textures within this first chapter), that same woman's voice valorizes male power as well. For it is Miss Rosa who speaks Sutpen's phallic potency and the power of his symbolic authority, as surely as she makes evident his rapacity and inhumanity—as surely as her lace triangle mirrors his own castration. "Making" and "unmaking" the Father, Rosa thus reads the mad male text ambiguously; for, as she herself knows so well (and this is what her story is about), she has herself been seduced by the godlike Father whose power can "overrun suddenly the hundred square miles of tranquil and astonished earth and drag house and formal gardens violently out of the soundless Nothing and clap them down like cards upon a table . . . creating the Sutpen's Hundred, the *Be Sutpen's Hundred* like the olden-time *Be Light*" (*AA* 4). Rosa's creation of the difference within the masculine is indeed so compelling that Quentin himself is split by it. He, like Rosa, is seduced and yet repelled by the power of the phallus. Hence there are "two separate Quentins now talking to one another in the long silence of notpeople, in notlanguage," talking of the Father (Sutpen) who raped the land and begot children, as Rosa says, "*without gentleness*" (*AA* 4–5), and yet who exerted masculine privilege and power in a culture maddened by its own desire for such.

This seductive power of the Father, that which makes his madness cut a dashing figure across the red clay hills of North Mississippi much like Faulkner's own grandfather the Old Colonel, is Rosa's creation and her question. It is the question which generates the novel, which writes itself in endless repetition off this book's last page, echoed as it is in Quentin's anguished cry, "*I dont hate it! I dont hate it!*" (*AA* 303). This is "the question underlying madness" which Felman says cannot be asked, for language is not capable of asking it; and thus the question Rosa insists must *write* itself upon the body of her (Faulkner's? our?) hysterical text and yet which is itself a reading of cultural madness. The key problem for feminist readers, as I've said before, is how woman can both *be* the text and still be herself. Doesn't one cancel the other, as it seems to do for Rosa? Or can woman somehow unhinge such oppositions by oscillating between them? For what we are coming to see are the multiple and proliferating texts of "madness," which exist, like literature, in their active resistance to interpretation. Rosa's "madness," her resistance to interpretation, is mysteriously wrapped around and folded into the text of cultural madness, which she, like us, reads hysterically. (We, of course, are reading her reading.) *Absalom, Absalom!* thus becomes a shifting, fluid mass of madness, a hysterical narrative . . . yet remains, we remember, a male text which "makes" woman, who "makes" and "unmakes" man even as she herself is being "made" and "unmade." Can we even expect conversation about madness (certainly we do not expect answers) from man himself, that is, from the male text?

At this hiatus, this disconcerting pause, we find hysterical symptoms (ours) erupting. Like Dora, we cough. Like Anna O., we do not speak our accustomed language. How can the text of madness write itself within this speechless space between us and Faulkner? How, within that second bisexual space between Faulkner and Rosa? between Rosa and the madhouse of "the Father," patriarchy's lockup? The question underlying madness proliferates across the narrative landscape on which Rosa sets Sutpen to ride so seductively and so treacherously. And he rides on, disappearing in a cloud of dust before we can discern his shape.

IV   *Race, Gender, and the Hysterical Intertext*

Perhaps history is not to be found in our mirrors, but in our repudiations: perhaps the other is ourselves.

James Baldwin

As the mad text(s) of *Absalom, Absalom!* begin to take life and fluctuate with their own rhythms, we may find ourselves, with Quentin, turning away from Sutpen's receding form to float back even further into the past and "watch resolving the figure of a little girl, in the prim skirts and pantalettes, the smooth prim decorous braids, of the dead time" (*AA* 14-15). As Faulkner's narrative surges toward the moment of this daughter's seduction by the Father—the real moment, I believe, when madness flashes across Rosa's hysterical text to speak itself—we may find ourselves likewise seduced by Rosa the woman-made-girl. We may find ourselves imitating her mode of listening to what she calls *"that other something"* beyond and between language, to that which is as much created by the listener's imagination as it is heard. Still reading hysterically, and so allowing Rosa's text to imprint itself upon us, we may lurk, as she does, "Cassandra-like" around corners and beyond closed doors to catch the sense of the sounds, the traces, the erasures, the whispers of meanings beyond and between the words we hear. What we seem to be listening for, and what we are moved by, are those ways in which Faulkner's text talks to itself: how it whispers its own divisibility. Yet, as we listen to the conversations between race and gender within *Absalom* itself, we also may catch snatches of a second, intertextual interchange: in significant ways *Absalom* and another of Faulkner's novels, *Intruder in the Dust*, seem to speak to and about the "fell darkness" of patriarchal constructs which measure human worth not only by race and sex but by madly complex expectations of what black and white men and women should be.

Listening to conversations between these two texts, we may become aware of standing *outside* Faulkner's personal cultural narrative — his ambivalent stance on racial issues[11] and his life experience as a white southern male. Yet, as may be obvious, part of my project here is to explore ways of *re*hearing authorial voice in what Mikhail Bakhtin would call its "dialogical" modes of discourse, that discourse which, as Stephen M. Ross explains in regard to Faulkner, "by its very nature takes other speech, other voices, into account" ("Oratory" 17). In this way we may hear Faulkner's cultural voice in an intertextual range, much as Robert Siegle has suggested we experience narrative itself, as "the central medium" through which culture naturalizes codes of reason while at the same time embodying a "reflexive dimension [that] works equally hard to show how such naturalization takes place" (11). This "reflexive dimension" of Faulkner's fiction, as it traces and retraces the meanings of race and gender in southern culture, peculiarly resonates in the space between *Absalom, Absalom!* and *Intruder in the Dust,* both of which also *talk to themselves* in cogent and provocative ways about the mystery of racism, the terror of racial encounter, and the urgency of cultural guilt. In these texts, and in between them, madness writes itself in all directions at once, and especially in the intensity of what I call, for lack of a better term, their *racial events* — those charged, expressive moments when racism speaks its own text of madness, when it says itself as mad, as stubbornly resistant to interpretation. These *racial events,* their mad texts, seem inescapably generated by gender-inflected discourses which spiral out to engage in intertextual conversation about the relationships of race and gender within patriarchy.

Let us begin by listening to a wise man. In *Intruder in the Dust* old Ephraim extols the value of intuition, that canniness of mind beyond ratiocination, a power which he says women and children have and men do not. "Young folks and womens, they aint cluttered," he tells Chick Mallison. "They can listen" (*ID* 71). Old Ephraim speaks the truth — it is the woman, Rosa, and the child-becoming-man, Chick, who listen, and who force us to listen, to the rhythms of their own mad texts of racism. In seeking out those rhythms we hover in the space between what seem to be the two most intense *racial events* in the Faulkner canon, and hence deep within the chasm southern culture created between blackness and whiteness. In *Absalom* Rosa's memory of herself and Clytie on the stairs of Sutpen's Hundred defines that chasm and, in so doing, reverberates in the cross-racial feminine space of cultural madness. When young Rosa destroys the alterity and generative power of that feminine space through her denial of Clytie (*"Take your hand off me, nigger!"*), she embraces the realm of the proper, which similarly has denied *her* humanity.[12] She becomes one of the boys.

Such a denial is implicit in Chick's encounter with Lucas Beauchamp in *Intruder in the Dust*. We, and he, hear and must continue to hear echoing through the discourse of the novel that clatter of coins dropped at Lucas's feet, "the four shameful fragments of milled and minted dross," in payment for those things for which there is no payment: hospitality, nurturance, common human decency. This is a moment frozen in the space between silence and sound. From the instant Chick extends the coins, he knows he has disrupted that language through which Lucas recodes a racist cultural economy. Chick is "forever now too late, forever beyond recall, standing with the slow hot blood as slow as minutes themselves up his neck and face, forever with his dumb hand open . . ." (*ID* 15). When Lucas rejects the money, he condemns Chick to re-enter that silence "for another eternity" until, shame turning to rage, the boy watches his own "palm turn over not flinging the coins but spurning them downward ringing onto the bare floor, bouncing and one of the nickels even rolling away in a long swooping curve with a dry minute sound like the scurry of a small mouse . . ." (*ID* 16). So Chick begins his painful journey toward expiation, toward diminishing the *sound* of his own smallness and perversity and, like the young seduced Rosa, setting forth to rewrite the interior narrative of self by "unmaking" the seducing Father within.

Although there are certainly other intense racial encounters in Faulkner's fiction, particularly in *Go Down, Moses*, the *idea* of racial encounter, which constitutes these two moments and moves in the space between and within these two narratives, becomes not just the reflexive dimension of a racist and sexist culture, but also a tracing and retracing of the mysterious and troubling connection between the human need for recognition and the human desire to reject that need. As Aaron

Steinberg points out, prevailing psychoanalytic theory makes this connection by seeing white racism as projecting upon the black subject unresolved unconscious conflict (121, n. 3). What these two racial encounters make us know is that the question underlying the madness of racism is as elusive as Felman says. What we hear between and beyond these texts is racism's power, not merely as an external construct, but as an intensely personal *event* in which one subject denies the status of subject to another, yet *in that act of denial* paradoxically splits one's own subjectivity, enacts one's own castration.

Racism is therefore one of the darkest and most self-destructive impulses. When Rosa rejects Clytie, she invalidates herself as a full, caring, significant woman — as the *Rosa* of Clytie's defining voice. This denial of Clytie, and the concomitant show of alliance with patriarchy, is precisely what leads the young Rosa to position herself as object within the realm of the proper. That position results in her eventual seduction by the Father; for, as is the case in all seductions, one first seduces one's self into being seduced. When Chick denies Lucas as a man, when he insists that Lucas "act like a nigger," he negates his own growth toward manhood. Yet, in the intensity of these racial events, those shells that we think of as encasing identity mysteriously dissolve: whiteness becomes blackness, for both are signs which suddenly shift and merge within the intensity of the moment. Rosa writes the moment across the female body: *"But let flesh touch with flesh, and watch the fall of all the eggshell shibboleth of caste and color too"* (AA 111). As John Irwin suggests, the confrontation of the other, "the self with a difference," is a painful, often terrifying act, a loss of control over the repressed "dark self" whom one would deny at almost any cost (92). Once that confrontation occurs and those barriers dissolve, however, there is no retreating from the connections forged. So, as Rosa is the uncanniness within the Father's House, Clytie is the uncanniness within Rosa, that which she has repressed in order to remain sheltered by the Father, whose madness she continues to articulate all her life. Just as Miss Rosa's white triangle constitutes to Quentin's male gaze the castration he fears, Clytie on the stairs of the Father's House embodies Rosa's complicity in the cultural text which she will grow to speak as madness. Likewise, although Chick may throw the four coins into the creek, he must live with the sound of their ringing on the floor and, we suspect, exhume their living mystery and treachery over and over, beyond youth and even through the remainder of his life.

As the black presence of Clytie and Lucas speaks to us in traces within the reflexive dimension of these narratives, they become exemplars of Baldwin's assertion, as Craig Werner interprets it, that "we seek answers to questions of cultural and personal identity in the ways in which we draw the lines of demarcation between self and other" (717). In this sense, indeed, "the other is ourselves." It is inescapable. It folds back upon the subject and reconstitutes it as social sign in a complex amalgam of cultural codes. Like Clytie and Lucas, it thus calls into question the cultural construction of subjectivity. In these racial encounters, the black subjects' demand that patriarchy reconstruct its notion of subjectivity, and the white characters' reification of patriarchal denial, are complicated by the fact that the two white participants are actively seeking gendered identities and that the two black characters in varying ways complicate that process. Considered together, these encounters converse with each other in peculiar ways, as they both focus and interpret multiple cultural experience and the intersections in southern culture of race and sex.

It is surely no accident that these, Faulkner's most powerful scenes of racial interaction, are between two females on the one hand and two males on the other. The white individual, confronting a black other (who is denying the objective position she or he is being placed in, and who is insisting on the position of subject and on a subject-to-subject relationship to whiteness), thus becomes inextricably connected not only to problems of race but also to the development of a gendered subjectivity within the Father's House. It is the difficulty associated with becoming a white man or woman in a patriarchal society which complicates, even formulates, Chick's and Rosa's denials of black humanity in these moments of connection and rejection which dislodge and then inevitably reconstruct psychological and cultural barriers between the races.

Werner argues that Faulkner allows only his white characters to excavate and reevaluate history, and that, out of their evaluation, Faulkner creates a "narrative of repudiation" (719). Although both *Absalom, Absalom!* and *Intruder in the Dust* are "narratives of repudiation," it seems to me that the excavation is a narrative process which subsumes both white and black text-making and which is produced out of sexual as well as racial difference. In Siegle's paradigm, reflexivity is the process of the narrative's "turn[ing] back on itself" while at the same time "looking all around itself" (2). This is indeed the process of these two narratives, although I believe that there resides in the space between them a kind of inter-reflexivity which allows them not only to turn back upon themselves while looking around themselves, but also to turn back upon and look around each other, an idea that Michel Gresset hints at when he reminds us of Faulkner's "capacity *to write his own work as an intertext*" ("Introduction" 7). Thus we may expect to hear provocative intertextual conversations *in the spaces between*. These spaces are variously constructed. They are, at once, the cultural texts of race and sex within these novels' mad narratives of patriarchy, the reflexive texts which *Absalom* and *Intruder* become in their own separate relationships to culture, and the inter-reflexive texts they become for each other in these separate reflexive roles.

Both Irwin and Lee Jenkins have remarked upon the connection within the white male unconscious between repressed fear of castration and blackness (another intertext between gender and race), and the referential burden the black subject/object bears as a projection of "the repressed impulses" of white male fear (Jenkins 54). In Irwin's schema, which links the observations of Freud, Otto Rank, and Carl Jung,

> The dark self is an involuntary repetition, an unconscious projection that has returned by means beyond the control of the conscious will. And when the repressed returns, when the unconscious projection rises to the level of consciousness, the conscious will immediately finds itself confronted by another force that attempts to overrule it—the supergo's demand that that which has returned be re-repressed. (92–93)

Irwin argues that this repressed fear of castration, i.e., femininization, motivates Sutpen's rejection of the "dark, feminine Bon" (93). Moreover, such fear, in the Freudian model, becomes by its very nature a fear of death. For, as Irwin points out, what is repression but a cutting off, a killing, of the part that evokes anxiety? (89–90) In Irwin's paradigm, the confrontational presence of blackness becomes excruciatingly threatening to the white male. This is particularly the case, as I will explain, for a young adolescent such as Chick, who is in the process of learning what it means to be a man in a culture which devalues its own difference.

Irwin and Jenkins follow the lead of Freud and Rank in concentrating on involuntary repetition and (in Rank's paradigm) on doubling as male phenomena.[13] In another context I have suggested that cross-racial female relationships within a cultural matrix demanding moral superiority from white women and sexual availability from black women present an even more volatile admixture of anxiety, terror, and sexual jealousy—one which informs Rosa and Clytie's early encounter and makes it a trope for examining black and white women's relationships in the Old South.[14] Rereading this crucial encounter, this moment of female flesh on female flesh, I envision Clytie on the stairs with Rosa's hysterical text written across her body. Thadious Davis points to the fact that the speakers of *Absalom* invent themselves out of their varying concepts of "Negro" (189). In this sense Rosa seems to write Clytie's black female body as the very site of her own denial of white female subjectivity, and so as the very *sign* of the question of cultural madness. Clytie is the "What" of "What is?"—the question which underlies madness and speaks itself in the hysterical narrative about patriarchy. In such a culture, one whose economic exchanges of women include as a factor racial difference, Rosa (like other women, black and white) can only, as Matthews points out, continually defer her desires (124). Rosa speaks her sexuality; her sexual desire becomes, as Foucault suggests about sex in general, the stimulus for "a regulated and polymorphous incitement to discourse" (History of Sexuality 34). Her discourse thus becomes, in the Foucaultian analysis, a cultural necessity, "something akin to a secret whose discovery is imperative, a thing abusively reduced to silence, and at the same time difficult and necessary, dangerous and precious to divulge" (35).

This precious and dangerous thing, this "scandal" as Spivak would say, is, of course, the plenitude of the female libidindal economy. Miss Rosa's continued insistence upon the "root and urge" of her youth compels her to write her own body before the male gaze and across the male text; and, as Cixous has said of the woman writer, "her flesh speaks true. She exposes herself. Really she makes what she thinks materialize carnally, she conveys meaning with her body. She *inscribes* what she is saying because she does not deny unconscious drives the unmanageable part they play in speech" ("Sorties," in Cixous and Clément 92).

Like Caddy, Rosa speaks the disruptive excess of the feminine, which, as Irigaray tells us, "jams" the machinery of the logos and dissolves binary modes of thought (*This Sex* 78) through its own desire to break open and split apart, as Cixous says, "without regret" ("Sorties," in Cixous and Clément 90). And so young Rosa, as re-created by the woman she is to become, climbs the stairs of the Father's House to participate in love and grief. She is a young woman whose desire is for *"a world filled with living marriage like the light and air which she breathes"* (*AA* 116), a world more *"true than truth."* That desire ties her to what Miss Rosa later will call *"that other something"* which makes her a female subject-in-process whose desire writes the *jouissance*

> *of all springs yet to capitulate condensed into one spring, one sum-*
> *mer: the spring and summertime which is every female's who*
> *breathed above dust, beholden of all betrayed springs held over*
> *from all irrevocable time, repercussed, bloomed again.* (*AA* 115)

In Rosa's remembering, Clytie's touch dissolves ego boundaries and allows free play between subject and object. The place of the touch becomes Kristeva's semiotic *chora*, in which a new feminine language is possible, a language which speaks *between*:

> *Because there is something in the touch of flesh with flesh*
> *which abrogates, cuts sharp and straight across the devious in-*
> *tricate channels of decorous ordering, which enemies as well as*
> *lovers know because it makes them both — touch and touch of*
> *that which is the citadel of the central I-Am's private own: not*
> *spirit, soul; the liquorish and ungirdled mind is anyone's to take*
> *in any darkened hallway of this earthly tenement. But let flesh*
> *touch with flesh, and watch the fall of all the eggshell shib-*
> *boleth of caste and color too.* (*AA* 111–12)

Why, then, does the young Rosa destroy that feminine space by denying its bearer, the black woman who, as Rosa herself remembers, *"did me more grace and respect than anyone else I knew"*? (*AA* 111) What is most frightening here is the double loss of female subjectivity at the hands of woman herself. Rosa denies Clytie hers and in the process loses her own. James A. Snead points out that Rosa, having herself been objectified, objectifies others (104). Yet the question remains: Why can she not see *Clytie* as female subject? Perhaps because they are both inside the Father's House, that "dim hot airless" vault which textualizes all southern women as objects. The house itself speaks (for) Clytie. *It* says:

> *'Dont you go up there, Rosa'. . . . it was as though it had not been she who spoke but the house itself that said the words—the house which he had built, which some suppuration of himself had created about him as the sweat of his body might have created, produced some (even if invisible) cocoon-like and complementary shell in which Ellen had had to live and die a stranger, in which Henry and Judith would have to be victims and prisoners, or die.* (*AA* 111)

Rosa's tragedy at nineteen is that she could not read what Johnson would call the difference *within* the cultural text, that which makes it speak against itself; in this case she could not read the possibility of cross-racial female relationships which would dismantle patriarchal constructs of racial interaction. As an old woman, she speaks from that feminine space which disrupts culture; yet she cannot help but speak her culture as well, with its voices of racial and sexual repressiveness. As she undermines the Father's systems and plays creatively with the language of desire and loss, she remains, in some sense at least, frozen on those stairs, her body, like the hysteric's, "a theater for forgotten scenes . . . bearing witness to a lost childhood that survives in suffering" (Clément, "Sorceress and Hysteric," in Cixous and Clément 5). The space between Faulkner and Rosa, then, may be less than we think; for he, like the feminine of his own creation, tells us that history can never be over, that "was" can never be "was," and that cultural madness writes itself . . . upon us all.

Like Rosa, Chick Mallison knows his own heart of darkness. We, if not he, recognize the pressures of gender expectation as powerful motivating forces for his racism. Chick's story is, I find, about the development of a masculine identity which comes to accept its own feminine elements, a painful process in a culture which, even as the New South, defines the masculine in terms of mastery and the feminine as the lack thereof. Chick's progress is measured by his learning to listen to the feminine elements within himself, and overcoming his fear of them. As old Ephraim intuits, "young folks and womens" are linked in this novel by their ability to listen to the difference within the voice of culture, i.e., within the voice of Lucas Beauchamp. His voice, like that of Clytie Sutpen, not only defines black will and black presence, but speaks what it is to be a man or a woman in a patriarchal society. The process of the story is the process by which Chick learns to hear this message, through and beyond the rhetoric of Gavin Stevens and through and beyond his adolescent fear of the feminine shadow self. Though Lucas's words are few, they are of utmost importance because they are articulations of individuation in a language the black voice has spoken in autobiography from the early slave narratives to the present. Chick, like his culture, devalues that language at first, yet he gradually learns what is essential for him to know: that Lucas speaks out of a sense of himself as a speaking subject commensurate with, indeed surpassing, Chick's own; and that that self is as bisexual as it is biracial.

Although, as Walter Taylor points out, Lucas of *Intruder in the Dust* is something of a model of black manhood (*Faulkner's Search* 149) and although he is associated with Chick's grandfather, his actions as recalled by Chick also reflect feminine characteristics. Indeed, Lucas reminds us of Maggie Mallison in his maternal insistence on caring for the cold wet Chick he finds at the pond's edge. By refusing his money, he shows Chick the intrinsic value of such nurturance and the complexity of human interaction. Later he demonstrates to Chick the invalidity of his desire for mastery. He shapes Chick into "not just a man but a specific man" (*ID* 151) who comes to acknowledge his kinship with women, with blacks, and with a human community of mixed virtue.

As the narrative progresses, Lucas's moral voice and its feminine element encircle Chick's imagination, much the way Chick's image of female creativity shapes the dust of Lucas's yard in the summer: "the dust each morning swept by some of Lucas' womenfolks with a broom made of willow switches bound together, into an intricate series of whorls and overlapping loops which as the day advanced would be gradually and slowly defaced by the droppings and the cryptic three-toed prints of chickens . . ."(*ID* 8). Chick's vision of patterns in the dust suggests the possibility of creative, repetitive, and I would suggest feminine, responses to moral issues deriving from cultural defacement, responses evoked by Lucas's demands upon him. Carol Gilligan's research shows that female responses to moral problems differ from male responses in that often, for women, "the moral problem arises from conflicting responsibilities rather than from competing rights and requires for its resolution a mode of thinking that is contextual and narrative rather than formal and abstract" (19). Women's construction of the moral problem is "as a problem of care and responsibility in relationships rather than as one of rights and rules. . ." (73). Male morality is, as we have seen, one "of rights and noninterference," whereas women's is "a morality of responsibility" (22). What *Intruder in the Dust* is about, it seems to me, is Chick's movement toward the latter type of morality.

Even so, in his early efforts to become what he thinks a man should be, the young Chick represses the feminine within. He recalls that his fall in the water was "something a girl might have been expected or even excused for doing but nobody else. . ." (*ID* 5). In a culture where a black man is expected to act "like a nigger" and "white folks . . . like white folks," Chick fears loss of control (*ID* 48). He fears his mother's control, despite the fact that he admires her more than he admires his father. He feels that Lucas, in his refusal to take his money, "had debased not merely his manhood but his whole race too" (*ID* 21). Chick assimilates the racial encounter with Lucas into the clearly sexual symbology of masculine desire, against which he is helpless: "the round hard symbol of the coin . . . to its gigantic maximum, to hang fixed at last forever in the black vault of his anguish like the last dead and waneless moon and himself, his own puny shadow gesticulant and tiny against it in frantic and vain eclipse . . ." (*ID* 21). He seeks (and connects) "reaffirmation of his masculinity and his white blood" in an erasure of the encounter of "his dead childhood" (*ID* 26).

Yet, out of his guilt and his need to expiate it, Chick learns that experience is indeed contextual, that he can deny mastery and appropriation as goals, that he can listen even beyond words to his own responsibilities in a complex culture. In the exchange of "gifts," Lucas begins to show him that mastery can always be mastered, that economic discourse constitutes more complex human interactions than those controlled by mere money. Lucas shows Chick new codes of exchange: the boy's purchases mean less than Lucas's human creation of "fresh home-made sorghum molasses." In this recoded language, Chick hears a new narrative of human interaction and moral responsibility.

And so when Lucas looks at him from his jail cell, Chick knows what that look says. He can read the hysterical text which Lucas writes upon himself as symptom. Chick understands that he must read the symptom, must listen beyond language, must excavate both himself and, as Aaron Steinberg suggests, the meaning of racial hatred (120). "All right. What do you want me to do?" he must say to Lucas (*ID* 68), because Lucas has taught him, as Gavin Stevens does not, that some things are indeed "mad." They are beyond words and so must be listened to in new ways. Like Eunice Habersham who must drive in circles to get home, Chick learns to act morally in madly circuitous systems of encounter. He learns that such systems contain multiple languages and that morality is often a matter of relationships rather than rules. He finds that human debts involve human economics, something Sutpen never learned: that digging up a grave may indeed become the fair exchange for eating *"that plate of meat and greens"* (*ID* 68). More than that, though, Chick learns to hear beyond the structures of language, to know how to listen when "language means more than it can say" (Matthews 62). He knows why Lucas has called on him to exhume what is assumed to be the body of Vinson Gowrie: that he alone, of all the white people available, would enter the jail cell with the ability to *listen* and hence "would hear the mute unhoping urgency of the eyes" (*ID* 69), and read Lucas's mad text.

It has been said that this novel is provincial (Volpe 253) and that the potential of its powerful racial encounter between young Chick and Lucas is ultimately lost in Gavin Stevens's "ceremonial pronouncements on 'Sambo' and world politics" (Sundquist 149). I would argue, though, that Stevens's talk shows simply that talk is cheap. As Olga Vickery points out, Faulkner is here "attempting to bridge the gap between words and deeds by sustaining the parallel between them" (144). What we hear from Lucas is that the language which *means* is not always the one we think we hear, or the one we want to hear, or even the one hearable over the demanding voices of societal expectation and individual desire. But by hearing traces of Lucas's mad text and by learning to read his own, Chick becomes a white man who allows himself an expansive moral dimension dependent upon and responsive to the polyphony of his own biracial and bisexual voices within. In so doing he comes to understand the non-negotiable responsibilities of human interchange. He learns what a receipt is. Unlike the protest novels disparaged by James Baldwin for their dishonest simplicity and "indecent glibness" (578), *Intruder in the Dust* thus moves toward rather than away from experiential complexity.

I would strive to continue with that movement in my listening between these texts. We proceed from silence to sound; perhaps, as Doreen Fowler suggests of Faulkner's works in general, from a despairing to an affirming vision (65–75). In *Absalom, Absalom!*, we leave the Rosa Coldfield of Quentin's narrative voice in front of Sutpen's Hundred, "struggling and fighting like a doll in a nightmare, making no sound, foaming a little at the mouth" (*AA* 301), and move through intertextual space into Gavin Stevens's office where we hear the insistence on human dignity implicit in Lucas's request, "My receipt" (*ID* 247), and the awareness of the human economics of morality such a request implies. Yet, as we read hysterically between these narratives we must listen as carefully to what Rosa cannot say as to what Lucas can, for both speak the language of complex and pain-filled cultural and psychological interactions not only of black and white but of race and gender. And somewhere in the intertextuality of saying and not saying, which as Faulkner knew is the realm of all experience; somewhere here in the spaces and even in the erasures of meaning *between*, resides a metalanguage of culture which is biracial and bisexual, naturalizing and reflexive. It speaks of and beyond itself, and therefore in many voices both defining and surpassing their creator's own.

V   *Seduction and Reading*

But it was not love: I do not claim that; I hold no brief for myself, I do not excuse it. I could have said that he had needed, used me; why should I rebel now, because he would use me more? But I did not say it; I could say this

*time, I do not know, and I would tell the truth. Because I
do not know.*

Rosa Coldfield

How to retrieve and rearticulate the feminine out of absence?

Rosa came to Sutpen, she says, *"like a whistled dog"* (*AA* 128). Forty-three years later she still struggles with the question underlying her own madness, her own continued resistance to interpretation as a female presence who chose to negate herself, to become an absence to be filled by the Father: to be *"whatever it was he wanted of me — not my being, my presence: just my existence, what it was that Rosa Coldfield or any young female no blood kin to him represented in whatever it was he wanted"* (*AA* 134). Rosa's questions, then, are ontological but gender-specific. How, and why, does the female subject erase herself? How does woman even begin to articulate the madness of such erasure? Can she reenergize subjectivity from *"the absence of black morass"* (*AA* 134), the nothingness woman may be seduced into embracing? These are the questions which flare briefly but brilliantly out of the darkness of Rosa's mad text of seduction. They lead us to wonder what are *Faulkner's* questions about Stupen's seduction of Rosa, and how they converse with Rosa's and with ours. For it may be that the question of the female subject's erasure has everything to do with the (male) writer's being seduced into becoming his text, and so disappearing into it. Again, then, we may perhaps look to the female character as the entry into the male text, and her loss as its productivity. In this case, Rosa's white triangle, her lack, becomes its pleasure, and ours.[15]

Between Rosa's insistent, maddening questions about her seduction and our reading of those questions, the question underlying madness creates its own resistance to interpretation; and, not insignificantly, in the process, questions the interpretability of Faulkner's text (and our own) through our questioning of Rosa's question. The question underlying madness thus writes itself. It belongs to no one — not Sutpen, not Rosa, not the cultural "them" Rosa speaks for and to. It becomes instead what Felman calls a "reading effect," which transfers itself to us by seducing us with its rhetoric (*Writing and Madness* 30–31). I have said that in a peculiar and mysterious way *Absalom* reads us. This is particularly true, I find, in Rosa's mad text of chapter five which seduces us into pondering what is unrepresentable about writing and textuality as surely as Sutpen's phallic power seduced her into that treacherous space of absence. We become, then, as Felman has suggested more generally, "unconscious textual *actor*[*s*] caught without knowing it in the lines of force of the text's '*pure rhetoric,*' of the *addressing power* of its signs, and of their reference to interpretants" (31).

This is, as Felman observes, a rethinking of narrative which posits reading as "the blind *repetition,* the performative enactment of the *rhetoric* of the text (and not of its meaning)" (31). In this way we, like Rosa, become signs of the text by performing its rhetoric, which is, in this case, the rhetoric of madness. Rosa—her rhetorical reproduction of self always dependent upon the rhetorical rhythms created by her own erasure—speaks the irrepresentable rhythms of her own fullness and emptiness, those "*things for which three words are three too many, and three thousand words that many words too less*" (*AA* 134). This is, as Felman might point out, the rhetoric of the mad text, whose reading is a "slippage . . . *between* the excessive fullness and the excessive emptiness of meaning" (254), whose fluctuations and forces we seek and find pleasure in, whose openings and gaps lead us to the Faulkner who, like Rosa and like us, is seduced by his own text and has disappeared into its femininity. And so again we enter a bisexual space connecting female character and male author and we find it, and them, reading us. As they read us and we read them, our multiple bisexual spaces become as unanalyzable as Rosa's seduction, and Faulkner's, and ours.

We move in many directions at once. We have approached Rosa the *character* as a cultural subject, in considering the intersection of race and gender in her encounter with Clytie, and the conversations their encounter may have with the encounter of Lucas Beauchamp and Chick Mallison in *Intruder in the Dust*. At this point, though, we may turn to explore Rosa's rhetoric of madness as *Absalom*'s deconstructive *energy,* which allows the book to make itself by unmaking itself, to enact its own castration but to rename castration as pleasure. Before we speak with the mad Miss Rosa, we may wish to remember that she speaks from the *inside* of madness, as the hysterical body which constitutes itself as a text of the unconscious. What she says has a power to articulate itself beyond and between whatever we may think of to say about it.

She speaks the rhythms of the unconscious in a feminine rhetoric which reenergizes the female subject. This is what calls us to its rhythms and so creates its seductiveness, what Felman calls its *"reading effect."* These rhythms out of which (in which?) (through which?) Rosa remakes herself whisper mysteriously about how subjectivity may reconstruct itself out of its own loss and, at the same time, out of its own rhetoric.

Cixous writes of women who live loss, who create and re-create the splitness of the subject by not resigning themselves to loss, by not mourning it; for mourning would make them whole. Their texts are the processes of "taking loss, seizing it, living it. Leaping" ("Castration or Decapitation?" 54). Rosa's text, it has been pointed out again and again, is generated by her unwillingness to let go of loss. She instead lives it. Recent critical thought about Faulkner has concerned itself with the pervasiveness of loss in his works and the ways in which loss initiates narrative desire — tracing and retracing in language those spaces created by absence.[16] Matthews has shown us, moreover, that this tracing does not reconstruct that which has been lost, but instead constitutes a fluid and creative play of differences which, in their very creativity and playfulness, dissolve the possibility of reconstruction or retrieval of the lost one or thing. Loss thereby triggers narrative desire, which in turn is both absorbed and regenerated in its own playful explorations of the infinite and mysterious spaces left by absence. As we know, these processes, as they become themselves by differing from themselves, signify *both* the constitutive and deconstructive qualities of a text.

I hasten to add that the loss which Rosa *lives* is not the loss of Sutpen. What most obsesses Rosa and what generates her narrative desire is the loss of her ability to write her own text, to produce *"l'écriture féminine,"* the writing of feminine desire. What she struggles to do in chapter five and in her whole narrative is to restore herself to her text and her text to herself, to say herself *both as woman and as women,* as the feminine whose desire generates language and as the female subject who creates language. What makes her text so powerful and so beautiful — and so madly seductive — is that, like the narrative of the hysteric, it follows the laws of its own desire and constitutes itself out of their free play. As I have said, Rosa writes the text as hysterical symptom upon us — we join her in becoming it. At the same time, Rosa speaks her desire to reconstruct in language *her* feminine body, that which she was seduced out of by the symbolic order of the Father. Clothed in the old stale female flesh which constitutes her absence to the male desiring gaze, Miss Rosa Coldfield speaks her sexuality, not just in the past, but in the present. In this way she turns absence back into presence by recreating (making, playing) female desire in the space (mad, unreadable, fluid) *between.*

> *But root and urge I do insist and claim, for had I not heired too from all the unsistered Eves since the Snake?*
>
> Rosa Coldfield

Rosa writes herself within woman's tradition of forbidden sexuality. Readers have marked the intensity of Rosa's descriptions of her youthful *"world of living marriage."*[17] Yet what may be most moving about Rosa's sexual text is its own present tense: her *"summer of wistaria"* is perennial, insistent upon its own *"root and urge."* Sutpen creates Rosa as absence; Quentin describes her body as "lonely thwarted old female flesh" (*AA* 9). Rosa overcodes these male texts with her own woman's text of herself as

> *warped chrysalis of what blind perfect seed: for who shall say what gnarled forgotten root might not bloom yet with some globed concentrate more globed and concentrate and heady-perfect because the neglected root was planted warped and lay not dead but merely slept forgot?* (*AA* 116)

Sutpen's interest in Rosa was in the emptiness she constituted: her womb.[18] In writing over his male text, as she does Quentin's, Rosa constructs the womb as part of her female subjectivity, as a *place* — rather than a *space* — of interiority, through which she as a girl viewed external reality:

> *I lurked, unapprehended as though, shod with the very damp and velvet silence of the womb, I displaced no air, gave off no*

*betraying sound, from one closed forbidden door to the next
and so acquired all I knew of that light and space in which people moved and breathed as I (that same child) might have
gained conception of the sun from seeing it through a piece of
smoky glass. . . . (AA 116)*

The "question underlying madness" of Rosa's text is, then, not so
much the question of what makes it impossible to interpret the historical text of the Father (Sutpen's text: who he was, why he did what he
did, etc.) but:

— How one can be seduced into losing one's own text.
— How one's own text can be rewritten out of its own loss, or miswriting;
  that is, how subjectivity can be erased and then reconstructed out of its
  own erasure.
— How rhetoric itself may generate that reconstruction.
— How such rhetoric, as it writes the female body, creates a bisexual space
  between male author and female subject.
— How the "in-between" of that space, its bisexual tension between the
  masculine and the feminine, seduces us (male and female readers) in
  a mysterious and uninterpretable way.

What is so resistant to analysis, so *mad* then, about chapter five is that,
within its bisexual space of reading, seduction creates both pain and
pleasure, both absence and presence, both deconstruction and reconstruction. Rosa's seduction by the Father, Sutpen, destroyed her life yet
creates her text as something so beautiful and powerful that it seduces
us into allowing it to write its madness . . . on us.

How is this madness written? It seems to me that, as Rosa is asking
"Why? Why? and Why?" (AA 135) she allowed herself to be seduced,
madness, with all its gaps and stoppages of meaning, writes itself across
her — and perhaps across us as well. Yet Rosa's hysterical narrative, which
remakes chronology in its play between the conscious and the unconscious, also remakes madness's texts. Sutpen, Rosa says, was *"mad, yet
not so mad,"* for madness *"has faster rules"* (AA 134). With their seductive rhetoric, those "faster rules" reweave Rosa's original and conventional definition of madness as insanity into a new theoretical fabric

which allows madness to write itself as indecipherable, unreadable. In Rosa's memory, then, madness writes its own text across Sutpen's words of insult, the *"blank naked and outrageous words,"* and across young Rosa herself, who was *"that sun, or thought I was who did believe there was that spark, that crumb in madness which is divine, though madness know no word itself for terror or for pity"* (AA 135).

I have been trying to show how madness creates itself in *Absalom, Absalom!* If we follow Rosa's text carefully at this point, we may read the process of madness's becoming. Rosa is here remembering the moment of her seduction, how *"that ogre . . . held out its hand and said 'Come' as you might say it to a dog, and I came"* (AA 135). Yet she has, she says, slain the ogre in her mind and made him into a mortal villain who is both pitiful and mad; for she has told herself through the years,

> *Why should not madness be its own victim also? or, Why may it be not even madness but solitary despair in titan conflict with the lonely and foredoomed and indomitable iron spirit: but no ogre, because it was dead, vanished, consumed somewhere in flame and sulphur-reek perhaps among the lonely craggy peaks of my childhood's solitary remembering—or forgetting; I was that sun, who believed that he (after that evening in Judith's room) was not oblivious of me but only unconscious and receptive like the swamp-freed pilgrim feeling earth and tasting sun and light again and aware of neither but only of darkness' and morass' lack—who did believe there was that magic in unkin blood which we call by the pallid name of love that would be, might be sun for him (though I the youngest, weakest) where Judith and Clytie both would cast no shadow; yes, I the youngest there yet potently without measured and measurable age since I alone of them could say, 'O furious mad old man, I hold no substance that will fit your dream but I can give you airy space and scope for your delirium.'* (AA 135)

I am quoting this passage so extensively because I believe it constitutes a rhetorical space in which madness actually moves about in rhetoric from one character to another. It writes itself as the Sutpen who seduces

Rosa. Then it moves to write itself as the Rosa who seduces herself into reifying his phallic dream and who thus becomes the absence, the *"airy space"* that dream desires to fill *yet all the time* continues, mistakenly, to construct herself as *presence*, as *"that sun"* whose presence is the quintessential presence to all earthy creatures, who is center and truth and Being for all life.

What Rosa "writes," then, in addition to female sexuality, is an intertext between female presence and female absence. And this intertext carries the chilling implication that, as a cultural presence, woman can *seduce herself* into thinking that objectivity is subjectivity—that she is *"that sun"* when she is actually nothing more than *"airy space."* Woman is thus seduced by madness, for she becomes the opposite of what she thinks she is; her text becomes uninterpretable, even to herself. Madness thus writes itself in an expansive and troubling way, for it shows us as feminist readers what we fear and what we are seduced by—and they are . . . the same.

So, as Miss Rosa Coldfield speaks her sexuality as that text which she still must write, madness writes its own intertext of the female subject/object. Woman's body thus generates the feminine libidinal energies of the novel, its "sex which is not one," its multiplicity and disavowal of linearity, its hysterical narrative that splatters its madness everywhere at once and nowhere in particular. Yet madness writes itself in other spaces. And these, it seems to me, are recoverable only through their rhetoric, Rosa's rhetoric of madness, which, like the feminine in Western culture, says *somewhere else,* and so subverts and disrupts all that its discourse reaches, by gazing over the brink of rhetoric at the unrepresentable. To the feminist reader Rosa's rhetoric may seem to gaze also at a state of female subjectivity which is frighteningly incongruent with its own self-construction, which is not what it thinks it is. The question underlying madness thus writes itself across Rosa's *"Why? Why? and Why?"* as it explodes out of the theoretical discourse of an old and difficult southern lady . . . who is called a ghost, but is anything but.

For the symbolic order to assert itself over the unrepresentable, it must silence its difference within.

It must shut the old lady up.

VI   *Shutting Rosa Up*

Because he was not articulated in this world. He was a walking shadow. He was the light-blinded bat-like image of his own torment cast by the fierce demoniac lantern up from beneath the earth's crust and hence in retrograde, reverse; from abysmal and chaotic dark to eternal and abysmal dark completing his descending (do you mark the gradation?) ellipsis, clinging, trying to cling with vain unsubstantial hands to what he hoped would hold him, save him, arrest him—Ellen (do you mark them?) myself, then last of all fatherless daughter of Wash Jones' only child who, so I heard once, died in a Memphis brothel—to find severence (even if not rest and peace) at last in the stroke of a rusty scythe.

Rosa Coldfield

Rosa's mad text made Sutpen; and here, at the end of chapter five, it unmakes him. Clinging to first one "fatherless daughter," Ellen, and then another, Rosa, and then a third, Milly Jones, this Sutpen of Rosa's unmaking fades into a castrated shadow of man, cut off from the object of his desire—his masculine replication in a son. If we continue to think of how "character" may be constituted, diminished, and dissolved in narrative, we may see how Rosa's text, as much as Wash Jones's scythe, slays the ogre, as surely as she conjured him initially, with his French architect and wild slaves, out of a whirl of North Mississippi dust. Her mad text thus seems to wind itself toward some sense of closure, albeit an illusory one, for it enacts the death of the Father, the demise of Sutpen and his realm of the proper.

Finally, though, I am not so much interested in how Rosa silences Sutpen (for, as we shall see, that too is an illusion) as I am in how she herself, as woman speaker constituted by her own voice, is shut up, shut down, and shut out by men. At this point I will issue a warning about what is to come: the last half of *Absalom,* as we know, is dominated by male voices. I believe that these voices encode the sexual politics of patriarchy by silencing women as speaking subjects within its narrative of mastery. If we continue to think of ourselves as reading hysterically from the analysand's position, we may find our space of discourse (Rosa/ Dora's space) shriveling. For these male voices speak from the position of the subject-presumed-to-know. They seize the narrative, and they speak with authority. In allowing them to speak at full pitch — and we must, for they do — we may find these conversations weighted down by male voices. We may find it difficult to keep up our end of the conversation. What we may *hope* to hear (I guarantee nothing), if we can survive the sheer weight of the communal patriarchal voice which silences Rosa Coldfield, is finally the mad voice of Faulkner's own text. This voice *speaks out of* its own uninterpretable ability to re-create woman as speaker. This Woman (I do not know her name) *speaks out of* a feminine silence which men created but which men cannot control. She speaks out of the spaces of rhetoric which are *somewhere else,* between and beyond what we think language is. If we continue to trust Faulkner as he drags us into this bog of male discourse, we must struggle to keep our heads up so that we can speak what that silence means.

I am beginning at the point of Rosa's text quoted in the epigraph so as to pay attention to *Absalom*'s narrative sequence between chapters five and six. Again the hysteric instructs us. Like Rosa's narrative, the story the hysteric tells in analysis usually wanders; yet its wanderings instruct the listener/reader "about the crucial role of sequence, at once foreseen and unforeseeable." The hysterical narrative, in literature and psychoanalysis, thus "derives its meaning from the temporal order which constitutes it; narrative exists in the time of its telling rather than the order of its events" (Jacobus 218). This idea seems essential to any understanding of *Absalom,* but particularly crucial to our reading of the text between these two chapters. This seems to be a space in which binary opposition does generate and regenerate itself along the lines of sexual difference. As such, this textual space of bisexual stress may be read as one of many such sites of the *production* of *Absalom*'s madness, its mysterious and ceaseless disruptions of meaning, its stubborn resistance to analysis. If we continue to approach the hysterical text as language's negotiation of an unrepresentable *space* in discourse, we may begin to experience the back-and-forthness, the *tautness* of this bisexual space in which the feminine and the masculine do battle.

Rosa, as we have seen, has her differences *within,* and they generate her own text's madness, *its* resistance to interpretation. She has been "seduced" as sexual object, evidenced in her acquiescence to Sutpen, and as ideological subject, as we see in her racist denial of Clytie's humanity. Now we may move outward from Rosa to read what Johnson refers to as "the difference *between* entities"—that is, binary oppositions created by sexual difference—and perhaps from that point to "the subtle, powerful effects of difference already at work within the illusion of a binary opposition" (*Critical Difference* x–xi): in short, the difference *within* the difference *between.*

To begin: as Rosa recounts Sutpen's death, she is completing her hysterical narrative, at least so it should seem to Quentin. This, of course, is the point in the psychoanalytic process (if all goes well) at which "reminiscence loses its grip on the present and life [supposedly] can begin again": the hysteric is cured; she should no longer suffer from the painful, and consequently repressed, scenes of her own history (Jacobus 219, 216). What happens next, though, is strangely provoking. Quentin the listener ceases to listen! He, like Freud in Dora's case, constructs his own male narrative; hence his re-creation of the scene of Judith, with her raised wedding dress, confronting Henry after he has killed Charles Bon. Is this creation simply the result of Quentin's obsession with the Judith-Henry confrontation and its implication of brother-sister incest? It is difficult to know. Twice we are told that Quentin "was not even listening" to this, the last gasp of Rosa's long history (*AA* 140). Is Quentin's problem perhaps more closely related to the fact that he simply cannot bring himself to participate in Rosa's killing of the masculine in her text, in her *speaking* the castration her triangle of lace constituted to the male gaze? He does not participate imaginatively in the "unmaking" of Sutpen's phallic power; for, as we have seen in his conflicted response to the Sutpen story, such power is what he both desires and detests. Yet Miss Rosa will not allow Quentin to write his own male narrative for long. She insists that he confront the *failure* of that "something" in the patriarchal house he calls home. She overcodes his male text of Judith and Henry; she persists; she will not be shut up. She says:

> "There's something in that house."
> "In that house? It's Clytie. Dont she———"

"No. Something living in it. Hidden in it. It has been out there for four years, living hidden in that house." (*AA* 140)

So ends the fifth chapter of *Absalom*. At the beginning of chapter six, Mr. Compson, who throughout the book attempts to diminish and silence Rosa's mad feminine text, takes control of the narrative and announces her death in his letter. In the same sense that she "killed" Sutpen, Quentin's father kills her. This is a "killing" seconded by Quentin's and Shreve's subsequent comments. Quentin, explaining his father's letter to Shreve and denying his own kinship to Rosa, kills her before her time. He names her as "neither aunt cousin nor uncle, Rosa. Miss Rosa. Miss Rosa Coldfield, an old lady that died young of outrage in 1866 one summer" (*AA* 142). To which Shreve responds, "You mean she was no kin to you, no kin to you at all, that there was actually one Southern Bayard or Guinevere who was no kin to you? then what did she die for?" (*AA* 142) Here, then, the denied kinship to woman, the repressed and feared female sexuality (why else the name Guinevere?), again the speaking of woman's death. And yet, Rosa/Guinevere rises out of the complicitous male narrative of her death—out of her early death in Quentin's consciousness, out of Shreve's misnaming (which he persists in throughout the book), out of the folds of Mr. Compson's sardonic letter proclaiming her death—to force Quentin to confront the "something in that house." Like Caddy, whose voice emerges and re-emerges out of the male discourse it is buried within, Rosa is reborn to move through "the moonless September dust" of Quentin's mind. Dressed in black, clutching her umbrella, "the implacable doll-sized old woman" rides the smothering dust cloud to lead him to the dark house and its "something," which is, not surprisingly, a double of himself—a man, a man cut off and dying (*AA* 142–43).

Let me restate the sequence of what we may construe as this space between chapters. 1. Woman's text "kills" man. 2. Men's texts kill woman. 3. Woman won't stay dead; she is reborn and eventually leads man to "the something" in the patriarchal house, which, it seems to me, is the vision of his own castration. As readers of the hysterical text that is *Absalom, Absalom!* we may be instructed by the chronology of this brief narrative space. What I have *not* paid much attention to until this point in my hysterical reading is the "difference *between* entities," specifically the bisexual space between the novel's male and female characters. In Cixous's vision of artistic bisexuality, as we have seen, the bisexual space of "in-between" consciousness is one in which female and male elements are exacerbated through interaction with each other; hence the permanent state of tension in thinking and writing generated in an ongoing exchange between the two. What we find illustrated by the narrative sequence just outlined, however, is another text of bisexual interaction. Rather than an exchange, it is a binary struggle for what we may think of as *narrative authority*. Rosa's woman's voice speaks, as we have noted, a hysterical text which itself becomes a metaphor for the resistance to interpretation, which reflects back upon itself and so becomes the reflexive dimension of culture's patriarchal text. On the other hand, the male voices of *Absalom* seem engaged in a constant struggle to distance and disavow woman's body and woman's text (which sometimes are one and the same).

Rosa tells men that they are all castrated. That they lack power, wholeness, Being. That their narratives lack authority. Yet she, we have observed, also reconstructs lack as pleasure, as the very beginning of desire, as the text's own desire for play and production: as the text's madness. Quentin, his father, and Shreve fear her feminine text, its resistance to interpretation, and its flow beyond patriarchal structures. They, like Sutpen, want to empower themselves both to control and to interpret experience. They want to erect *their* grand narrative, *their* Sutpen's Hundred, and so encode the authority of their cultural story. Like Freud, they must erase the hysterical text which reads them too well. Had they been asked, they might indeed have agreed with Freud and asked Dora: Is Herr K. really so bad after all? Is Rosa's ogre really such an ogre? Are not Dora's and Rosa's hysterical texts themselves aberrant? Is not the presence of madness (coded female) simply the proof of sanity and rationality (coded male), rather than that which questions the very bases on which the notions of sanity and rationality are constructed? (At this point my text feels weighted by men's questions. It is a struggle to continue to speak.)

Since Rosa threatens and disrupts all that controls and orders southern patriarchy, it is no surprise that the novel's males are often engaged in overcoding her feminine text with masculinist texts which marginalize and diminish it. This overcoding of the feminine in *Absalom* has proven an irresistible enterprise for some critics as well, who, in interpreting Rosa and other female characters, take their lead from Mr. Compson, Quentin, and Shreve.[19] As John N. Duvall points out about Faulkner studies in general, "Such interpretive moments are a strategy of containment," pointing to the lack of "a self-reflectivity that would call into question its assumptions when speaking about gender" (47). Within a context of questioning our own questions as well as our assumptions, we may inquire not only where Faulkner figures in this textual war of the sexes, this difference *between,* but also, as Johnson asks us to consider, how binary difference in this case may be seen as functioning in unpredictable ways. What "subversions" are "logically prior to it and necessary in its very construction"? (*Critical Difference* xi) From within Quentin's imagination at the end of the novel, Rosa's helpless silenced woman's body can write itself only as obscenity in the feminist consciousness. How then do we read Faulkner's stance toward "the realm of the proper" and the shutting up (in? out? down?) of Rosa Coldfield? This is the hardest question, and one which turns around to question us about the way we have until this point conducted our own readings. Again a discomfiting silence, a gap in the critical text. Again the question: can we continue to trust Faulkner in these conversations?

Can we trust ourselves?

> Ellen had lost some flesh of course, but it was as the butterfly itself enters dissolution by actually dissolving: the area of wing and body decreasing a little, the pattern of the spots drawing a little closer together . . .
>
> Mr. Compson

Let us begin by thinking about Mr. Compson's male gaze and how it pins down the feminine.[20] Like Nietzsche, Mr. Compson appreciates and insists upon the construction of distance, which allows the male gaze to configure its own representation of woman: she is (and must be) "an effect at a distance" (Derrida, *Spurs* 47). Within such a construction, Mr. Compson's text freezes the feminine and activates the masculine; he "makes" the feminine as No One, as absence. Consider how he constructs woman's image: Ellen, the fading butterfly, "the substanceless shell, the shade impervious to any alteration of dissolution because of its very weightlessness: no body to be buried: just the shape, the recollection . . ." (*AA* 100). Judith, "the blank shape, the empty vessel" of her brother's male texts (*AA* 95), the "bucolic maiden" who read Bon's letters without understanding them (102). The nameless octoroon, "a woman with a face like a tragic magnolia, the eternal female, the eternal Who-suffers . . ." (*AA* 91). And seventeen-year-old Rosa Coldfield, the "Southern Lady" who feeds upon others of her own blood "like a vampire . . . with that serene and idle splendor of flowers abrogating to herself . . ." (*AA* 68). Mr. Compson's male gaze is as innovative as it is deadly. It fixes femininity as a butterfly pinned to a paper, flapping feebly, eventually becoming still, flat . . . analyzable.

In writing about Italo Calvino's *Invisible Cities,* Teresa de Lauretis discusses how the city of Zobeide, depicted therein, was built by men of various nations out of an identical ongoing dream in which they pursued a naked woman who, running through the dark streets of an unknown city, always escaped them. The men came together and constructed a city with spaces and walls different from the ones dreamed, so that the fugitive woman of the dream could not escape. The city itself, as de Lauretis points out, "tells the story of male desire by performing the absence of woman and by producing woman as text, as pure representation" (*Alice Doesn't* 12–13). This is the same narrative process that Mr. Compson initiates when he answers Quentin's first question about Rosa Coldfield ("But why tell me about it?" [*AA* 12]) with the statement that southern women are ghosts. Shreve and Quentin together take up this male story and participate in the complicitous male struggle for narrative authority over Rosa's woman's text. This is the difference *between* which generates *Absalom.* Yet, as I have suggested, there is a difference *within* the difference *between.* Up until now we have tried to read some of that difference in Rosa's mad text. Now, as we read the struggles of the male texts to overcode woman's reading and speaking of the cultural madness within and without, we will attempt to discover where they falter, where they gape and sputter, where they cannot pin woman down or keep her at a distance.

For illustration let us look again at how Mr. Compson constructs Rosa as a girl. Placed in "that grim tight little house with the father," nurtured by the "outraged female vindictiveness" of the aunt, the young Rosa of Mr. Compson's creation lurks and eavesdrops outside closed doors in the "mausoleum" inhabited by father and aunt (*AA* 47). As a girl she sits at the table with Sutpen and his family, her small body "with its air of curious and paradoxical awkwardness like a costume borrowed at the last moment and of necessity for a masquerade which she did not want to attend . . ." (*AA* 51). Mr. Compson writes a text in which young Rosa is silent. He derides her "schoolgirl's poetry about the also-dead" (*AA* 65). She is the watcher, the listener—always outside, always on the other side of the closed door or across the way. Yet the difference *within* her silence, as it is created by Mr. Compson, is its (and her) uncanny, and empowering, ability to listen beyond language. This Rosa, as she sits across from Sutpen, has extrasensory powers of perception "as though she actually had some intimation gained from that rapport with the fluid cradle of events (time) which she had acquired or cultivated by listening beyond closed doors not to what she heard there, but by becoming supine and receptive, incapable of either discrimination or opinion or incredulity, listening to the prefever's temperature of disaster . . ." (*AA* 51–52). She is frozen in silence, but her silence bespeaks an ability to listen, like Cassandra, beyond the teleologies of time and space to what has yet to happen.

Of course, no one wanted to hear what Cassandra knew. De Lauretis points out that we may not be surprised at depictions of history in which women are absent as subjects. Calvino's absent woman "is thus an accurate representation of the paradoxical status of women in Western discourse: while culture originates from woman and is founded on the dream of her captivity, women are all but absent from history and cultural process" (*Alice Doesn't* 13). Mr. Compson constructs women who are absent to their own historical voices. For the most part, they are seen, gazed upon; but, like Cassandra, avoided when they have something to say. We may recall the striking visual moments women constitute in his text, with their strange postures: young Rosa sewing "tediously and without skill" (*AA* 61), Judith's "impenetrable and serene face" (99) (It is only Quentin's grandmother's story, emerging through Mr. Compson's, that permits Judith to speak.), the voluptuous octoroon with her tragic magnolia face, Ellen the butterfly pinned to the patriarchal board.

And yet, even within the tight grim house of Mr. Compson's narrative, the feminine oozes and flows up and out of containment, much as Caddy Compson emerges over and over out of her brothers' voices. Gail Mortimer points out that Faulkner's female characters have an "affinity for flowing, touching, doing, and being . . ." (*Faulkner's Rhetoric of Loss* 90); and that Faulkner's association of woman with water expresses his "anxiety about the eruption of her placid surface into something threatening annihilation"—an anxiety which leads him to image woman as a vase or urn, "an emblem of desire and a work of art" ("The Smooth, Suave Shape of Desire"151). Certainly within *Mr. Compson's* consciousness (which seems to distinguish itself from Faulkner's in many ways), the flow of female sexuality, like encroaching lava, is both seductive and ominous. His description of Judith's sexual development seems to become, in itself, a kind of liquid solution of femininity which both threatens and beckons, that which Jardine would call the feminine space over which narrative (in this case the patriarchal voice) has lost control and which threatens to overflow its bounds at any moment (something Faulkner's text does do in *The Wild Palms*, as I shall discuss in the following chapter). Judith, Mr. Compson tells his son, has arrived at

> that state where, though still visible, young girls appear as though
> seen through glass and where even the voice cannot reach them;
> where they exist . . . in a pearly lambence without shadows and
> themselves partaking of it; in nebulous suspension held, strange
> and unpredictable, even their very shapes fluid and delicate
> and without substance; not in themselves floating and seeking
> but merely waiting, parasitic and potent and serene, drawing
> to themselves without effort the post-genitive upon and about
> which to shape, flow into back, breast; bosom, flank, thigh. (*AA*
> 52–53)

This is the feminine about to overflow, the unrepresentable about to become the uncontrollable, female sexuality *becoming*. We are reminded of Rosa's "summer of wistaria," her feminine space of desire. Unlike Rosa, Mr. Compson writes woman's desire as other. He "makes" (in every sense of the word) woman in the same way he describes the thousand white men of New Orleans who "made" the female octoroons, who constructed them as pure representation of male desire ("made them, created and produced them") in order to access and appropriate "a female principle" which those men constructed as being implicit in black female sexuality and as constituting what Mr. Compson calls (with relish) the "strange and ancient curious pleasures of the flesh" (*AA* 92). As Mr. Compson tells his son, these women were bred for pleasure and sold for a price, "accepted or declined through a system more formal than any that white girls are sold under since they are more valuable as commodities than white girls, raised and trained to fulfill a woman's sole end and purpose: to love, to be beautiful, to divert . . ." (*AA* 93). Woman's sexuality is thus bounded and bargained for; it is the commodity which fuels the economy of the realm of the proper.

It is difficult to know how to converse with Mr. Compson's own "making" of woman. He writes a masculinist text which challenges Rosa's story for narrative authority. He distances her text and diminishes her. She is a ghost, a vampire, a girl with dangling legs that never grew. Yet his self-consciousness about the cultural representation of gender, his sardonic awareness of *what* he says about women in general, gives us pause. What we know is that Quentin's father, even as he tries to pin down the feminine, also recognizes, as Nietzsche, Derrida, and Freud did, his own inability to do so. For woman, even as Mr. Compson freezes her with the male gaze, continues to hold at least the *potential* for overflowing the male text and becoming Rosa Coldfield, who just won't shut up, who *talks and talks*. And so, it seems to me that in a subversive way, the feminine seeps silently through the rational and controlled surface of Mr. Compson's talk, which shuts up its own feminine voice as it seeks to order experience by putting people in their proper places, by naming woman in terms of her usage ("ladies, women, females" or "ladies or whores or slaves"). Although he speaks of what men do to women and, by his self-consciousness, distances himself slightly from the cultural values he is explaining (and transferring) to Quentin, we sense his participation in the masculine "we" that he describes as creating women as commodities.

Mr. Compson thus comes to reify patriarchal narratives of mastery, in which feminine desire such as Rosa's, or perhaps Judith's or the octoroon's (the difference within his text — that which he is pulled toward yet repelled by), is objectified and pinned down. We are reminded, in fact, of how Rosa describes her moment of seduction:

> *And then one afternoon (I was in the garden with a hoe, where the path came up from the stable lot) I looked up and saw him looking at me. He had seen me for twenty years, but now he was looking at me; he stood there in the path looking at me, in the middle of the afternoon.* (AA 131)

Mr. Compson's male gaze does what Sutpen's did: it sees woman in terms of pure representation, as the vehicle of male desire. Like Sutpen, Mr. Compson only wants Rosa to shut up, to be true to his own configurations of her, as the child with dangling legs, as the lurker behind doors, as the "Southern Lady" vampire, as woman on the outside. But "this other-than-themselves,"[21] this Rosa Coldfield, won't stay in *or* out of the Father's House; she won't shut up and she won't stay put. The male gaze seeks to pin her down and keep her still. It seeks to silence her difference. Its failure to do so ultimately results in the fall of the Father's House, that "gray huge rotting deserted house" that Sutpen built (*AA* 153).

Maybe we are both Father.

Quentin Compson

The perimeters of Mr. Compson's gaze extend farther than we think. His voice reverberates through the chill New England air of Quentin and Shreve's dark room. Shreve is right when he says to Quentin, "Dont say it's just me that sounds like your old man" (*AA* 210). For, as Quentin himself realizes, his father's way of seeing and his father's voice contain "*the old ineradicable rhythm*" which they both, as males, move to. Walter Brylowski finds that these rhythms constitute a shared mythic consciousness which may be connected to Rosa's mythologizing of Sutpen ("Faulkner's 'Mythology'" 123–24). I, on the other hand, believe that Quentin and Shreve participate in, and come to construct, a shared *male* consciousness. Irwin reads these male relationships as highly competitive and structured upon the Oedipal model of father-son struggles for dominance (122). Certainly this is true of Sutpen and Charles Bon, and, less obviously, perhaps, of Mr. Compson and Quentin. Yet what may strike us as much more important are these men's *shared narratives of mastery,* handed down by men to men, sometimes all the way from Sutpen himself to Grandfather to Father to Quentin and Shreve, the latter four saying and resaying the story back and forth to one another. This is a community of male telling. *"Yes,"* Quentin thinks, *"we are both Father. Or maybe Father and I are both Shreve, maybe it took Father and me both to make Shreve or Shreve and me both to make Father or maybe Thomas Sutpen to make all of us"* (AA 210).[22]

In the final third of the book particularly, these male voices merge and mingle as if they were multiples of one voice. Mr. Compson's presence is everywhere. His voice, his gaze, layer Quentin's story of Grandfather's story of Sutpen's story. We may, in fact, think of Quentin's father's talk as an ongoing narrative act that runs under the whole last section of the book, sometimes emerging to speak in its own voice but mostly speaking through other male voices. This shared (white) male discourse reifies itself again and again until it arrives at the pure language of the Father. This is, I find, that point in the text which records Sutpen's bald statement of patriarchal quest, related through Grandfather Compson's/Mr. Compson's/Quentin's voice(s):

> "You see, I had a design in my mind. Whether it was a good or a bad design is beside the point; the question is, Where did I make the mistake in it. . . . I had a design. To accomplish it I should require money, a house, a plantation, slaves, a family — incidentally of course a wife. I set out to acquire these, asking no favor of any man." (AA 212)

I am not arguing that all the male speakers in *Absalom* approve of what Sutpen did. Nevertheless, as male subjects constituted by a cultural order that privileges man, they engage in a common discourse, in a "man talk" that *enables* Sutpen's voice to emerge and speak patriarchy's narrative of mastery; in this sense they reify patriarchy's authority at the same time that they construct their own. Myriam Díaz-Diocaretz has discussed how woman in some of Faulkner's stories and novels becomes "a *repeatable* text" created by Faulkner's strategic consciousness in combination with the voice of "cultural belief" (258). Her argument has particular application to our conversations at this point. Despite their judgments upon the blatancy of Sutpen's phallic order, Grandfather Compson, Mr. Compson, Quentin Compson, and Shreve all seem to articulate the "cultural belief" of patriarchy—belief which legitimizes itself by excluding the feminine, by placing women outside the symbolic order, and by thus diffusing women's potential to disrupt that order's authority *while at the same time* positing the female body as a commodity of exchange whose valuation or devaluation fuels the symbolic order's inner workings. In the mutuality of their male conversations, Faulkner indeed teaches us about the ongoing quality of the grand narrative of patriarchy—how it passes itself along; how, like Mr. Compson's voice and gaze, it can be always moving under the surface of how men "talk" to one another, and particularly of how they join together in a symbolic order which configures woman as other; how the *exclusion of the feminine,* as Ruth Salvaggio points out in her provocative *Enlightened Absence,* actually becomes the necessary element for the masculine to order itself and its interactions.

In considering what is necessary to legitimize cultural narratives, Lyotard suggests that people actualize such narratives "not only by recounting them, but also by listening to them and recounting *themselves through them*; in other words, by putting them into 'play' in their institutions—thus by assigning themselves the posts of narratee and diegesis as well as the post of narrator." Through this process, narratives of culture "thus define what has the right to be said and done in the culture in question . . ." (23). Matthews has remarked on how "marriages of speaking and hearing" in *Absalom* show "that the truth of a narrative arises from the way it is created and shared, and not strictly from its content" (151). Within the *male* interchanges we are exploring here, cultural narrative legitimizes itself as a process of listening and recounting stories which *do not tell about or do not listen to* the culture's own feminine voice, or put another way, disallow *women's* positions as speakers. This "man talk" empowers Thomas Sutpen to speak by shutting Rosa Coldfield up. And I am not speaking metaphorically. We have heard Sutpen's voice. Now we move toward Rosa's final silencing.

This silencing of woman's cultural narrative figures itself as a process of devaluation ("It wasn't a son. It was a girl.") which is most obvious in Sutpen's systematic use of women and denigration of the female body, but which forms all the male texts. Rosa is its primary target, for she is, as we have seen, the hysteric who erases the boundaries between the conscious and the unconscious and so shows the Father to himself in disconcerting ways. As a result, much of the tension in Quentin and Shreve's talking seems to be generated out of two bisexual spaces: one which contains their continual struggle to legitimize their (Mr. Compson's, Sutpen's, Grandfather's) own cultural narrative by silencing Rosa's/woman's; and the other, that space in which the feminine text writes what patriarchy *does not know* and does not *want* to know across the man talk of the dormitory room.

Shreve, as I mentioned earlier, consistently distances and diminishes the authority of Rosa's narrative by misnaming her. Despite Quentin's attempts to correct him, he calls her, at various times, "this old dame" (*AA* 143); "this old gal, this Aunt Rosa" (175); "the old dame, the Aunt Rosa" (143, 258, 279, and *passim*); "the old Aunt Rosa" (260). In chapter eight he explodes into a Mr. Compson–like misogynistic tirade of male entrapment, as he envisions Charles Bon's leaving the octoroon without saying goodbye, and for good reason:

> Because you cant beat them: you just flee (and thank God you can flee, can escape from that massy five-foot-thick maggot-cheesy solidarity which overlays the earth, in which men and women in couples are ranked and racked like ninepins; thanks to whatever Gods for that masculine hipless tapering peg which fits light and glib to move where the cartridge-chambered hips of women hold them fast);– not goodbye: all right: (*AA* 249–50)

Appropriating Mr. Compson's male gaze, Shreve goes on to speak of woman (Judith, in particular) as a cup of sherbet which man can either pass up, or suddenly desire and take. Yet, at the same time, Shreve seems oddly fascinated by Rosa's own fascination with what is at the very margins of meaning. He asks Quentin, "What was it the old dame, the Aunt Rosa, told you about how there are some things that just have to be whether they are or not, have to be a damn sight more than some other things that maybe are and it dont matter a damn whether they are or not?" (*AA* 258). Again, in the final chapter, he associates Rosa with what we might call "the essential unknowable": like madness, the essential unknowable is consistently uninterpretable, yet its (her) *very resistance to meaning* is paradoxically and mysteriously crucial to meaning. To Quentin he says:

> "Yes. You dont know. You dont even know about the old dame, the Aunt Rosa."
> "Miss Rosa," Quentin said.
> "All right. You dont even know about her. Except that she refused at the last to be a ghost. . . ." (*AA* 289)

Shreve seems, then, to find Rosa's mad text of castration, of *not knowing,* fascinating, terrifying, and seductive.[23] He leans ambivalently toward, then away from, her feminine text as it speaks the uninterpretable pleasure of giving up mastery as a goal, of calling into question, as Gallop would say, "the phallic illusions of authority" (*Reading Lacan* 20), and thereby nudging out the boundaries of meaning.

Quentin's fear of losing control, his desperation to cover up his inadequacies (I am thinking of *The Sound and the Fury* as well as *Absalom*), dictates finally that he allow his father's voice of mastery to take hold of his own (Quentin's) consciousness and speak a male discourse of empowerment. Finally, with his father's voice ringing in his head as it did in *The Sound and the Fury,* Quentin shuts Rosa up for good. Let us plunge into a strange bisexual space of Quentin's and his father's shared narrative. In the sixth chapter, Mr. Compson, speaking through his son's memory, says, "They lead beautiful lives—women. Lives not only divorced from, but irrevocably excommunicated from, all reality" (*AA* 156). Quentin's father then goes into his story about his aunt whose main worry was that she would be buried in the wrong dress, and so on. How do we read within this space of the male text in which woman is both freed from fear of death, which is, as Freud tells us, the ultimate castration, at the same time she is denied full participation in life? Woman is not alive; thus she need not fear death. This narrative sequence, constructed between Quentin and his father denies women as subjects in history. Within his son's memory, Mr. Compson offers his description of the octoroon visiting Bon's grave, a "magnolia-faced woman a little plumper now" but still the sexual object of the male gaze; wearing, Mr. Compson says with relish, a "soft, flowing gown designed not to infer bereavement or widowhood but to dress some interlude of slumbrous and fatal insatiation, of passionate and inexorable hunger of the flesh" (*AA* 157). This description of the octoroon is followed by Mr. Compson's depictions of Clytie and Judith as Charles Etienne's jailers (162); and of the animalistic qualities of Charles Etienne's "ape-like" and "kenneled" wife (167). There is a fear of woman's subjectivity, her potential to *mean,* which runs at the bottom of all of these descriptions, carried on by Quentin's participation in his father's mythologizing of woman as absence, and of women's lives as a charade of what living really is.

The fact that Quentin knows his father's/Shreve's narratives before hearing them should not be surprising. For what Mr. Compson articulates is Western culture's systematic devaluation of women, a devaluation which, as I said at the beginning of this book, is intimately related to the way the feminine is placed outside the realm of those essential interactions which legitimize cultural narrative. What Quentin's father says does not, as Quentin knows, tell him anything new, but strikes *"word by word, the resonant strings of remembering"* (*AA* 172). Quentin's father places *women* either outside the realm of those essential interactions which create and reify cultural narrative, or he articulates *woman* as a sign in social discourse, further encoding the narrative of mastery so matter-of-factly stated by Sutpen, and handed down through three generations of Compson males. This mythologizing of feminine devaluation reaches a crescendo in three male voices which merge in Quentin's text of woman as absence, articulated in thought as a response to his father's and Shreve's complicitous narratives. Hearing Shreve's retelling of Judith's death, conjuring Rosa's inscribing of Judith's tombstone, Quentin thinks,

> *I didn't need to listen then but I had to hear it and now I am having to hear it all over again because he sounds just like Father: Beautiful lives—women do. In very breathing they draw meat and drink from some beautiful attentuation of unreality in which the shades and shapes of facts—of birth and bereave-*

> *ment, of suffering and bewilderment and despair—move with*
> *the substanceless decorum of lawn party charades, perfect in*
> *gesture and without significance or any ability to hurt. Miss Rosa*
> *ordered that one.* (*AA* 171)

This, finally, is how woman is shut up. She is (note the passive voice) stripped of substance. She is placed on the periphery of culture. Her feminine narrative is judged illegitimate and unreadable. In this way, systems of mastery assert themselves by placing their own difference within *outside* themselves—in other words, configuring difference within (the cultural self) as difference between cultural self (constructed as male) and cultural other (constructed as female). Like the "balloon-faced nigger" at the front door of the plantation, like Sutpen, like three generations of male Compsons, like a Canadian Harvard man, they prescribe and validate their own systems of order by keeping difference out.

What Rosa Coldfield wants is to get in. What she wants Quentin to know is what it feels like to be out, how that kind of pain must be articulated. But he cannot converse with her loss and her desire, not really; because it speaks his own too clearly, because it writes the hysterical text of repressed fear, because it says the terrible pleasure of writing such a text. His imagination silences her in front of the big house. It makes her a "light thin furious creature making no sound at all now, struggling with silent and bitter fury, clawing and scratching and biting at the two men who held her . . ." (*AA* 300).[24] And his father's letter, read in Shreve's voice, buries her, with the sardonic hope that she will be reborn in an afterlife which allows *"the privilege of being outraged and amazed and of not forgiving . . ."* (*AA* 301).

What happens when difference becomes the subject? When it writes upon *us* the terror of its madness, its resistance to interpretation, its desire for play, its *difference*? As I feel the madness of my hysterical reading spinning with the rhythms of Faulkner's mad text of *Absalom,* rhythms which move on and on past his text or mine, what seems most *true* is perhaps what has been obvious about this book all along. And that is its very real terror. I have written about this terror as being everywhere at once. Yet at the end of the book it becomes larger and denser. It imbues Shreve's description of the horror of sameness in a way which recalls Melville's descriptions of whiteness. *Absalom* shows the terror of disallowing difference, of creating cultural narratives which insist upon mastery as a goal, which say no to all but one story—which, in Shreve's words, "bleach out" the world. When Quentin says he doesn't hate the South, he speaks an ironic truth; for what he has done is kill that part of it (and of himself) he hates, that bisexual space in the text between himself and an angry old woman. In doing so, however, he has killed his own difference within. Locked in a chain of constituted codes of sameness, he himself becomes culturally constituted by those codes and so loses that quality of subjectivity which can speak the unrepresentable mad text of Rosa Coldfield.

Yet what is so astonishing, and so brilliant, about *Absalom* is that, paradoxically, while Quentin allows himself to be encoded by one master narrative of culture, while he denies bisexuality, difference, madness, woman, *his own text speaks against him.* He says, "*I dont. I dont! I dont hate it! I dont hate it!*" (*AA* 303). But what he also says is the cost of writing the narrative of mastery. That cost is the silencing of Rosa Coldfield who speaks difference from the position of subject, and so who writes upon Quentin, and upon us, what it is to be pure representation, to be constituted as absence. In this way *Absalom, Absalom!* writes its own difference. In Rosa's talking, Quentin's hearing, and the tension between their two narratives, it writes the gaps and ruptures within patriarchal culture. This tension in turn creates a bisexual space in the novel, which, like the hysteric, emerges to write its own mad text of alterity. *That* text, Faulkner's text, curls around upon us in a mysterious yet highly political way, to affirm its own madness by affirming the difference it configures as feminine.

4 *Flooding and the Feminine Text*

Q. What did the tremendous wave signify? What caused it?

A. That simply is a physical fact in that country when a levee breaks. The water rushed through the crevasse and it came to the lowest place, which was a stream which up to that time had been flowing toward the river. This wave of water — at that time the river, the Mississippi, was forty feet higher than the country and when that levee gave way that mass of water that came through had to go somewhere and it broke on the east side of the river so that wave of water simply continued to go east until it spent itself and in this stream, which up until that time had been flowing placidly west, it turned around and went backward. That's just a physical fact of hydraulics and levee.

William Faulkner,
Faulkner in the University

Can one write water, can one read water? How can one do it? That is precisely the question of this text. One can only do it by throwing oneself into the water, by becoming one with the water.

Hélène Cixous, quoted in Conley,
Hélène Cixous: Writing the Feminine

I *Flooding and the Question of Positionality*

In this inconclusive concluding chapter I want to think about how Faulkner's narrative floods, and whether that flooding may be read as feminine. Faulkner had his own ideas about "writing water." At the

University of Virginia he spoke of narrative's power to represent "the furious motion of being alive, that's all any story is. You catch this fluidity which is human life and you focus a light on it and you stop it long enough for people to be able to see it . . ." (*Faulkner in the University* 239) (editor's ellipsis). In these conversations, though, the question we may well ask is how, indeed, does the writer "catch" and "focus" and "stop" fluidity's "furious motion," and at the same time allow it to move and flow, sometimes even to flood over its own bounds to *somewhere else*? Bleikasten suggests that Faulkner writes out of a narrative desire for masculine authority, the authority of the father-author, in "what is perhaps the ultimate stake of the writing game: mastery" ("Fathers in Faulkner" 145). Yet there are obvious limitations to thinking about narrative in general, and Faulkner's writing in particular, as a vehicle toward authorial empowerment; our readings up to this point have, in fact, suggested just the opposite—that Faulkner the author disperses himself into the writing, dissolving into the spaces of his narrative which are sometimes marked by woman.

To master fluidity is inevitably to control its motion and to encase it in solid linguistic structures, which, like a river's levees, direct its flow. Can we characterize Faulkner's narrative in this way—in terms of how successfully the author has managed to control and master its own flow? Do we wish to? Certainly Faulkner is the stylist *par excellence*—"a careful craftsman, conscious of the need for calculation and design" (Reed 7). Yet, as I have suggested in other contexts, Faulkner's narrative art seems to distinguish itself from what it may have set out to be and becomes most beautiful and mysterious and compelling *not* when it is most ordered and focused and controlled but rather when it somehow slips out of its own self-constructed levees and "becomes one with the water." When it privileges *its own* "oceanic feeling,"[1] its own dangerous and exhilarating desire for *the escape of* fluidity; that is, for an experiential excess which dissolves ego boundaries and allows movement between itself as text and the otherness of the reader. When it *floods*.

His statement about catching and focusing and holding fluidity notwithstanding, what Faulkner seemed to *practice* in his art is the knowledge that the freezing of fluidity is like the freezing of water: it creates a hard opaqueness which becomes something else altogether. Keats's Grecian urn, which so fascinated Faulkner, embodies the dilemma of art in that it freezes *the image* of fluidity, of desire, but cannot preserve its motion. It is this sensation of "furious motion" (which Charlotte Rittenmeyer so valued) and its attendant "experience of temporality" (Pearce xiii)—in, for example, Keats's twittering sparrows of "To Autumn" and Stevens's deer roaming those mountains *beyond* the outer boundaries of "Sunday Morning"—which defy that freezing point by mysteriously continuing to remain kinetic. Such poems become fluid—in Cixous's phrase, "one with the water"—by producing themselves over and over within a space which is itself in constant flux, a space whose boundaries are always being eroded and reformed by the sloshing of its own fluid movements. The poet thus creates form *in motion*. The aquatic life of such poetry swims everywhere and so retains flexivity within one fluid space, which itself becomes oceanic in always remaking its own shoreline.

Although I do not wish to draw too fine a metaphoric distinction between the fluidities of poetry and narrative, it seems to me that fiction, specifically Faulkner's fiction, because it is narrative, must do something else—that is, must have a different way of remaining fluid. Because it is *story,* and thus has a beginning and an ending, it cannot preserve fluidity by allowing it to move under the surface of one *place,* one body of water: one lake. Its narrativity requires that it flow sequentially from one place to another. Its "space," as Gérard Genette points out, is actually "the time needed for *crossing* or *traversing* it, like a road or a field" (34). This is obviously true, to a degree, of all writing. Genette notes, "one cannot read a text backwards, letter by letter, or even word by word, or even sentence by sentence, without its ceasing to be a text" (34). More specifically, however, narrative is, as Ronald Schleifer says, "*temporizing* in both senses of the word: both *passing* and *gaining* time so that the endless displacements and endless destructions of time can be deferred" (875). Yet, in the way that Frank Kermode suggests, narrative texts have their "secrets" which may be very much at odds with sequence (138). In this sense much of what compels us in Faulkner's narrative art is not its sequential flow in time, but rather its overflow in space—those places where it pushes out its own boundaries, where it spills out over its own "levees." At the same time, though, it, like the river, builds up natural levees to control and direct its fluidity—which must, however, inevitably *overflow* what it has itself created. In this sense, as we have experienced in *The Sound and the Fury* and *Absalom, Absalom!*, Faulkner's art often seems to strain against its desire to direct its own narrative flow, forcing itself along toward those inevitable points which exceed containment. Then it oozes or gushes or floods over boundaries in ways that are hard to recognize, yet are always already in motion.

This is a multiple and mutual process of reproduction. As Faulkner himself well knew, a river—particularly the Mississippi River—reproduces itself by flooding, creating new flows. In this way land and water cross-fertilize each other, land by allowing itself to be liquified and washed away to enrich the river, water by depositing sediments from other lands which themselves have been enriched by earlier floodings. Similarly, certain *overflowings* in Faulkner's art reproduce themselves by creating new channels which seem to move the narrative, and even the idea of narrative, *somewhere else*, thereby recreating itself in new and non-linear flows which spread lavalike in many directions at once. In this sense Faulkner's books, by mysteriously exceeding their own spaces, expand our sense of how and where narrative may *move*. Because they "flood" in this way, they indeed defy consumption by infinitely deferring the space necessary to accomplish it in. In one sense, then, Faulkner was right about the fluidity of experience. At times he could and did contain, stop, catch, focus it. At other times, though, as we have seen in *The Sound and the Fury* and *Absalom, Absalom!*, it would overflow its own levees and flood.

This engagement of containment and flooding is, I think, what Faulkner's most fluid book, *The Wild Palms*, is about. It is, moreover, an engagement crucial to the dilemma of narrative art, which must *contain* fluid, but also *be* it. The reader of fluids faces a subsequent dilemma. Cixous also asks, we will recall, "how can one *read* water?" (my emphasis). It is essential, I think, to read flooding in the same way Faulkner writes it: to be aware of that which contains and directs its flow, but also to recognize that there are times when containment breaks down and that it is then incumbent upon us to learn how to read the fluidity of those moments—to learn to submerge ourselves in such watery places of the text. For what happens at such points is that the text mysteriously dissolves boundaries between writing and reading and, in its fecundity and ability to rechannel itself, may also rechannel the relationship between itself and . . . us. As I have said already, Faulkner's texts sometimes move to read us. At these "flood stages," narrative moves of its own volition to create new ways of flowing from text to reader, thereby fertilizing itself with its own flooding, and so becoming bisexually self-generating out of (and in) its own excess. In this final chapter I will be attempting to read flooding as crucial to our thinking about the bisexual nature of Faulkner's art. As I converse with this narrative of Faulkner which floods the most, I want to move toward the questions of where and why *The Wild Palms* floods, and how that flooding may be read *as itself* feminine and, moreover, *may* be read, with a peculiar difference, by . . . a woman.

At the base of this study have been the issue of positionality and the premise that women read differently than men. There is perhaps no better illustration of sexual difference in interpretation than that between male and female responses to the word *flooding*. What *flooding* means to a woman is quite different from what *flooding* means to a man. This difference became clear to me when I asked a class of male and female students to define *flooding*. The males spoke, as I have been doing in the introductory part of this chapter, of *something* overflowing, of rushes and gushes of rivers and streams: of water. Women, on the other hand, were silent, flushed, knowledgeable. Reluctantly they spoke of their own bodies, of *feeling* flooding, of *being* overflowing, of experiencing the seeps, drips, gushes of menstruation and miscarriage, childbirth and lactation, of exceeding boundaries: of blood and milk (theirs). I want to think about the flooding of Faulkner's narrative in both senses, but especially in the second, woman's way. For is it not woman who experiences flooding, "the secret irreparable seeping of blood," from the position of subject? Whether from natural or unnatural causes, woman has special expertise: Temple Drake and Charlotte Rittenmeyer know what it is to flood. They have no need to pose the male question, "Where do women bleed?" (*WP* 17). Such female "flooding" seems an untidy subject for critical discourse. Yet its very untidiness, its fluidity, may be a way of getting at that *something more* of Faulkner's art which is itself profoundly untidy as it seeps between the conscious and the unconscious, between language and what it can say, between the subject and the otherness of the world.

We may thus think of flooding in this second, woman's way as a trope for the very process of the subject's deployment into the world through language. The space of that deployment is, of course, that in-between space which unhinges our notions of what subjectivity is. For flooding is like language if one is doing it: it transports one into the otherness of the world, it transgresses and dissolves boundaries between inside and outside. Woman's body's flooding is thus (about) *something more,* as is, I think, Faulkner's narrative's flooding. That *something more* of Faulkner's writing, as I have said before, will always exceed what we have to say about it; for even as it speaks it is always still flooding beyond what it can say. Its language never catches up to its flooding, for its excesses are always slipping away before words can move to speak them. Like Faulkner's tremendous wave, the force of that excess creates channels which constitute new places for language to speak from.

In thinking about how flooding and femininity may merge in *The Wild Palms,* I will be continuing to attempt to read and write woman as subject. Barbara Johnson, in a critique of her own work, points to the difficulty of doing this within the ideological frames of the world we live in. It is not easy, she writes, "to assert that the existence and knowledge of the female subject could simply be produced, without difficulty or epistemological damage, within the existing patterns of culture and language" (*A World of Difference* 40) — an observation which seems particularly relevant to reading a male text, not to mention one which ends in the words, "Women, [shi]t!" Thus, as I begin by posing questions about how *The Wild Palms* floods, and hence about how Faulkner's narrative may exceed its own boundaries in mysterious and provocative ways, I would caution that I am leaping into treacherous waters which may turn back upon feminist readers in disconcerting ways, which indeed may reveal exactly what flooding *costs.*

Yet *The Wild Palms,* whatever else it does, explores the expansive powers of female desire: Charlotte Rittenmeyer flows throughout this text; both sympathetic and unsympathetic critics note her ubiquity.[2] Faulkner is writing woman's body's desire, whose excessiveness floods this narrative in much the same way that the narrative's excessiveness floods *itself* and creates new channels which break down boundaries between what it is — a narrative system which flows sequentially this way and that — and what it sometimes becomes — a narrative flood which washes away landmarks of reading. Such a flood forces us to read fluid space, the semiotic *chora*, where the mysterious beginnings of language float without form.

To begin articulating the crucial questions about *female* desire and the flooding of this text, let us turn to a remarkable study of *male* desire and its relationship to feminine fluidity on the one hand and fascism on the other. In *Male Fantasies: Women, Floods, Bodies, History,* Klaus Theweleit thoroughly documents a lineage of associations between women and water—in history, art, literature, popular culture, and so on. In all European literatures and other literatures influenced by them, he writes, "desire, if it flows at all, flows in a certain sense *through* women. In some way or other, it always flows in relation to the image of woman" (272). In his examination of male texts, Theweleit uses scores of examples from literature, art, and popular culture to demonstrate not only how woman is objectified as the image of male desire, but also how "that image lives in water" (273). What is at work in all of these forms, particularly in literature, he argues, is a specific form of oppression of women: oppression through a reduction to a principle—"the principle of flowing, of distance, of vague, endless enticement" (284). Throughout history, male writers have "encoded their own desire, their own utopias, their own yearning to be free of boundaries, with the notion of an 'endlessly flowing woman.'" Thus Theweleit argues that male desire did not emerge in relation to actual women, but as a part of man's search for "a territory of desire." Male desire therefore suppressed and negated female desire (380–81). (The whole Theweleit argument leads, of course, to the fascist fear of dissolution and flowing, hence of woman.)

Throughout these conversations I have tried to pose, with some insistence, certain troublesome questions about the condition of female subjectivity in Faulkner's texts. In regard to *The Wild Palms,* the key question may well be whether Faulkner is following the pattern documented by Theweleit of creating a territory of male desire by objectifying woman as its flow. Put another way, is the feminine allowed to flow and flood . . . *herself,* or is this feminine fluidity of *The Wild Palms* simply a continuation of the "repeated dramatization of woman as simulacrum, erasure, or silence"? Gail Mortimer finds that female characters in Faulkner's texts often are depicted as images associated with water, and that women who are sexually threatening to male characters are seen as "bodies of water in turmoil." Caddy Compson is thus "imaged as a river when [Quentin] begins to believe that incest between them is possible," Eula Varner and Charlotte Rittenmeyer evoke a feeling of drowning, and "[t]he raging flood in [*The Wild Palms*] is a highly comic enactment of man's helplessness in the presence of an overwhelming feminine threat of engulfment" ("Smooth, Suave Shape" 150–51).

In *The Wild Palms* in particular, Mortimer sees flooding associated with the threat of feminine sexuality, motherhood, and woman's threat to ego boundaries ("Ironies" 32–34). In her comments on Faulkner's texts in general, Mortimer again posits the widely held notion that Faulkner's female characters are often stereotypes reflecting "a mythic or primitive imagination." These characters are "incarnations of such qualities as fecundity, serenity, sexual desire, death, or evil. Because we view them only through the (often troubled) consciousness of his male characters and narrators, they attain a degree of reality determined by the quality of the male's awareness that they exist, and they embody characteristics that are essentially projections based on his own needs and anxieties" ("Smooth, Suave Shape" 149). Within this schema, women are often depicted either as bodies of water (often threatening) or urns/vases which contain and cover over feminine threat (151).

Although my conversation with femininity and flooding distinguishes itself from Mortimer's water/urn dichotomy in ways similar to my differences with other more general studies of Faulkner's female characters discussed in my introductory chapter, here perhaps I should stress a difference in positionality. As I have made clear by my untidy mention of female flooding, I want to read flooding as the language of the speaking subject — hence, as the artist's way of speaking the *something more* of art, as that fluidity of language which is neither inside nor outside text and reader but always in motion *between*. Flooding, in my thinking about this text, is not something *done to* men which frightens and alienates them — a "something" named woman. It is rather how this male text speaks itself as something more than itself — as something feminine which derives from a male author (one accused at times of misogyny), and so as something which unhinges those systems of binary representation which make one thing "masculine" and another "feminine." Even when that something more is indeed contained and covered over, as it sometimes is in Faulkner's books, it may still be read from the inside out—from its position *inside* the urn. To read that something from the outside alone is, it seems to me, to see only the exterior of the urn, thus the frozen image of woman but not her motion and temporality.

To try to read from inside is to squeeze into what I continue to call an in-between space in Faulkner's narrative. This is a space which, because of the excessiveness of the sometimes-contained feminine, is always a flood zone. It is never a safe place. Yet we may remind ourselves, as we continue to read from this (non)position, that language itself, like flooding, is both inside and outside the subject. That in-between space where flooding occurs may offer a new way of thinking about the process of language's containment and overflow of its own "stories," a process that Faulkner's writing embodies—sometimes quite literally. I am, in short, thinking about the *feminine body* of Faulkner's art, about how that body writes herself into and out of the watery and bloody text of *The Wild Palms,* and, moreover, about how that writing of the feminine body traces the very process whereby difference, therefore language, is produced.

And where she writes *from* and *of* is that untidy, oozing, constitutive place where narrative left a *stain* as the trace of its mysterious transgression between inside and outside, between our reading of it and its of us.

II   *Geography and the Question of Excess*

Formerly, the River was confined in its channel by natural levees, but during flood times, the stream departed from this confinement wherever a portion of the natural levee had caved into the stream and thus lowered the height of the levee or formed a notch or crevasse. The stream passed through this newly formed gap with a tremendous rush of water and cut a channel on the back side of the slope away from the stream and finally a great portion of the stream was diverted into this new channel. Because of the fact that the Mississippi River had built up natural levees and because the height of the river surface was well above that of the surrounding ground during flood stage, the River tended to rush with some force into this lowland and flood it. If there was a more or less unbroken access to the sea, the River developed a new channel along these lines or joined with its own bed at a lower elevation farther downstream.

William G. Haag,
"The Geography and Cultural Anthropology of the
Mississippi River"

Q. How do you pronounce the name of your mythical country?

A. If you break it down into syllables, it's simple. Y-o-k, n-a, p-a, t-a-w, p-h-a, YOK [Yock]-na-pa-TAW-pha. It's a Chickasaw Indian word meaning water runs slow through flat land.

William Faulkner,
Faulkner in the University

I will begin by trying to think of *The Wild Palms* geographically, and by imagining how the book, with its two parallel narrative flows, floods *itself*. But I begin simultaneously with a contiguous, perhaps obvious observation: this is a book which is not merely *about* desire, but one which is itself desiring. In *The Sound and the Fury* and *Absalom, Absalom!,* desire is "spoken" through the otherness of woman's silence and woman's talk, both of which in their own ways shatter any boundaries we may seek to construct around what language can accomplish—what a text has the capacity to become. If we listen within and around those ruptures of language, we hear Caddy Compson's silence resonate *into* language and Rosa Coldfield's hysterical voice narrate the female body's otherness to the patriarchal culture which shuts out and shuts in and eventually shuts up the woman who dares articulate herself as a desiring subject. What sets *The Wild Palms* apart as a discourse of desire is that it is a text which is primarily engaged in wanting its other, and yet, because of the book's splitness, that other is *it*.

This production of desire at the textual level propels "Wild Palms" and "Old Man" to overflow at times their own narrative spaces and to flood inward toward each other, momentarily blurring the boundaries constructed between the two narrative sequences.[3] In this capacity to flood into itself, *The Wild Palms,* as the split subject *par excellence,* becomes a "traversal" of the process of difference[4] through the building of tensions created by desire, tensions which involve not only the difference between two narrative sequences, but the continuous over-turning of the reader's desire for one over the other. Again, of course, we find ourselves within a Cixousian space of bisexual writing, marked by the mutual engagement of difference — the text's difference from itself and the repeated patterns of desire that difference precipitates. *The Wild Palms* is not just *about* desire and loss; but the book itself, in its own splitness, constitutes and traverses the productivities of desire and thus impels the reader to read desire at the very site of its production, which is, of course, within the subject. And, for our purposes in reading *The Wild Palms,* that subject may be constructed not only in the more ob-vious ways — as author, as character, as reader — but also as the book itself, that is, as the bisexual narrative subject which reproduces itself by desiring itself.[5]

To continue our conversations with Faulkner at a fathom where it is possible to note his disappearance into (and between) the linguistic structures of his own creation, we may engage *The Wild Palms* as a *nar-rative* subject which, like the human subject (indeed like its human author), is divisible and whose divisibility and the reader's response to that divisibility generate what we may think of as the *something more* of the text, that excess which is located in what we may envision as fluid spaces within the text — spaces which are created by each story's desire for the otherness of the other. *The Wild Palms* thus remains from begin-ning to end *unhinged* between self and other, subject and ob-ject . . . always in motion between the structures which contain its stories and the flooding which creates new channels to connect them. To begin, then, with geography is simply to launch ourselves from a relatively safe, dry place — but one we must inhabit in order to know the difference between it and the fluidity we are trying to read. If we are to experience the flooding of this text, to "become one" with its fluidity, then we may find landmarks between such distinctions as presence and absence, land and water, becoming strangely obscured by our own desire to "read water"—our willingness to *be* flooded.

The Wild Palms has been critically configured as two thematically related but noncontiguous parallel flows, like a double version of the upper headwaters of the Mississippi, which flow in a relatively straight, narrow channel. *Two* of these would look like this:

"Wild Palms" and "Old Man" have been thought of as two such parallel flows which contain like elements, and which should be read, as they were written, for what Faulkner himself called their "contrapuntal quality" (*Faulkner in the University* 171). Thomas L. McHaney points out that the novel gains its intricate coherence from structural, thematic, and symbolic repetitions within each of its two narratives—for example, circular journeys, captivity, a wasteland atmosphere (39–41). I configure the "geography" of these narratives differently, for I am not seeking to uncover new repetitions in two separate stories but rather to understand how "Wild Palms" and "Old Man" almost literally touch each other, how they flood into each other in ways difficult to analyze. Just as important, I am exploring those spaces where their separateness actually creates such desire in the *reader* for the continuation of one narrative's flow over another's that the reader must create new ways of reading which spill over from one text to another and forge new channels between reader and texts. The way in which desire actually creates a *something more* to this already plural text by a process of containment and flooding makes something slip or elide at the textual level of *The Wild Palms*. This *something more* includes not only the interchange between the two stories, but also the book's complex, shifting lay of land which makes those stories flow and stop flowing, and thus causes the desiring reader—the reader hungry for The Story—to read on.

Instead of thinking of "Wild Palms" and "Old Man" as two noncontiguous but thematically similar flows of narrative sequences, as shown in figure 1, let us imagine the two stories flowing *together* as one river in a geographical pattern similar to that of the lower Mississippi River. In the essay "The Geography and Cultural Anthropology of the Mississippi River," quoted at the beginning of this section, William G. Haag describes how the lower Mississippi flows from Cairo, Illinois, to the Gulf of Mexico. The direct distance between those two points is only about 450 miles; yet, in contrast to the upper Mississippi, which flows swiftly and straight within rocky banks, the lower part of the river follows a circuitous route that stretches the 450 miles to nearly 1,100. Because the actual fall of the land from Cairo to the Gulf is only about three inches per mile, the lower river meanders from side to side of the alluvial valley—always a "restless stream that constantly shifts its bed from one area to another" (Haag 173). This almost horizontal pattern of flow is obvious from a map, which shows the Mississippi doubling back upon itself over and over as it moves south. At many points the river looks like this:

Or this:

The Mississippi River—which so captured Faulkner's imagination, as he recounts in his essay "Mississippi," and into which Faulkner flushed the tall convict without his even knowing it—has altered its course many times, through various processes (Haag 174). When it floods, however, as this section's epigraph relates, the river tends to rush into lowlands, make new channels by forging its way through breaks and gaps in the natural levee, and develop a new flow which rejoins the original channel further downstream. Part of an original channel which might have looked like this:

then would be transformed into this:

In this most fluid of Faulkner's books, then, it may be helpful to figure the two narrative sequences as a single meandering flow of the same river, one which moves back and forth on an almost horizontal path. Like the Mississippi, whose flooding is so much a part of its own "story," *The Wild Palms* sometimes floods, causing an excess which must go somewhere else but which eventually returns to its original channel and is reappropriated—though always with a difference. Through this process, *The Wild Palms* mysteriously becomes itself by differing from itself, all the while flowing and flooding in discernible and undiscernable ways.

How does this book flow? How does it flood? And what happens then? Derrida, as we know, writes of the ways that language is always already creating itself by deferring and differing from itself. In its narrative application, the deconstructive process of *The Wild Palms* may be described in two ways: first, as a turning process which is observable in the bends or folds of this meandering riverlike text—bends at which our desires are deferred by being turned to another narrative sequence; and, second, as a process of overflow which floods between stories and between text and reader to allow excessive desire to go *somewhere else,* to differ from itself. This second process is clearly more radical because it allows language both to flood itself, *and* to become flooded by its own flooding and so to dissolve back into the fluid, womblike space which houses language before it is fully formed—before it can speak. *That* space emerges in the text when the reader's desire to read *between* the two stories, to flood over and create new channels between them, becomes stronger than the text's ability to restrain and redirect that desire.

There is, however, another factor in this peculiar effect of *The Wild*

Palms to reabsorb its own language and to flood itself in such a way that language dissolves into this prenatal space. This is the effect *upon the book itself* (as well as upon the reader) of the book's splitness. As I have said, this splitness transforms the book into a desiring subject itself, and compels it to want that part of itself which is not momentarily being narrated — to become bisexual writing as Cixous defines it: as *one* practice of writing generated by the tension between difference. In *The Wild Palms,* then, there are intercalary spaces in which narrative turns, like the lower Mississippi River, to flow in an almost opposite direction. And there are *other* spaces, created by the book's splitness, where flooding occurs and breaks through the established patterns of flow to carve alternate channels which flow in ways we may not know how to read.

In the first instance, in those "bends" in the river, what occurs is not so much *difference within* narrative flow, as it is *displacement* of that flow. We actually may read the process of that displacement by pausing to "read" our own response to sequentiality, that is, our own narrative desire to make the story flow. What occurs in *The Wild Palms* is therefore more than the contrapuntal effect which Faulkner said he was trying to achieve; the novel flows sequentially until the reader's desire for the story reaches a point of fullness, beyond which it cannot go without flooding: "'You can come in now,' he said" ("Wild Palms" *WP* 22). Then the book stops to absorb and contain the flow of desire by folding back upon itself to proffer another story: "Once (it was in Mississippi, in May, in the flood year 1927) there were two convicts" ("Old Man" *WP* 23). The book must meander within the terrain between what story the reader desires and what story the narrative gives; to arrive at what the reader wants is not only to extinguish the reader's desire (all novels have this problem), but also to dissolve the bisexual desire of the split text for its other, that which it floods *toward.* And to do the latter would allow desire to reach its goal, thereby representing itself as a form rather than a force and so drying up its flow in the very act of constituting it in a system of signs.

To experience this narrative flow as it meanders back and forth in this way, let us explore some of those intercalary spaces which are the "bends" of its turning from one story to another. Throughout this study

I have attempted to converse with textual spaces which may not be imprinted by linguistic codes, but which, like Kristeva's maternal *chora,* are, in their very flexibility and instability, crucial to the evolution of meaning. In *The Wild Palms,* some of these spaces are located, as might be expected, between chapters. These are spaces where one narrative flows toward its other and is received in various ways. The two sentences quoted above may serve as examples. At the end of chapter one of "Wild Palms," Charlotte is painfully hemorrhaging. As she floods, so does her story begin. To Harry she says, "Oh you damned bloody bungling—— No no no no. Quick. There I go again. Stop me quick. I am hurting. I cant help it. Oh, damn bloody bloody—" (*WP* 21–22). Like the doctor, we are trying to "read" the situation; like him, we desire more information; like him, we are ready to "come in now." The abrupt shift to "Once . . . there were two convicts" marks the sudden containment of the first story, just as our desire for it is aroused. Faulkner has indeed stopped and focused our attention on the fluidity he has created, the flow of his own narrative. At this point we are forced to regard the narrative's flow as "the form of a force" created by the master-author who can cut it off as well as turn it on. At the same time, though, in the space between the first and second chapters, as we begin again to read the "Old Man" sequence, we become aware that we have merely turned a bend and that a new flow is starting.

Again, between chapters two and three, the same situation: In "Old Man" the levee has broken. Like Charlotte's flooding at the end of chapter one, there is no stopping the flow of what is about to happen. All that the convicts can do is to follow the deputy's order to turn out: "Get up out of it!" (*WP* 30). Again we want to know more: *This,* then, is The Story, we think. Again, in the space between, a bend in the text. Our desires are deferred and turned back to the original flow with the enticing redirection of the first line of chapter three: "When the man called Harry met Charlotte Rittenmeyer . . ." (*WP* 31). And so the narrative meanders.

As a split subject, then, the book insists repeatedly on its own displacement and deferral, and so prevents our settling into any kind of logocentric reading of it. Its admission of its lack of wholeness becomes The Story which writes our own lack of mastery as readers. It thus folds back upon us to read us as readers who, as Jane Gallop would say, "are inevitably bereft of any masterful understanding of language, and can only signify ourselves in a symbolic system that we do not command, that, rather, commands us" (*Reading Lacan* 20). We read our own inability to read.

Yet this rhythm between narrative flow and its stoppage is not as predictable as these initial examples indicate. Something extra, something excessive, is always *added* by the repression of desire. Our desire for one narrative's flowings over another's, and Faulkner's containment and redirection of that desire, eventually must flood over and become *something more*. This *something more* is not containable. It overflows through those bends of the chapters' intercalary spaces and makes new channels which enable the two stories of this book to speak together like the lips of one mouth. It (the book) thus speaks itself as Not One — as that which always already contains its other. As I have pointed out, Irigaray describes female sexuality in similar terms in *This Sex Which Is Not One*. Because of the multiple nature and placement of her sex organs, woman's pleasure is based on an autoerotic nearness which undermines the linearity of desire, "diffuses the polarization toward a single pleasure, disconcerts fidelity to a single discourse . . ."—which is never "simply one" (30–31).

Irigaray insists that it is only in such a position of multiplicity, and within a feminine libidinal economy which allows the production of excess, that the female imaginary can deploy itself in language. Female sexuality has obvious pertinence to character in *The Wild Palms,* as I hope to show in my final conversations with Charlotte Rittenmeyer. Yet the flooding of a feminine libido within this particular male text seems also to have peculiar *structural* effects. For example, the end of the third chapter actually seems to move *into* the beginning of the fourth, making the two speak together the flooding(s) of desire. Let us follow the sequence from one chapter to the other. At the end of the third chapter, Charlotte, as she leaves her husband to go with Harry on the train, has recognized that she must *do* something to seal her fate with Harry. She takes him to their drawing room on the train. As he turns from fumbling with the lock, she reveals herself to him:

When he turned she had removed her dress: it lay in a wadded circle about her feet and she stood in the scant feminine underwear of 1937, her hands over her face. Then she removed her hands and he knew it was neither shame nor modesty, he had not expected that, and he saw it was not tears. Then she stepped out of the dress and came and began to unknot his tie, pushing aside his own suddenly clumsy fingers. (*WP* 60)

This is the end of a chapter, but not another bend in the river. For, within the space between the two chapters, and it is space—there is nothing *written* there—excessive desire seems to break through the chapter boundaries and flood over into the introductory clause of "Old Man." "When the belated and streaming dawn broke . . ." (*WP* 61), an almost literal climax of the sexual act described as being initiated in the preceding chapter. In this space between chapters, the text has broken from its regular "bend," and flooded. As dawn breaks, the convicts see for the first time the "flat still sheet of brown water" which covers everything indiscriminately, whose *excess* dissolves boundaries between land and water, stillness and motion:

It was perfectly motionless, perfectly flat. It looked, not innocent, but bland. It looked almost demure. It looked as if you could walk on it. It looked so still that they did not realise it possessed motion until they came to the first bridge. There was a ditch under the bridge, a small stream, but ditch and stream were both invisible now, indicated only by the rows of cypress and bramble which marked its course. Here they both saw and heard movement—the slow profound eastward and upstream ("It's running backward," one convict said quietly.) set of the still rigid surface, from beneath which came a deep faint subaquean rumble which (though none in the truck could have made the comparison) sounded like a subway train passing far beneath the street and which inferred a terrific and secret speed. (*WP* 62)

Like the real flood, Charlotte Rittenmeyer's desire, which Harry reads on her face, mysteriously extends across the levees between it and the convict's story, and is read *out of* that "other" narrative. In this way Faulkner's text creates a new channel *between* stories out of the flooding of female sexuality. Such a channel looks like this:

We may "see" such a channel geographically, but how do we conceptualize the flooding which creates it? How do we "read water"? In the essay "The 'Mechanics' of Fluids," Irigaray speculates that the "solid" ways in which language and thought have been systemized in Western culture make it almost impossible to conceptualize fluidity. In accounting for the historical lag in developing a scientific theory of fluids, she argues that the properties of fluids actually constitute a physical reality which resists symbolization. In this way thought has been systematized along "solid" lines — in structures and categories which deny the workings of the fluid unconscious, hence denying the flow of desire (*This Sex* 110). Fluid, like desire, is "always in a relation of excess or lack vis-à-vis unity." It eludes placement and identity (117).

Irigaray believes that this conceptual failure of science and philosophy relates to how the feminine does not "fit" into the conceptual models which privilege form over process. Within such a theoretical system, the feminine, like fluidity, becomes unthinkable. Woman does not exist. (This view, of course, reminds us of Johnson's comment about the difficulty of speaking of woman as subject within ideological patterns which deny the humanity of real women, and de Lauretis's similar quandary in thinking about the relationship between women as historical subjects and woman as sexual object.) As we try to read the flooding of *The Wild Palms,* we may realize that we are moving away from the dry safe grounds of cultural models of reading, models dependent upon what Irigaray calls "a teleology of reabsorption of fluid in a solidified form" (*This Sex* 110), a teleology which formulates rather than frees reading and writing — a teleology inevitably figured by the symbolic authority of the phallus.[6]

To say that Faulkner's writing is fluid, then, is to speak to his willingness to subvert his own authority as master-author for the purpose of participating in a different economy of desire—one which is based not on a premise of give and take but on a promise of excessiveness which compels writing and reading to go *somewhere else.* He has written flooding in much more than the literal sense, for his texts, and particularly this one, are always allowing desire to write its own flows and streamings across those levees which he himself is so carefully constructing. I use the progressive mode purposely, for *The Wild Palms* is always in motion, especially when, like the flooding river, it may *appear* "perfectly motionless, perfectly flat" while at the same time, below the "bland and unhurried surface," it rushes onward with "a terrific and secret speed" which may defy our capacity to read (*WP* 62). The questions then become: How do we read that which makes all reading speculative? How do we read something so much in motion?

Let us make another attempt at "reading water." Between "Wild Palms," chapter seven, and "Old Man," chapter eight, we may try to experience the aquatic movement of this flooding narrative, that which is unreadably present between what language speaks. In "Wild Palms," Harry has been imagining the meeting between Charlotte, Rat Rittenmeyer, and their daughters, when Charlotte arrives in a cab to pick him up. In the cab she asks him to promise that he will obtain medical care for her and then disappear when her condition worsens, so that he will not be held accountable for the botched abortion which she knows will cause her death. The exchange is as follows:

> "Dont be a fool now. There's no time now. You'll know in time. Get to hell out, do you hear?"
> "Out?"
> "Promise me. Dont you know what they'll do to you? You cant lie to anybody, even if you would. And you couldn't help me. But you'll know in time. Just telephone an ambulance or the police or something and wire Rat and get to hell out fast. Promise me."
> "I'm going to hold you," he said. "That's what I'll promise you. They were both well?"

"Yes," she said; the scaling palm trunks fled constantly past. "They were all right." (*WP* 227–28)

Thus ends the "Wild Palms" chapter.

"Old Man," too, begins with a woman's request. The woman of the narrative asks the convict to bring a knife to cut the umbilical cord which still links her to her newborn child. The convict is greatly affronted by this latest request from the woman whom he has rescued. He feels, in fact, so outrageously affronted by the demand that it takes him a full minute to respond to her cry, "The can! The can in the boat!" (*WP* 229). Under her direction, and ignorant of what he is doing, he manages to cut the can into a jagged piece of tin and help her separate her child from herself. How do the end of the "Wild Palms" chapter and the beginning of "Old Man" speak together? In both stories women ask men to do something for them. Charlotte wants Harry to save himself by severing himself from her death; the woman wants the convict to save her and her child by severing the child from her. Yet there is more here than corresponding action. The act of severance requested of Harry by Charlotte is *carried out* by the convict in his response to the woman's request. As narrative *act,* then, a new channel forms itself to speak to the problem of excess. Charlotte's request is in excess of what Harry can promise. Her desire, as I will suggest in the next part of this chapter, is always in excess of his. Her ultimate loss of self, her own death, is in excess of any loss he may experience. Her "tremendous silence . . . roar[s] down upon him like a wave, a sea" (*WP* 307). It is, however, *she* who is silenced. He has the luxury of saying, "*between grief and nothing I will take grief*" (*WP* 324). Charlotte takes nothing; she is dead.

A question posed, then, by these intercalary spaces in *The Wild Palms,* and by the book as a whole, is the question of excess. Excessive desire, excessive love, excessive loss—what, indeed, does one do with *excess* and its inevitable flooding? The channel between these two chapters tells us that excess must go *somewhere else* to write another story. But what is that new story? These are questions posed by the structure of this book. This is a structure which deconstructs its own design, for its boundaries and demarcations between narrative sequences are created to break down under the instability of the excessive desire they generate, both within and without. What Faulkner has done is to create a textual geography in which excess has nowhere to go. There is no place for spillage. But where does excess go when it has nowhere to go? Does it, like the river, sometimes run backward? Or does it cut new channels to flow in the spaces which lie *between* what language can say and which hence remain ultimately unreadable? Or may we read excess in some *other* place in this text?

We have peered between narrative structures (chapters, stories) into the spaces where excess *goes.* Geography, however, enables us merely to see new channels, not to plunge into their waters. Where we may take that plunge and read what flooding *feels like* may be at the level of the desiring character, rather than the desiring text. For it is one thing to observe a flood, but quite another *to flood,* to enter the tropology of flooding at the level of its production — in the text of *The Wild Palms,* at the level of the female subject's sexual desire, her *jouissance.* "These rivers," as Irigaray says, "flow into no single, definitive sea. These streams are without fixed banks, this body without fixed boundaries. This unceasing mobility" (*This Sex* 215).

This is the scandalous Charlotte Rittenmeyer who does not know the difference between inside and outside and doesn't much care — whose flooding woman's body splatters its own text in all directions at once, and so obscures geographical distinctions.

III   *The Overflow of Difference*

> She doesn't hold still, she overflows. An outpouring that can be agonizing, since she may fear, and make the other fear, endless aberration and madness in her release.
>
> Hélène Cixous, in
> *The Newly Born Woman*

The Wild Palms is crucial to an understanding of Faulkner's art because its binary structure compels us to read nonlingual spaces. These spaces are sites of, as Kristeva would say, "the very act of naming" (*Desire* 210), where "language" is still an unstable nonentity which sloshes about between one sign and another and which sometimes mysteriously exceeds itself in its own production. In these spaces, language overflows whatever markers we have for safe and solid ways of reading, and forges new channels whose depth and direction we have yet to measure. My purpose throughout these conversations has been not only to re-vision Faulkner's writing but also to rethink our ways of reading it. This is a feminist project, not because it empowers woman reader over male writing, but because it enables us to *read* silence and hysteria and flooding at a site of a production which I believe may be named feminine. Such re-visioning also enables us to retrieve a female subject from Faulkner's writing, a "woman" who can speak. This presence of the feminine in Faulkner, the "she" who sometimes articulates the *something more* which is at the very heart of his works' motion, problematizes the whole notion of gender opposition and offers the possibility of bisexual spaces in other literature written by men and women—spaces whose differences we have only just begun to discern.

Jessica Benjamin sees the feminist enterprise as pulled among three tasks: "to redeem what has been devalued in women's domain, to conquer the territory that has been reserved to men, and to resolve and transcend the opposition between these spheres by reformulating the relationship between them" ("A Desire of One's Own" 78). Such a reformulation of the whole notion of difference outside the compartments of phallocentric thought, the third task Benjamin delineates, seems to lie at the very heart of Faulkner's art, and especially of *The Wild Palms,* whose binary structure is deconstructed over and over. To consider the radical implications of this reconceptualization of difference, let us continue to think in spatial terms about *The Wild Palms,* specifically about Charlotte Rittenmeyer's desire. Within these "geographies," whose contours I shall be drawing primarily from psychoanalysis, I want to try to move into a space of female overflow in *The Wild Palms*— again, a space *between,* which not only reflects language's position as being "neither inside nor outside the subject" (Johnson, *A World of Difference* 6), but which also reveals how woman's body may come to mediate the very motion of difference itself.

When Harry turns to look at Charlotte's face as she removes her clothing, what he sees there is pure desire, a feminine space which he enters willingly and lovingly. Faulkner's creation of Charlotte as a desiring subject seems unusual in a number of ways—so unusual (compare it, for example, to Hemingway's of Catherine Barkley) that, in exegesis, it becomes a threatening and, to some critics, even an unreadable phenomenon. The problem—Benjamin has stated it more generally—is that woman in Western culture is not, and has not been, "culturally articulated as a sexual subject" ("Desire" 83). In Theweleit's terms, woman has been objectified as the flow of male desire in culture, art, and literature; as a cultural icon, she is the voiceless embodiment of sexual desire. This is "the problem of woman's desire"—that there has been no "female image or symbol that would counterbalance the monopoly of the phallus in representing desire" (Benjamin 83). As Benjamin points out, the closest we have come may be motherhood and fertility—certainly neither is representative of sexual agency (and both are firmly eschewed by Charlotte Rittenmeyer). Johnson, as we have seen, views the problem in its larger context by offering the chilling speculation that existing systems of thought which repeatedly dramatize woman "as simulacrum, erasure, or silence" may and often do preclude our thinking about her (writing her or reading her) in any other way (*A World of Difference* 40).

Within such phallocentric structures, the problem of the artist, female or male, becomes how to represent female desire as emanating from a subject. Giovanni Bellini, as Kristeva points out, represented female desire in spatial terms—in the strangeness of a maternal space which moves beyond the child object to go *somewhere else,* and which thereby "retain[s] the traces of a marginal experience, through and across which a maternal body might recognize its own, otherwise inexpressible in our culture" (*Desire* 243). For feminist readers, however, the problem of woman's desire is how to retrieve its expressibility out of (or at least how to note its displacement within) a cultural paradigm resting on a binary model, a "male/active equals female/passive" equation which makes woman's lack of sexual agency seem part of the natural order. Cixous's "Sorties" is about finding such a "way out" of binary modes of thought which organize the discourses associated with *masculine* and *feminine* into hierarchical, active/passive structures.

The ubiquity of such reified oppositional patterns of thought may explain many readers' aversions to Charlotte Rittenmeyer. My project here is not to critique other readings of *The Wild Palms,* but it may be enlightening to note the vehemence with which some readers have chastised Charlotte for her sexuality. For Thomas McHaney, there is something very wrong with such a woman. He finds that "carnality kills Charlotte"; she cannot hold to her own ideal of romantic love because she "likes 'bitching' too much" (*William Faulkner's* The Wild Palms 99–100, 52). Her death, McHaney strongly implies, is necessary if Harry is to become "the master of his world" by choosing life over death—"the only decision a man who would be a man can make" (194). Edmund Volpe complains that Charlotte's "aggressive sexuality" lacks "romantic appeal" (216). Mortimer, as we have seen, agrees with Volpe's assessment of the threatening nature of the feminine in the novel: Volpe finds that the pregnant woman and Charlotte "seem to embody the extremes of 'the female principle': the mother and the Lilith. Between these alien forces—oppressive responsibility that he does not want, and bewitching seduction that destroys him—the male seems to be trapped. Like Adam, both of Faulkner's heroes are dragged from the serene security of Eden to face the outrages of a fearful and violent existence" (217). What is important in both stories, W. T. Jewkes writes, is "the problem of masculinity," the male choice between "purity and compromise" embodied in the sex act. Jewkes believes that, in the end, in a "final reverie [which] is clearly a dream of masturbation," Harry finds a way around "the problem": "And though punished, at the end he has a real phallus in his hand; the convict only waves a cigar" (50–52). Even woman-centered readings find Charlotte Rittenmeyer's vision "flawed" and her character likewise marred by "contradictions—the fusion of her masculine and her all-too-feminine qualities is just one example" (Bernhardt 364). Although Charlotte is the artist figure of the book, according to Laurie A. Bernhardt, her "most important flaw—her inability to see love, like art, as a creative, life-giving act—leads to her tragedy" (364).

Is it possible to re-vision the feminine space of Charlotte Rittenmeyer? Cleanth Brooks's observation about the tradition of romantic love and *The Wild Palms* may provide a starting point. Brooks sees the lovers as participating in "the ancient erotic heresy of the West" ("Tradition" 266)—what Denis de Rougemont in *Love in the Western World* defined as chivalric love or romantic love, its mode "a serious and dedicated adultery"—which usually results in exile from community and even death (Brooks, "Tradition" 269). Obvious examples are Tristan and Isolde. In *Women: The Longest Revolution* Juliet Mitchell traces this Western tradition of romantic love in psychoanalytic terms and from a different point of view. She poses a two-part argument. In love narratives of the romantic epics and lyrics of the twelfth and thirteenth centuries, the male lover was the focus and "subject of the passion." By the beginning of the seventeenth century, however, the woman became the focus of romantic stories, but only, Mitchell hastens to point out, as feminine *object* (108). Throughout Western history, according to Mitchell, the common assumption is that the lover is male, and that he is seeking "the lost feminine part of himself" (109). "Romantic love," she continues,

> is about the self, it is erotic, but does not have a sexual object that is ultimately different from itself. The lady of the courtly epic, Goethe's eternal feminine, Cleo the poet's muse, the feminine principle of *fin de siècle* artists, are all, in the last resort, metaphors for the lost female part of the original, psychologically bisexual self. That is the general distinguishing quality of romantic love as such. But there is an important assumption here . . . that assumption is that the romantic lover is male. (112)

One might say, then, that the flow of desire in the romantic narrative, regardless of the focus of the love story, traditionally has been *from* male subject *to* female object (*A Farewell to Arms,* whose connections to Faulkner's novel are a matter of record, may serve as example).[7]

Where does Charlotte Rittenmeyer fit into this schema of Western romantic love? The fact is that she doesn't. Her own desire initiates the love affair. If we read Charlotte Rittenmeyer as the unhinging of a dichotomous model and, moreover, continue to think of *character* as a process which enacts unconscious drives and their cultural construction, we may begin to read Charlotte's desire, and even its failure, as connected, first, to the way Faulkner radically problematizes the very binary structure he creates in *The Wild Palms,* and, second, to the way we read the book's escape from its own structure. Reading Charlotte, however, we also may come to see, as I believe Faulkner did, that what is possible in art may have far different consequences in life. Like books, human beings may indeed flood beyond themselves. The problem, as Charlotte's story shows, may not lie in writing fluidity—the overflowing of boundaries—or even in reading it. The problem comes, as Faulkner knew well enough, in living it. For if the shores of one's own subjective space are no longer discernible, or, more radically, are dissolved, then, like Charlotte, one may drown.

This, indeed, as Benjamin observed in her psychoanalytic practice, is "the problem of woman's desire" in relation to cultural constructions of "ideal love" which valorize male control and female abandon (80). As Benjamin so shrewdly points out, the question of desire runs parallel to the question of power (78). In the beginning, of course, the love affair does subvert the sexual politics of Western constructions of heterosexual love. Charlotte's desire is a source of power in that it is an active force which propels events along. She makes the arrangements, and the sacrifices. In the end, though, love turns upon her and leads to her own powerlessness. Her own inner space, like her infected uterus, is filled up with an excessive fluidity which kills. That space becomes the site of the Bad Smell. She *is flooded.* And yet, like the hysterical Rosa, Charlotte speaks out of that position—from fathoms deep, under blood and water. She is herself spilling and being spilled, painfully, passionately. Her overflow, desire's flooding, is figured in her female body.

>   "Then why the doctor? Why the five dollars? Oh, you
>   damned bloody bungling—No no no no. Quick. There I
>   go again. Stop me quick. I am hurting. I cant help it. Oh,
>   damn bloody bloody—" (*WP* 22).

The Wild Palms begins with Charlotte Rittenmeyer's hemorrhaging from infection brought on by a bungled abortion. Directly after the abortion she bled profusely. Then the flooding stopped abruptly, and infection set in. Now the release of blood, sudden and frightening but not cleansing, comes from the putrefaction within her body. It is a sign of her death, a sign of her body's irreparable failure to flow properly. As a final irony, she and Harry have used some of their last funds to buy her a nightgown, so that, with their luck, she will ruin it with her flow. But it is too late, for gowns or doctors. At the beginning of the book, Charlotte is doomed. Its beginning is her end. Her female anatomy becomes, quite literally, the fluid space in which sequentiality dissolves. She is the book's ending and its beginning. Her dying body is written from cover to cover.

When the doctor moves through the female anatomy of the damp leaky cottage, down its brown-stained stairs and hall, to treat her, Charlotte is already in the space between life and death. Alternately unable to bleed and bleeding profusely, she knows she is dying. As she is trying both to bleed and to hold back bleeding, to flood and to stop flooding, her own female anatomy becomes the peculiar constitutive space between the book's representations of life and death. In that space, representation breaks down; life and death become one thing. At the same time, Charlotte speaks the terror of a flooding which is excessive, that breakage of self in the space between itself and the otherness of the other in which love and suffering, as she knows, do indeed become the same thing. She speaks "the secret irreparable seeping of blood" (*WP* 5), the "damn bloody, bloody—," which may, and in Faulkner's personal life certainly did, accompany such breakage. What Faulkner was able to do in his book *structurally* — that is, in the creation of structures which are again and again washed away — now becomes painfully problematic at the level of female characterization in "Wild Palms." Here the flood waters of "Old Man" turn to blood. The uterus which contains and produces life in one story becomes the site of the Bad Smell in another.

How does this happen? To continue to think about female desire in psychoanalytic terms, we may envision Charlotte's desire as being produced within what Benjamin calls "inner space." What Benjamin has found in her psychoanalytic practice to be "experientially female is the association of desire with a space, a place within the self" which contains "a force imbued with the authenticity of *inner* desire." According to Benjamin, "[t]his space is in turn connected to the space between self and other" (97). If we are able to "read" Charlotte's body, we may see how she tries to extend her inner space into what Benjamin calls a relationship between subjects rather than a (male) subject–(female) object relation "that idealizes one side and devalues the other" (98). Through most of the narrative, Charlotte's body extends to become the fluidity that she loves—"the motion, the speed" (*WP* 100) of the art she wants to make. She seems most herself swimming nude in the Wisconsin lake, sketching, sunbathing. She extends her body into the world through her sexuality and by making things with her hands. When she dies, it is a total collapse "as undammed water collapses" (*WP* 306), and her silence roars down upon Harry "like a wave, a sea" (307). The "*I*" of her self, as Harry sees it, is like "watching a fish rise in water—a dot, a minnow, and still increasing" (*WP* 285). We are reminded of Quentin's last moments before he drowns, the movement of the self into the fluid shadow, into another space, the moment of liquefaction.

If, as Benjamin says, woman's desire is created within an inner space whose force propels the desiring subject into a relationship, and if that same female desire nevertheless finds itself objectified and specularized in a relationship defined by the phallic model of thought, what happens then? Does that inner space of desire flood itself? Does it stop up and become a Bad Smell? This, again, is the question of excess: Where does excess go when it has nowhere to go? This seems to be the question of this love story. For, until Charlotte's death, Harry seems unable to disengage himself from a phallic model of desire which posits woman as the object (albeit beloved) of romantic narrative. To him, Charlotte's "inner space" is a vessel which receives him, into which he ejaculates: "the pervading immemorial blind receptive matrix, the hot fluid blind foundation—grave-womb or womb-grave, it's all one" (*WP* 138).[8] This male-constructed matrix has no desire of its own. It is formless and blind: penetrable. In this sense, as Harry tells McCord, Charlotte is both mother and lover to him (*WP* 141). The "receptive matrix" is multi-purposed. Woman can be anything man wants her to be.

It is Charlotte's death, the last flicker of the yellow eyes, which finally compels Harry to "read" her feminine text of desire (posthumously) as having emanated from an inner space with a force of its own. This force, as Harry comes to realize, is of the body, "the broad thighs and the hands that like bitching and making things," but also floods beyond it (*WP* 324). This is a force that we (and Harry) may name as feminine because of its intimate connection to the spatiality of the female body and, through that spatiality, to the possibility of a *something more*, an expansiveness. Certainly we see the embodiment of this expansive space in the body of the unnamed pregnant woman of "Old Man." In the end, Charlotte tries to reclaim her inner space: she tells Harry to "take the knife and cut it out of me. All of it. Deep. So there wont be anything left but just a shell to hold the cold air, the cold—" (*WP* 286). Charlotte's body, and her desire, suggest the possibility of an "intersubjective space"—which is both, at once, inside and outside the self, and which links self to self in ways that flood inner spaces of desire.

This may be why Charlotte is frightening; for, as the tall convict well knows, the female body—with its inner space's potential for fullness—says that desire can take on a life of its own. We are reminded that Derrida, in writing about "irreducible difference," reverts to the metaphor of a woman giving birth to a "formless, mute, infant, and terrifying form of monstrosity" (*Writing and Difference* 293). Such an excess can flow into spaces which human beings cannot structure or contain, and language as we know it cannot speak. This is what Faulkner knew, and seems to have been writing about in a painful and personal way: in more common terms, the simple geographical facts of flooding—that it comes and goes, and not always when one wishes it to, that it creates new topographies and new channels, that its smooth surfaces hide currents which move with "terrific and secret speed." It is in no way surprising that woman's body comes to speak "the difference within" this text of flooding, that which makes it speak against itself. Charlotte Rittenmeyer bleeds into these pages the unresolvable pleasure and terror of the flooding of self. In the end Charlotte's "*I*" floats away like flotsam. We are left to read its indecipherable traces in the dark stain of her woman's blood.

To return to the split structure of this book, and its implications to Faulkner's narrative art, I would suggest that both Charlotte's and the book's floodings raise the question of where stories are really located. Faulkner's narrative, and not just *The Wild Palms,* is often like the flooding river which suddenly reverses itself in one huge crashing wave and sweeps us, blinded and drenched, *somewhere else. The Wild Palms* shows us how Faulkner's art moves between points, how it is indeed located not here or there, not in water or on solid ground, but in the force that moves between. That force turns upon the velocity of difference's motion, difference's flowings and overflowings which relocate the text, the real story, again and again.

More generally, what is crucial to this process, this *fluctuation* of Faulkner's writing, is his willingness to allow the feminine her own inner space, her own desire. Faulkner writes woman, but she writes him too. Flooding out of that inner space in the male creative consciousness, "She," like Caddy-Rosa-Charlotte, questions the opposition of the masculine and the feminine, and so suspends our belief in "the discourse of patriarchy which defines women and men, identifies them not only as different but antithetical" (McLeod 41). "She" gives us a way out.

Barbara Johnson has suggested that critical reading should be willing to encounter and generate "the surprise of otherness" (*A World of Difference* 15). In reading Faulkner, we are given no choice in the matter, for he is always placing himself, and us, in the position of being surprised by an otherness who tells different stories. This is how his writing floods. This is why his levees won't hold. In these texts, that otherness speaks with a woman's voice. "She" speaks a discourse of difference. Her silence resonates. Her madness questions. Her woman's blood floods these pages, and seeps beyond them into places we do not know how to name.

It is She who reads us. It is She who creates the possibility of our own difference.

Epilogue:
Hearing the 'I'/
Beginning Again

> I would be I: I would let him be the shape and echo of his word.
>
> Addie Bundren

We return to questions: how can we read bisexuality within a text—and beyond that, how can we read bisexually? The former is impossible without the latter. The real issue, though, is not whether bisexuality *can* be read but whether it is worth the struggle *to* read. In short, why bother? What I have suggested in regard to Faulkner is that bisexuality can indeed be read, but only if the reader is willing to experience a text's interior otherness. Such reading requires listening—sometimes in awkward and unaccustomed positions or circumstances—to the voices of the bisexual text's multiple, often *multiplying,* sexual identities. These voices, as they emerge through character, language, and structure, both disclose and reproduce the intricate workings of male/female difference *at the same time* their very presence in a text dismantles binary ways of thinking, speaking, and reading sexual difference.

In the context of Western culture, the binary opposition of male/female always reifies male power. Therefore, to read difference rather than opposition, in literary *or* cultural texts, is a radical act which itself questions how knowledge and meaning have been constituted and transmitted through language. As I have already suggested, such an act, not to speak of the methodologies it requires, is a form of struggle. This is not the struggle of the feminist resisting reader *against* the male text but that of the feminist reader who follows the tension of the bisexual text where it takes her, who deliberately resists closure and the empowerment of one form of difference over another. The result of such reading should not be to entrap the reader in the web of the text but rather to expand the web by spinning new strands in many different directions.

In that linear and time-bound narrative *As I Lay Dying,* it is a struggle to hear the 'I' in Addie Bundren's "I would be I." That 'I' and the dead woman who utters it cut across the opposition of life and death. From inside the coffin in which patriarchy has sealed her, Addie Bundren rethinks subjectivity as a female space—"[t]he shape of my body where I used to be a virgin . . ." (*AILD* 165). Her woman's voice and woman's desire emerge out of that space, resisting the image of the phallus, the language of the Father and its appropriative gesture, the symbolic authority of the word. How do we hear Addie's 'I' which resists language, which is the word's own otherness? What do we listen *for?*

It is possible to hear the female voice of a bisexual male text if we understand that we are listening for the process of difference in the act of articulation. In a culture which historically has valorized male texts, silenced or muted women's literary voices, and denied the existence of bisexual subjectivity altogether, such listening/reading is a revolutionary act. For those who would revise cultural narratives of sexual difference, bisexual reading becomes an imperative act. For, if feminist theory posits the compelling necessity of restructuring the social relations between the sexes, then feminist praxis—literary or otherwise—must concern itself with deconstructing the hegemonic structures of opposition and domination and constructing methodologies for reading difference as subject, for hearing the 'I' of difference—for believing in the presence of difference within us all.

Only then will we liberate those categories we call female and male. Only then will we free ourselves to begin again.

Notes

1. Beginnings

1. See Luce Irigaray, *This Sex Which Is Not One* 31. In "The Laugh of the Medusa" Hélène Cixous argues that, "far more extensively and repressively than is ever suspected or admitted," writing is generated by a libidinal and cultural economy which is marked as masculine and which, because of exaggeration and oppositional thinking, often has become "a locus where the repression of women has been perpetuated" (249). The idea of excessiveness and expansiveness being marked as feminine pervades the thinking of Cixous, Irigaray, and Kristeva, influenced as they are by psychoanalytic theory. Woman nourishes life, Cixous writes; she gives without measuring how much; she creates "an 'economy' that can no longer be put in economic terms" ("Laugh" 264). Likewise, Irigaray argues that woman's libidinal plurality creates a feminine discourse of desire which replenishes itself, which is "always something more" (*This Sex* 29). And similarly, Julia Kristeva writes that it is probably necessary to be a woman to push theoretical reason beyond its limits and thus to create a linguistics of "heterogeneous economy" which is capable "of accounting for a nonetheless articulated *instinctual drive,* across and through the constitutive and insurmountable frontier of *meaning*" (*Desire* 146).

2. As Lisa Appignanesi points out in *Femininity and the Creative Imagination,* the link between the idea of the feminine and the creativity of the male writer is not new and is readily observable in the writings of Goethe, Baudelaire, Mallarmé, Gautier, Joyce, Flaubert, James, and Proust (2–9).

3. Two recently published theoretical projects which explore these connections and which I believe have provocative implications for *both* feminist methodology and Faulkner studies are Baker, *Blues, Ideology and Afro-American Literature,* and Siegle, *The Politics of Reflexivity.* Baker proffers "the blues matrix," with all its decentering inventiveness, as a vernacular trope for approaching culture and literature. Siegle shows that narrative becomes the central medium that works both to naturalize cultural models and to reveal the process of that naturalization. Narrative voice thus may be heard as cultural voice and narrative itself as constituting cultural experience.

4. Like Cixous, Showalter stresses the cultural role of literature in creating women's sense of alienation from their own experience: "Women are estranged from their own experience and unable to perceive its shape and authenticity, in part because they do not see it mirrored and given resonance by literature" ("Women and the Literary Curriculum" 856).

5. In a paper entitled "In Praise of Helen," presented at the 1985 Faulkner and Yoknapatawpha Conference, André Bleikasten bravely confronted an even more problematic issue by asking, "How does a man read as a woman?" That paper, with the question omitted, is published in article form in Fowler and Abadie, *Faulkner and Women*, 128–43.

6. I am, of course, borrowing Annette Kolodny's memorable term, although I contend, and I suspect Kolodny would agree, that in this case the "minefield" is composed of more than male fear. See Kolodny, "Dancing through the Minefield: Some Observations on the Theory, Practice, and Politics of a Feminist Literary Criticism."

7. I wonder, in fact, what the term "agreement" means. Does the fact that my thinking about Emily Grierson is somewhat different from Fetterley's mean that I do not "agree" with hers, or she with mine? Is "agreement" desirable? Do we not grow in our understanding through disagreement and multiplicity, in "playful pluralism," as Kolodny has suggested? These are rather basic questions, but ones which are stumbling blocks to my "agreement" with this measure of feminist methodology.

8. I should add that Cixous's "bisexuality" differs from androgyny, defined by Carolyn Heilbrun as that which "suggests a spirit of reconciliation between the sexes" (*Toward a Recognition of Androgyny* x).

9. This essay by Myriam Díaz-Diocaretz, "Faulkner's Hen House: Woman as Bounded Text," was presented in shortened form at the 1985 Faulkner and Yoknapatawpha Conference.

10. It should not be necessary to point out that this determination to subvert and expand is what American feminism is all about, not to mention what the resisting reader may be up to if she follows Fetterley's approach. As Jardine herself notes, this conceptualization of woman, as "the effects of the human subject's *inscription* in culture through language" (my emphasis), may be helpful in a number of ways (42). We need to "understand how the feminine operates in culture" as alterity, "the relationship of women writers and theorists as subjects to cultural production, [and] the real political implications bound to the interrelationships among these conceptions, language, and sexual difference" (47). With such understanding, we may recognize that "the status of women is determined not only at social and political levels, but by the very logical processes through which meaning is produced" (44).

11. The patriarchal order of southern culture and its relegation of women to marginal status have been foci of several book-length studies, including those of Clinton, Angela Davis, Gwin, Anne Goodwyn Jones, Lebsock, and Scott.

12. At the base of such a description is the Derridean notion of the unconscious of the subject as nonpresence, a pattern of differences which do not, as Freud would have it, constitute the processes whereby the conscious is realized but which relay a "radical alterity," the traces of which are beyond "the metaphysical speech of phenomenology." The unconscious, according to Der-

rida, "can no more be classed as a 'thing' than as anything else; it is no more of a thing than an implicit or masked consciousness" (*Speech and Phenomena* 152). Deconstruction, perhaps even more than psychoanalysis, challenges the concept of Being as presence. In his essay "Structure, Sign and Play in the Discourse of the Human Sciences," Derrida finds that the rupture in Western metaphysics has resulted from its confrontation with this very issue, the problematic nature of consciousness, including "the Freudian critique of self-presence" (*Writing and Difference* 280). Being is thus inscribed in a system of differences and in the play of presence and absence: "Being must be conceived as presence or absence on the basis of the possibility of play and not the other way around" (292).

13. A persuasive example is Régis Durand's suggestion that narrative analysis may seek the subject in a new way by employing the Lacanian notion of the "fading" of the subject, or *aphanisis* (865).

14. In *Faulkner's Rhetoric of Loss*, Gail Mortimer argues that Faulkner's protagonists respond to loss by erecting various kinds of defenses which allow them to feel that they are exerting control upon "the dissolution that is the normal state of things" and that Faulkner's rhetorical strategies mirror the tensions between control and lack of it (4–5). In this schema women represent a lack of control and a projection of male fear. They become "distorted or mythicized beings, the projection of a masculine consciousness at its most vulnerable" (122). My project suggests that loss and desire are productive generators of the narrative process, which is itself linked to the feminine in Faulkner's texts.

15. See, for example, David Williams, *Faulkner's Women: The Myth and the Muse,* which approaches the female characters as Jungian archetypes; and chapter four of Mortimer: 97–129, which, along with David L. Minter, *William Faulkner: His Life and Work,* approaches the female characters as projections of Faulkner's dis-ease with female sexuality.

16. Those who view Faulkner as a misogynist see his female subjects as lustful, devouring, destructive creatures, "a constant source of evil" which thwarts the active, positive male principle and reflects "the moral vacuum in society itself" (Kenneth Richardson 66–67). The other side of the coin is the Brooksian school, which asserts that Faulkner admired women who did what they were supposed to do—who reproduced and nurtured. This type of woman, according to Cleanth Brooks, possesses "natural force of tremendous power" ("Faulkner's Vision" 697) but, like the earth, lacks self-consciousness.

17. As I have pointed out, two summaries of critical inquiries into the nature of female characterization in Faulkner's fiction are Judith Wittenberg, "William Faulkner: A Feminist Consideration"; and Carol Ann Twigg, "The Social Role of Faulkner's Women: A Materialist Interpretation." Wittenberg and Twigg divide critics into those who consider Faulkner a misogynist and those who believe him to be a gyneolatrist. Both views, they point out, dehumanize the characters. For my own listing of critics in both schools, see Gwin, *Black and*

White Women of the Old South: The Peculiar Sisterhood in American Litera-ture 191–93, n. 9. Critics are beginning to move outside these categories; see, e.g., Díaz-Diocaretz, Duvall, Sensibar, and Snead.

18. In an analysis of *Absalom, Absalom!* Thomas Lorch carries this andro-centric model to the extreme by arguing that the novel "presents male aspira-tion and will and the passive, enduring, absorbent Female in more closely balanced conflict than we find in Faulkner's other novels." Thomas Sutpen is Faulkner's most powerful male figure, Lorch finds, but he is brought to destruc-tion by society and women, who "absorb and stifle his creative spark." "Female nature" in Faulkner's fiction is "necessary and good," but only "because it pro-vides the living material for the male to shape and elevate" (38–41). For a cri-tique of this kind of approach, see Elisabeth Muhlenfeld's review essay, which chastises Page and other critics for simplifying and objectifying Faulkner's fe-male characters (*"Faulkner's Women"*).

19. John T. Matthews has applied the Derridean model in an illuminating study of the structures of Faulkner's language. He argues that the language of the narratives "produces meaning from *différance*" and hence "meaning arises from the lack of authoritative, unique, absolute, or central significance," rather than from any sense of conclusiveness or closure (*The Play of Faulkner's Language* 31).

20. Judith L. Sensibar points out, rightly, that Joe also initiates the play-acting, "that he is equally steeped in the trappings of romance and melodrama" (*" 'Drowsing Maidenhead Symbol's Self' "* 125).

21. Again, see Chodorow on woman's merger of ego boundaries.

22. In "The Bounded Text," chapter two of *Desire in Language,* Kristeva describes the text as a productivity within a structure:

> The text is therefore a *productivity,* and this means: first, that its rela-tionship to the language in which it is situated is redistributive (de-structive-constructive), and hence can be better approached through logical categories rather than linguistic ones; and second, that it is a permutation of texts, an intertextuality: in the space of a given text, several utterances, taken from other texts, intersect and neutralize one another (36).

Díaz-Diocaretz carries this concept forward by thinking of how women are con-tained in Faulkner's texts. I would carry this thinking another step by suggest-ing that Caddy *becomes* the productivity of the text while at the same time being bounded by it.

23. "Pleasure," the English equivalent for *jouissance,* is inadequate to de-scribe rich nuances of the French term. In a lengthy note to the volume *New French Feminisms,* Marks and de Courtivron explain the term and its connotations:

The verb *jouir* ("to enjoy, to experience sexual pleasure") and the substantive *la jouissance* ("sexual pleasure, bliss, rapture") occur frequently in the texts of the new French feminisms. We have constantly used the English words "sexual pleasure" in our translations. This pleasure, when attributed to a woman, is considered to be of a different order from the pleasure that is represented within the male libidinal economy often described in terms of the capitalist gain and profit motive. Women's *jouissance* carries with it the notion of fluidity, diffusion, duration. It is a kind of potlatch in the world of orgasms, a giving, expending, dispensing of pleasure without concern about ends or closure (36–37, n.8).

Toril Moi's description of Irigaray's thoughts on *jouissance* seem to describe Caddy's position: "Woman's form is repressed by patriarchal phallocentrism, which systematically denies woman access to her own pleasure: female *jouissance* cannot even be thought by specular logic" (142). However, Cixous and Clément broaden the definition of *jouissance* in an extended glossary entry in *The Newly Born Woman,* in which they maintain that the word contains "*simultaneously* sexual, political, and economic overtones. Total access, total participation, as well as total ecstasy are implied. At the simplest level of meaning—metaphorical—woman's capacity for multiple orgasm indicates that she has the potential to attain something more than Total, something extra—abundance and waste (a cultural throwaway), Real and unrepresentable" (165). Likewise, in an introductory glossary to Kristeva's *Desire in Language,* Leon S. Roudiez emphasizes the totality of enjoyment signified as *jouissance* in Kristeva's use of the term (15–16). All of these related definitions lead to the feminine economy to which I referred at the beginning of this chapter, and which I believe operates not only in relation to Caddy's generative power but in relation to Faulkner's as well.

24. As Michel Foucault's *The History of Sexuality* shows us, sexual desire may become the stimulus for "a regulated and polymorphous incitement to discourse" (34).

25. In "Laugh of the Medusa" Cixous posits the concept of *l'écriture féminine,* the writing of the female body so as to transcend the masculine libidinal economy which lies at the heart of Western thought and literary practice. As Ann Rosalind Jones points out in her essay "Writing the Body: Toward an Understanding of *L'Écriture Féminine,*" Irigaray and Kristeva share Cixous's opposition of women's bodily experience "to the phallic-symbolic patterns embedded in Western thought." The immediacy of that bodily experience "promises a clarity of perception and a vitality that can bring down mountains of phallocentric delusion. Finally, to the extent that the female body is seen as a direct source of female writing, a powerful alternative discourse seems possible: to write from the body is to re-create the world" (Jones, 366). Indeed, *l'écriture féminine* may be seen as a response to the question posed by Sandra M. Gilbert and Susan Gubar in *The Madwoman in the Attic*: "If the pen is a metaphorical

penis, from what organ can females generate texts?" (7). Adrienne Rich, however, like the French feminists, envisions woman's writing of the body in more general terms, as touching "the unity and resonance of our physicality, the corporeal ground of our intelligence" (*Of Woman Born* 62). See Showalter, "Feminist Criticism in the Wilderness," and Ann R. Jones, "Writing the Body," for assessments of what they perceive as theoretical problems in the concept of *l'écriture féminine.*

26. As I suggest in the chapter section entitled "Race, Gender, and the Hysterical Intertext," Faulkner's cultural consciousness may be sought in the complex interactions between race and gender within and between his texts.

27. Derrida has said that "woman is writing and style must return to her" (*Spurs* 57). What happens here goes beyond the relationship Derrida posits.

28. This is a relationship similar to that posited by Robert Con Davis in his assessment of Lacanian interpretation: "Text and hermeneutics, while separate, are mirror images of each other" (*The Fictional Father* 187).

29. Two examples are Gresset and Polk, *Intertextuality in Faulkner,* a collection of papers presented at the Second International Colloquium on William Faulkner; and Parker, *Faulkner and the Novelistic Imagination.* Several essays in Gresset and Polk explore "spaces between" and within texts — even, as in the case of Polk's essay "The Space between *Sanctuary,*" spaces between versions of the same text. Parker, on the other hand, seeks a secret "something" as the central yet hidden meaning of four Faulkner novels. Although these two volumes are dissimilar in many important ways, they share an interest in hidden space in and around Faulkner's texts.

2. Hearing Caddy's Voice

1. I am using Robert Con Davis's terms to describe Lacan's model of narrative as a split process which "never reaches a point of stability or wholeness" and which therefore "poses a serious threat to the empirically-based tradition of interpretation as a transparent and focusable lens, an open subjectivity, through which a detached investigator peers into a stable (possibly pictographic) narrative structure ("Introduction," *Lacan and Narration* 857).

2. Certainly, however, we gain a sense of the dimensions of that space through these various approaches to Caddy. Sweeney's bibliography shows their diversity. For discussions of Caddy as a southern woman whose culture forces her into self-destructive patterns of rebellion, see Kerr, *Yoknapatawpha* 155–73; and see Simpson's analysis of Caddy's historical connection to the South and to "the modern drive to control history through the power of the human will" identified with Nazi imperatives (67). Millgate, on the other hand, emphasizes that Caddy is herself a symbol of cultural disruption (97). For mythical approaches, see Milliner, who calls Caddy a "third Eve," and David Williams, who

sees her not only as Eve but as the Great Mother, the anima, and the "archetype of life" (62–83). In his article "Caddy and Quentin: Anima and Animus Orbited Nice," Carter thinks of Caddy in terms of Jungian archetypes; and, reading Freud and Otto Rank along with Faulkner, Irwin connects the two siblings as doubles, with Caddy as the feminine within Quentin.

Although most critics accept Caddy's centrality to the novel, many see her as an image within her brothers' minds and thus as eternally other. Bleikasten's argument to this effect in *The Most Splendid Failure* is passionately articulated and seems to imply a central question posed by my project: how does a female reader's response to Caddy differ from a male's? In another provocative and skillful reading, Douglas Hill explores the complexity of readers' responses to Caddy. He, like Bleikasten, seems to presuppose a male reader, one who Hill says conspires in Quentin's role "in his own imagination, in his own private emotional response to Caddy" (31). Here I am reminded of Robert Moore's paper, "Desire and Despair: Temple Drake's Self-Victimization," presented at the 1985 Faulkner and Yoknapatawpha Conference and published in Fowler and Abadie, *Faulkner and Women,* in which Moore said that we as readers become voyeurs of Temple's rape and thus, "disgusted and fascinated," we participate in her defilement (115). Bleikasten and Hill also offer insight into Caddy's mysterious "capacity to draw and hold the reader" and show how her presence in the novel is central to its meaning. Bleikasten's reading of the novel is particularly illuminating in regard to Quentin.

Three female readers have offered appraisals of Caddy as a realistic female "character" and found her "feminine" characteristics to be admirable but destructive; as Baum says, "A large part of the reason for Caddy's damnation is found in herself. Ironically enough, those qualities in her character that are admirable are the ones which lead to her fall: her complete selflessness, which leads her to be indifferent to her virginity and to what happens to her; her willingness to put the other person's interests first; and her great desire to communicate love" (38). Like Page, Gregory mourns Caddy's inability to fulfill "her natural feminine role" (101). My project sees Caddy's feminine force more positively and defines the term "feminine" differently.

Several general studies of Faulkner which take post-structural approaches to *The Sound and the Fury* have been particularly helpful for their methodologies as well as their insights. I am indebted to Irwin's and Matthews' readings of Faulkner's narrative in conjunction with psychoanalytic and theoretical texts, as well as to Sundquist's cultural readings and Kartiganer's study of a form which does not insist upon order.

As an alternative approach for our conversations with Caddy and the feminine within Faulkner's text, we may turn for guidance to Kristeva, who, in explicating Barthes' project, suggests that critical discourse become experiential so as to enlarge its capacity "to capture the law of desire that makes music, that produces writing. But it is also to experience the desire of the one who reads, to find its code and to note it down" (*Desire* 120). Barbara Johnson pursues this notion of an open-ended critical discourse when she defines *difference* not as that which distinguishes one identity from another, but as "that which subverts the very idea of identity, infinitely deferring the possibility of adding the sum of a text's parts or meanings and reaching a totalized, integrated whole" (*Critical Difference* 4). Johnson insists upon "the importance of the functioning of *what is not known* in literature and theory." For, as she so shrewdly observes, "Far from being a negative or nonexistent factor, what is not known is often the unseen motivating force behind the very deployment of meaning" (*Critical Difference* xii).

3. Faulkner's statements about Caddy often have been reprinted and quoted. Caddy, he said at the University of Virginia, is "what I wrote the book about" (*Faulkner at the University* 6). To repeated questions about the "real meaning" of the novel, he answered in much the same way: "I was just trying to tell a story of Caddy, the little girl who had muddied her drawers and was climbing up to look in the window where her grandmother lay dead" (17). In an interview with Maurice Coindreau, he admitted, moreover, that he "fell in love" with Caddy: "I loved her so much I couldn't decide to give her life just for the duration of the short story" ("Preface," in Cowan, *Twentieth Century Interpretations of "The Sound and the Fury"* 30). And, of course, in the 1933 introduction to the novel, he went even further, to say that Caddy in the pear tree was "the only thing in literature which would ever move me very much" (Bleikasten, *William Faulkner's "The Sound and the Fury"* 9). Caddy became, he wrote, his daughter, his sister, the art object he wore thin by kissing. He had, he said, "made something you can die with," a doomed child with a muddy bottom climbing a tree (14). His statements about the novel, collected in both Bleikasten's and Cowan's anthologies of critical and textual essays on the novel, come back to the same point—that *The Sound and the Fury* is about Caddy Compson. It is interesting, in fact, to contrast Faulkner's insistence on this point to the absence of essays about Caddy in these two volumes. The Meriwether collection includes Eileen Gregory's "Caddy Compson's World" (89–101).

4. This elusiveness occurs quite often on the literal level (if there is such a thing in *The Sound and the Fury*). In Benjy's monologue, in particular, Caddy's space converges upon and fades into other spaces. Just one example: the girl Caddy climbs the fence to deliver Maury's letter, only to fade (in Benjy's discourse) into the eyes of the doomed Mrs. Patterson, eyes which forecast the despair to be seen later in Caddy's eyes as she stands in the door with Benjy pulling on her dress and bellowing.

5. See Durand's "On *Aphanisis*: A Note on the Dramaturgy of the Subject in Narrative Analysis," in Robert C. Davis, ed., *Lacan and Narration* 860–70, in which Durand shows how Lacan's theory of the fading of the subject provides insights into Thomas Pynchon's *Gravity's Rainbow*.

6. For example, see Foucault's observation that authors may be responsible for

more than their own texts ("What Is an Author?" 132) and Albert J. Guerard's assertion that Faulkner "cracked" the form of narrative with the writing of this text ("Faulkner the Innovator" 85).

7. In this connection we are reminded of Shoshana Felman's statement about the interconnectedness of the modern texts of literature and psychoanalysis.

8. In his influential essay "Time in Faulkner: *The Sound and the Fury,*" Sartre says that the true subject of the novel is the human dilemma of being placed in time. Messerli focuses on Caddy as "the *character* of time" (37) and finds that "in her pure dynamism, in pure becoming is life itself without human order" (41). Messerli's essay provides a full summary of other thinking on the subject of time in the novel.

9. We have been taught to listen to the power and the mystery of sound and voice reverberating through Faulkner's texts. As Karl F. Zender suggests, sound in Faulkner "is a mysterious, almost tangible force. It appears to be ubiquitous and sourceless, even when its source is known" (89). Voice—for example, the electrifying voice of Rev. Shegog—may in fact transcend vision and "engender a communion not only beyond the need for words but beyond the site of fiction's language" (Ross, "Rev. Shegog's Powerful Voice" 16). *The Sound and the Fury,* Matthews tells us, is about "the nature of articulation" (65) and "the recognition that the act of articulation cannot successfully reappropriate what has been lost" (114).

In the most extensive treatment of voice in Faulkner's work, Warwick Wadlington's recent *Reading Faulknerian Tragedy* explores how the activity of reading "contributes to the audience's potential voicing and witnessing of the text" (88). Texts such as *The Sound and the Fury* and *As I Lay Dying,* Wadlington writes, "by their distinctly styled or character-labeled sections . . . , accentuate the novel's rhetorical character not only as narrative but as a set of scripts or scores for the reader's enactment" (88). *Absalom, Absalom!,* according to Wadlington, "sharply accentuates voice itself, with all its conflicted accommodations and dependencies." The novel gains its "rhetorical power and risk" from a "tonic provocation" brought about by a battle between monologue and dialogue (173). More generally, reading Faulkner is often, according to Wadlington, a performative act (46).

10. More optimistically, Matthews finds that loss opens the way to "the fun of writing" and its continual deferment, its "play of failures" (73).

11. As Sundquist points out, many incidents in Quentin's monologue, other than the conversation with his father which Faulkner said was meant to be imaginary, may have never actually happened.

12. Polk, in his essay by the same name, points out that the image of Caroline Compson as a jailer is reinforced by her carrying the keys to the house. Her whining and general repressiveness make "of the house itself a prison, the grounds a fenced compound . . ." ("The Dungeon" 62).

13. In this respect, Faulkner's original title "Twilight" seems more apt.

14. Irwin makes a similar point when he says that Quentin needs to accept the feminine within himself (33).

3. *The Silencing of Rosa Coldfield*

1. Wadlington points to Faulkner's rewriting of classical and Shakespearean tragedy in *Absalom, Absalom!* and "its economy of the pure House, the un-mixed people, within a modern world struggling with the reality of human heterogeneity and mixed voices." In *Absalom*, as well as in *Oedipus* and *King Lear*, "the father's pure House" is subverted by the daughter (178). I would differentiate my term "the Father's House" as the conceptualization, not so much of racial purity, but of *male* power enacted through the making of value based upon class and sex as well as race. More generally, Wadlington describes "the House" of *Absalom* as that which insists upon monologue rather than dia-logue. Again, my reading of the novel points to the masculinity of that in-sistence—"the Father's House" with a capital *F.*
My interpretation of Rosa's narrative, and her relationship to the Father's House, is far grimmer than that of Matthews, who finds that her "narrative—as it voices her desire and articulates its objects—does not merely express her iden-tity; rather, her language constitutes her selfhood" (151).
2. The painting is reproduced in Garner, Kahane, and Sprengnether, *The (M)other Tongue* 108.
3. Philip M. Weinstein, who places Faulkner's female characters as irretriev-ably *other* in relation to the narrative voice of the fiction (and, I might add, in relation to the analytic stance of the critic), mentions that Rosa's "voice verges on a state of feeling all too easily associated with the female: hysteria" and adds that her "utterance courts hysteria because it is so inattentive to its audience as a *participant,* so unaware of its status as a *narrative*" (92). I am using the term *hysteria* in a totally different sense, as I explain in the text of this chapter. And obviously my critical position vis à vis Rosa, Faulkner's female characters, hysteria, and the feminine within Faulkner's texts is diametrically opposed to Weinstein's thesis. As I see it, the problem with positing woman as other in Faulkner's texts is that it leaves little avenue for exploration of the feminine, since it denies female subjectivity before exploring the possibility of its existence. To say that woman is other is to render her silent. My project, to the contrary, is to hear her speak; or, failing that, to reconstruct the process of shutting her up. I take an approach to Rosa which in some ways is similar to that taken by Judith Bryant Wittenberg to Temple Drake in *Sanctuary*. Tem-ple, according to Wittenberg, is like Freud's Dora, in that she is devalued and objectified by patriarchy ("A Feminist *Sanctuary* for Temple Drake?" Modern Language Association, 1985). Unlike Temple, however, Rosa, as I hope to show, writes the hysterical symptom upon us as readers—even as patriarchy is writing it upon her.

4. From its very etymological origin in the Greek word for uterus, hysteria has been associated with female deviance. See Mitchell's discussion of hysteria, femininity, and feminism in *Women: The Longest Revolution* (115–20). Furthermore, as both Mitchell and Charles Bernheimer point out, psychoanalysis itself came into being on the basis of Freud's clinical experience with hysterical patients, almost all of them women. See Bernheimer's brief history of hysteria, especially his analysis of Freud's complex responses to his hysterical patients (Bernheimer, "Introduction: Part One," in Bernheimer and Kahane, *In Dora's Case* 1–18). In a larger context, Mitchell suggests that psychoanalysis started from an understanding of hysteria, in the sense that it "led Freud to what is universal in psychic construction and it led him there in a particular way—by the route of a prolonged and central preoccupation with the difference between the sexes" (*Women* 300–301).

We may also think, with Claire Kahane, of hysteria as a trope for woman's "dis-ease" with patriarchal culture ("Introduction: Part Two," in Bernheimer and Kahane, *In Dora's Case* 31); or, with Mary Jacobus, as evidence of the uncanny return of the repressed (248) (in Rosa's case both views are pertinent).

5. Philip Weinstein says that, in addition to talking at great length, Rosa talks *at* and *through* Quentin—in contrast to Mr. Compson, who talks *to* him. "Since [Rosa] only talks *through* others," Weinstein argues, "it is hard to avoid reading *through* her" (91). Again, I think that Weinstein is reading *through* the feminine voice I am attempting to hear.

6. As Sprengnether points out in a note to her essay, "Enforcing Oedipus: Freud and Dora," there is an extensive body of commentary on Dora. For a list of these readings, see n. 2 to the Sprengnether essay in Gerner, Kahane, and Sprengnether, *The (M)other Tongue* (51–52), rather than the parallel but less extensive n. 1 in the first printing of the same essay in Bernheimer and Kahane, *In Dora's Case* (271–72). For a brief history of Dora's case, her real identity and familial situation, see Kahane, "Introduction: Part Two" and "Biographical Note: Dora's Family" in *In Dora's Case* (19–34).

7. As we have seen, Jane Gallop says this in another context in *Reading Lacan*: that, conversely, the attempt to hide a lack of mastery, one's own "castration," "necessitates a violent reduction of the contradictory plurality and ambiguity [of Lacan's text], just as the assembling of a coherent self necessitates repression" (20).

8. I am quoting from de Lauretis' translation in *Alice Doesn't.*

9. This is, of course, a paraphrase of the title of Gilbert and Gubar's *The Madwoman in the Attic.*

10. Page believes that Rosa still calls her sitting room the office because she cannot escape the past (104).

11. The contradictory nature of Faulkner's public statements about race is a matter of record. For a detailed summary, see my *Black and White Women of the Old South* 190–91, n. 5.

12. As Langford shows, Faulkner revised the 1865 scene four times to intensify its impact. Moreover, the interconnection of Rosa and Clytie is obvious from a textual history of *Absalom*. In her introduction to *William Faulkner's* Absalom, Absalom!: *A Critical Casebook,* Muhlenfeld shows how the character of Raby Sutpen, the vocal slave woman in *Absalom's* precursor story, "Evangeline, was, indeed, a combination of Rosa and Clytie, whom Faulkner split into two characters. Clytie and her silence in the novel therefore "carry the symbolic weight of all the tragic ramifications of slavery far better than the more voluble Raby," Muhlenfeld argues. "And Rosa . . . could carry much of the narrative burden which had been Raby's" (xxiv).

13. As I have suggested previously, Otto Rank, in *The Double,* conceives of the *Doppelgänger* in male terms.

14. In *Black and White Women of the Old South,* I have discussed how this encounter dramatizes biracial female experience under southern patriarchy. My project here is to reread this incident as an important generator of Rosa's hysterical narrative and as a "mad," hence uninterpretable, space of intertextual conversation about race, gender, and patriarchy. I am rereading my own reading of Rosa's narrative.

15. More generally, Matthews observes that Faulkner's narrative is produced by language's naming of absence (20).

16. As we have seen above in ch. 1, n. 11, Mortimer argues that in Faulkner's narrative women are constructed as representing a lack of control and a projection of male fear, as "distorted or mythicized beings, the projection of a masculine consciousness at its most vulnerable" (*Faulkner's Rhetoric of Loss* 122). My argument is that their loss generates narrative desire, hence the play of Faulkner's texts; hence our pleasure. In a provocative chapter entitled "Significant Absences," Mortimer points to the phenomenon in Faulkner's works of absence encased in shape. She cites both Rosa's "small body" and Ellen's "substanceless shell," as well as the description of Cora Tull by her husband as "a tight jar" (*Faulkner's Rhetoric of Loss* 87). I would differentiate my remarks from Mortimer's in that I am showing how male subjects create woman as absence — how they, like Sutpen, see woman for what her space represents. What I find most intriguing, though, is how Faulkner enables woman to speak out of these tight (non)places and how her desire to do so manifests itself as textual production.

17. Page, for example, believes that young Rosa "falls in love with love" and eventually transfers her desire for "normal fulfillment of herself in love and marriage" from Bon to Sutpen. Her remaining years, Page finds, "are spent in hopeless virginity and furious hatred" (105–107).

18. For an alternative view of Sutpen's identity and motives, see "'Strange Gods' in Jefferson, Mississippi," in which Richard Poirier finds that the multiple perspectives of *Absalom* suggest that "the act of placing Supen in the understandable context of human society and history is a continually necessary act, a never-ending responsibility and an act of humanistic faith" (21). Neither Rosa

nor I have trouble placing Sutpen, though we both may be guilty of positing his otherness in the same way I have discussed in regard to Weinstein's position vis à vis Faulkner's female characters.

19. See, for example, Lorch's "Thomas Sutpen and the Female Principle," which argues that in *Absalom* and elsewhere, Faulkner "recognizes female nature as necessary and good, because it provides the living material for the male to shape and elevate" (42); and, more recently, Philip Weinstein's gentler argument that, as other, and as hysterical other at that, Rosa is limited to producing a narrative which "can receive the living speculations of others only as an object receives them, unresponsively, rather than as a subject does, dialectically altering in relation to what she hears" (92). Again, I find Weinstein's position antithetical to mine. For a detailed summary of other critical responses to Faulkner's female characters, see my *Black and White Women of the Old South* 191–93, n. 9.

20. Although it is beyond the purview of this study to discuss film criticism in any detail, the gendered construction of the gaze is an important element in feminist film theory which informs my thinking. See de Lauretis, *Alice Doesn't*, and, more recently, Tania Modleski's "Rape versus Mans/laughter: Hitchcock's *Blackmail* and Feminist Interpretation." In the previously mentioned essay "Temple Drake's Self-Victimization," Robert R. Moore seems unaware that looking may be sexually differentiated. He says, "We find ourselves on a roller coaster ride of ambivalence as we respond to Temple. If she demands our sympathy and protective impulses, she is also fair game for our sexual fantasies" (114). And later he argues that Faulkner creates us as an audience of readers who, through our voyeurism, participate in Temple's rape, in "the defilement" of "the self" (the female self, one assumes) (116). This perhaps exaggerated example of the male gaze at work in criticism leads us to ponder, as Modleski does, the problematics of being cast as woman into a critical demeanor constructed by male sexuality.

21. This is Jardine's term (*Gynesis* 25).

22. I am reading this passage much more literally than Irwin, who argues that it is evidence of a cycle of revenge among father, son, and father-substitute (122).

23. Unlike Irwin, who associates castration with repression (88–89), I am more inclined to mediate between Mitchell's figuring of castration as the splitting of subjectivity, and Gallop's redefinition of castration as a theoretical position which frees itself by playing within the uncontrollable spaces between language and subjectivity.

24. Although I think that J. Gary Williams is correct in saying that Quentin is profoundly influenced by Rosa, I disagree that his "seeing" her at the end is an act of creating her as "a living person" (346).

4. *Flooding and the Feminine Text*

1. Wilhelm Reich uses the term *"ozeanische Gefühle"* ("oceanic feelings") in connection with the idea of the "streaming" of emotions—"the feeling of unity between you and Spring and God, or what people call God, and Nature. . . ." He criticizes Freud for allowing his work to become so intellectualized that it did not recognize this "biological activity . . . which is part of the universe" (*Reich Speaks of Freud* 93–94).

2. Several critics see Charlotte's ubiquity in the text as related, at the level of plot, to an unnatural disempowerment of her male partner. Pitavy, for example, finds that "Harry is dominated by the masculine Charlotte" (122) and so "drowns in the furious waters of love and sex" (120). Meindl believes that Charlotte, by making love her object, "ironically reduces her lover to less than an object: a tool" (90); and Howe characterizes Charlotte as "a young woman of powerful ego and compulsive sexuality" (233). McHaney envisions Charlotte as a seductress who ensnares "the innocent Wilbourne into her scheme" (31); even when she is dying and Harry is trying to "retreat" from her, Charlotte's "omnivorous yellow eyes" manage to "catch and retain him" (159). Bernhardt, Cushman, and Millgate, who view Charlotte more sympathetically, find her an active, creative presence in the text. Bernhardt and Cushman point to her creativity and its effect upon Harry and the reader, and Millgate shows how her strength sets the pattern of life (and disaster) for the couple. McHaney, Gary Harrington, and others point to Charlotte's connection to water. Bernhardt summarizes other comments about Charlotte not mentioned here (351–52).

3. Those who have been particularly interested in the structure of *The Wild Palms* include Howe, Moldenhauer, and Moses. Howe's focus is the interweaving of narratives, and Moses's is thematic mirroring. Moldenhauer finds that episodes of "Old Man" parody aligned episodes of "Wild Palms" and that the convict's story "serves as the antithesis" of the lovers' narrative (321). In a discussion of "Old Man" alone, Cumpiano finds that there are two reading levels for the convict's story, which "is like that of the flood itself, composed of distinct strata, flowing in opposite directions" (185). Cumpiano believes that we should read both "the familiar surface story of man's eternal quest to return to his homeland" and a "deeper, more violent current" revealing "a contrary view of the virtues of the hero and a reversal of the myths of man's drive to return to his source" (187). I am suggesting that *The Wild Palms* may be read as a "flooding" narrative which itself dissolves the binary oppositions evolving out of structure, theme, or characterization.

4. I am using Kristeva's term "traversal" ("Oscillation" 165).

5. The fact that desire floods all levels of discourse in *The Wild Palms* hardly should be surprising. As Judith L. Sensibar's recent work reveals, Faulkner's erotic life was always in crisis and always fueling his fiction ("'Drowsing Maidenhead'"). Both Minter and Wittenberg point out that *The Wild Palms* was writ-

ten during a period of intense feeling arising out of Faulkner's passionate affair with Meta Carpenter. In assessing the effects of Faulkner's love affair upon *The Wild Palms,* Wittenberg points out that the book emerges out of and overflows with Faulkner's own suffering and conflict. As such an expression of personal trauma, *The Wild Palms* presents a "dualistic vision of the difficulties, even destruction, wrought by the journey toward or away from love" (*William Faulkner* 172).

6. For a "phallic" reading *par excellence,* see Jewkes's interpretation of *The Wild Palms* as dominated by "the problem of masculinity" figured in the phallus and resolved by the metaphor of masturbation at the end of the book. The "problem" is that men, by having sex with women, lose their connection to "Mother Earth" by choosing "compromise" over "purity" (50). Yet "Harry's failure is only temporary" because he regains what he has lost and so "discovers his manhood in choosing to suffer. And though punished, at the end he has a real phallus in hand; the convict only waves a cigar" (52). More recently, Zender finds that "Harry's act of masturbation expresses Faulkner's understanding of the transgressive character of his art, of its need to break through the barriers of shame and propriety and establish contact with its disorderly source" (28).

7. For an extended discussion of the connections between *The Wild Palms* and *A Farewell to Arms,* see McHaney 3–24. In "The 'Hemingwaves' in Faulkner's *Wild Palms,*" H. Edward Richardson argues that, because Hemingway was famous and Faulkner neglected, *The Wild Palms* (specifically "Wild Palms") was "an independent satirical comment upon Hemingway himself" (360). In "Water, Water Everywhere: 'Old Man' and *A Farewell to Arms,*" Moses finds parallels between the "Old Man" narrative and Hemingway's book, particularly in the "master image" of water (172).

8. McHaney interprets this passage in Schopenhauerian terms. The "grave-womb or womb-grave" symbolizes birth/death as the dual condition under which the will to live remains viable (103).

Selected Bibliography

Abel, Elizabeth, ed. *Writing and Sexual Difference.* Chicago: Univ. of Chicago Press, 1982.

Appignanesi, Lisa. *Femininity and the Creative Imagination: A Study of Henry James, Robert Musil, and Marcel Proust.* London: Vision, 1973.

Auerbach, Nina. *Woman and the Demon: The Life of a Victorian Myth.* Cambridge, Mass.: Harvard Univ. Press, 1982.

Baker, Houston A., Jr. *Blues, Ideology, and Afro-American Literature: A Vernacular Theory.* Chicago: Univ. of Chicago Press, 1984.

Bakhtin, Mikhail. *The Dialogic Imagination.* Ed. Michael Holquist. Trans. Caryl Emerson and Michael Holquist. Austin: Univ. of Texas Press, 1981.

Baldwin, James. "Everybody's Protest Novel." *Partisan Review* 16 (June 1949): 578–85.

Barthes, Roland. *The Pleasure of the Text.* New York: Hill & Wang, 1974.

———. *S/Z.* Trans. Richard Miller. New York: Hill & Wang, 1974.

———. *Writing Degree Zero.* New York: Hill & Wang, 1967.

Baum, Catherine B. "'The Beautiful One': Caddy Compson as Heroine of *The Sound and the Fury.*" *Modern Fiction Studies* 13 (Spring 1967): 33–44.

de Beauvoir, Simone. *The Second Sex.* Trans. and ed. H.M. Parshley. New York: Knopf, 1978.

Benjamin, Jessica. "A Desire of One's Own: Psychoanalytic Feminism and Intersubjective Space." In *Feminist Studies/Critical Studies,* ed. Teresa de Lauretis, pp. 78–101. Bloomington: Indiana Univ. Press, 1986.

Bernhardt, Laurie A. "'Being Worthy Enough': The Tragedy of Charlotte Rittenmeyer." *Mississippi Quarterly* 34 (Summer 1986): 351–64.

Bernheimer, Charles, and Claire Kahane, eds. *In Dora's Case: Freud—Hysteria—Feminism.* Gender and Culture Series. Gen. Ed. Carolyn G. Heilbrun and Nancy K. Miller. New York: Columbia Univ. Press, 1985.

Blassingame, John W. *The Slave Community: Plantation Life in the Antebellum South.* New York: Oxford Univ. Press, 1972.

Bleikasten, André. "Fathers in Faulkner." In *The Fictional Father,* ed. Robert Con Davis, pp. 115–146. Amherst: Univ. of Massachusetts Press, 1981.

———. "In Praise of Helen." In *Faulkner and Women,* ed. Doreen Fowler and Ann J. Abadie, pp. 128–43. Jackson: Univ. Press of Mississippi, 1986.

———. *The Most Splendid Failure: Faulkner's "The Sound and the Fury."* Bloomington: Indiana Univ. Press, 1976.

———, ed. *William Faulkner's "The Sound and the Fury": A Critical Case-*

book. Garland Faulkner Casebooks 1. Series Ed. Noel Polk. New York: Garland, 1982.

Brooks, Cleanth. "Faulkner's Vision of Good and Evil." *Massachusetts Review* 3 (Summer 1962): 692–712.

——. "The Tradition of Romantic Love and *The Wild Palms.*" *Mississippi Quarterly* 25 (Summer 1972): 265–87.

——. *William Faulkner: The Yoknapatawpha Country.* New Haven: Yale Univ. Press, 1963.

Brylowski, Walter. "Faulkner's 'Mythology.'" In *William Faulkner's* Absalom, Absalom!: *A Critical Casebook,* ed. Elisabeth Muhlenfeld, pp. 109–34. New York: Garland, 1984.

——. *Faulkner's Olympian Laugh: Myth in the Novels.* Detroit: Wayne State Univ. Press, 1968.

Carter, Steve. "Caddy and Quentin: Anima and Animus Orbited Nice." *Hartford Studies in Literature* 12 (1980): 124–42.

Cash, W.J. *The Mind of the South.* New York: Knopf, 1941.

Chodorow, Nancy. *The Reproduction of Mothering: Psychoanalysis and the Sociology of Gender.* Berkeley: Univ. of California Press, 1978.

Cixous, Hélène. "Castration or Decapitation?" *Signs* 7 (1981): 41–55.

——. "The Character of 'Character.'" *New Literary History* 5 (1974): 383–402.

——. "The Laugh of the Medusa." Rev. version. In *New French Feminisms,* ed. Elaine Marks and Isabelle de Courtivron, pp. 245–64. Amherst: Univ. of Massachusetts Press, 1980.

——. "Sorties: Out and Out: Attacks/Ways Out/Forays." In Hélène Cixous and Catherine Clément, *The Newly Born Woman,* pp. 61–132. Minneapolis: Univ. of Minnesota Press, 1986.

Cixous, Hélène, and Catherine Clément. *The Newly Born Woman.* Trans. Betsy Wing. Foreword by Sandra Gilbert. Theory and History of Literature Series 24. Minneapolis: Univ. of Minnesota Press, 1986.

Clarke, Deborah L. "Familiar and Fantastic: Women in *Absalom, Absalom!*" *Faulkner Journal* 2 (Fall 1986): 62–72.

Clinton, Catherine. *The Plantation Mistress: Woman's World in the Old South.* New York: Pantheon, 1982.

Conley, Verena Andermatt. *Hélène Cixous: Writing the Feminine.* Lincoln: Univ. of Nebraska Press, 1984.

Cowan, Michael H., ed. *Twentieth Century Interpretations of "The Sound and the Fury."* Englewood Cliffs, N.J.: Prentice-Hall, 1968.

Culler, Jonathan. *On Deconstruction: Theory and Criticism after Structuralism.* Ithaca: Cornell Univ. Press, 1982.

Cumpiano, Marion W. "The Motif of Return: Currents and Counter Currents in 'Old Man' by William Faulkner." *Southern Humanities Review* 12 (Summer 1978): 185–93.

Cushman, William Price. "Knowledge and Involvement in Faulkner's *The Wild*

Palms." In *Faulkner: The Unappeased Imagination,* ed. Glenn O. Carey, pp. 25–38. New York: Whitson, 1980.

Davis, Angela. *Women, Race and Class.* New York: Random House, 1981.

Davis, Robert Con, ed. *The Fictional Father: Lacanian Readings of the Text.* Amherst: Univ. of Massachusetts Press, 1981.

———, ed. *Lacan and Narration: The Psychoanalytic Difference in Narrative Theory.* Baltimore: Johns Hopkins Univ. Press, 1983.

Davis, Thadious. *Faulkner's "Negro": Art and the Southern Context.* Baton Rouge: Louisiana State Univ. Press, 1983.

Derrida, Jacques. "Implications: Interview with Henri Ronse." In Derrida, *Positions,* pp. 1–14. Trans. Alan Bass. Chicago: Univ. of Chicago Press, 1981.

———. *Of Grammatology.* Trans. Gayatri Chakravorty Spivak. Baltimore: Johns Hopkins Univ. Press, 1976.

———. *Speech and Phenomena and Other Essays on Husserl's Theory of Signs.* Trans. and intro. David B. Allison. Preface by Newton Garver. Evanston: Northwestern Univ. Press, 1973.

———. *Spurs/Éperons.* Chicago: Univ. of Chicago Press, 1978.

———. *Writing and Difference.* Trans. Alan Bass. Chicago: Univ. of Chicago Press, 1978.

Díaz-Diocaretz, Myriam. "Faulkner's Hen House: Woman as Bounded Text." In *Faulkner and Women,* ed. Doreen Fowler and Ann J. Abadie, pp. 235–69. Jackson: Univ. Press of Mississippi, 1986.

Dinnerstein, Dorothy. *The Mermaid and the Minotaur: Sexual Arrangements and Human Malaise.* New York: Harper & Row, 1976.

Donovan, Josephine, ed. *Feminist Literary Criticism: Explorations in Theory.* Lexington: Univ. of Kentucky Press, 1975.

Du Bois, W.E.B. *The Souls of Black Folk.* Chicago: A.C. McClurg, 1903.

Durand, Régis. "On *Aphanisis*: A Note on the Dramaturgy of the Subject in Narrative Analysis." In *Lacan and Narration,* ed. Robert Con Davis, pp. 860–70. Baltimore: Johns Hopkins Univ. Press, 1983.

Duvall, John N. "Faulkner's Critics and Women: The Voice of the Community." In *Faulkner and Women,* ed. Doreen Fowler and Ann J. Abadie, pp. 41–57. Jackson: Univ. Press of Mississippi, 1986.

Eco, Umberto. *A Theory of Semiotics.* Bloomington: Indiana Univ. Press, 1979.

Fant, Joseph L., III, and Robert Ashley, eds. *Faulkner at West Point.* New York: Random House, 1964.

Faulkner, William. *Absalom Absalom! The Corrected Text.* New York: Random House, 1986.

———. *As I Lay Dying.* 1930. New York: Vintage, 1964.

———. *Collected Stories of William Faulkner.* New York: Random House, 1950.

———. *Essays, Speeches and Public Letters.* Ed. James B. Meriwether. New York: Random House, 1966.

————. *Faulkner in the University.* Ed. Frederick L. Gwynn and Joseph L. Blotner. New York: Vintage, 1965.

————. *Intruder in the Dust.* New York: Random House, 1948.

————. *Light in August.* 1932. New York: Vintage, 1972.

————. *Lion in the Garden: Interviews with William Faulkner, 1926–62.* Ed. James B. Meriwether and Michael Millgate. New York: Random House, 1968.

————. *Requiem for a Nun.* New York: Random House, 1951.

————. *Sanctuary. The Corrected Text.* New York: Vintage, 1987.

————. *The Sound and the Fury.* 1929. New York: Modern Library, 1966.

————. *The Unvanquished.* 1938. New York: Vintage, 1966.

————. *The Wild Palms.* 1939. New York: Vintage, 1966.

Feaster, John. "Faulkner's *Old Man* [sic]: A Psychoanalytic Approach." *Modern Fiction Studies* 13 (Spring 1967): 89–93.

Felman, Shoshana. *Literature and Psychoanalysis: The Question of Reading: Otherwise.* Baltimore: Johns Hopkins Univ. Press, 1982.

————. "Rereading Femininity." *Yale French Studies* 62 (1981): 19–44.

————. *Writing and Madness.* Trans. Martha Noel Evans and Shoshana Felman. Ithaca: Cornell Univ. Press, 1985.

Fetterley, Judith. *The Resisting Reader: A Feminist Approach to American Fiction.* Bloomington: Indiana Univ. Press, 1977.

Fiedler, Leslie. *Love and Death in the American Novel.* New York: Criterion, 1960.

Fishburn, Katherine. *Women in Popular Culture: A Reference Guide.* Westport, Conn.: Greenwood, 1982.

Flieger, Jerry Aline. "The Purloined Punchline: Joke as Textual Paradigm." In *Lacan and Narration,* ed. Robert Con Davis, pp. 941–67. Baltimore: Johns Hopkins Univ. Press, 1983.

Flynn, Elizabeth A., and Patrocinio P. Schweickart, eds. *Gender and Reading: Essays on Readers, Texts, and Contexts.* Baltimore: Johns Hopkins Univ. Press, 1986.

Foucault, Michel. *The History of Sexuality.* Vol. 1. Trans. Robert Hurley. New York: Vintage, 1980.

————. "What Is an Author?" In *Language, Counter-Memory, Practice,* ed. Donald F. Bouchard, 113–38. Trans. Donald F. Bouchard and Sherry Simon. Ithaca: Cornell Univ. Press, 1977.

Fowler, Doreen. *Faulkner's Changing Vision: From Outrage to Affirmation.* Ann Arbor: UMI Research Press, 1983.

Fowler, Doreen, and Ann J. Abadie, eds., *Faulkner and Women: Faulkner and Yoknapatawpha, 1985.* Jackson: Univ. Press of Mississippi, 1986.

Freud, Sigmund. "Femininity." *Standard Edition of the Complete Psychological Works of Sigmund Freud,* ed. James Strachey. 22: 112–35. London: Hogarth, 1964.

————. "Fragment of an Analysis of a Case of Hysteria." *Standard Edition* 7: 7–122.

———. *The Interpretation of Dreams. Standard Edition* 5: 339–627.

———. "Three Essays on the Theory of Sexuality." *Standard Edition* 7:135–243.

———. "The 'Uncanny.'" *Standard Edition* 17:217–52.

Gallop, Jane. *Feminism and Psychoanalysis: The Daughter's Seduction.* Ithaca: Cornell Univ. Press, 1982.

———. *Reading Lacan.* Ithaca: Cornell Univ. Press, 1985.

Gardiner, Judith Kegan. "Mind Mother: Psychoanalysis and Feminism." In *Making a Difference,* ed. Gayle Greene and Coppelia Kahn, pp. 113–45. London: Methuen, 1985.

Garner, Shirley, Claire Kahane, and Madelon Sprengnether, eds. *The (M)other Tongue.* Ithaca: Cornell Univ. Press, 1985.

Genette, Gérard. *Narrative Discourse: An Essay in Method.* Trans. Jane E. Lewin. Foreword by Jonathan Culler. Ithaca: Cornell Univ. Press, 1980.

Gilbert, Sandra M., and Susan Gubar. *The Madwoman in the Attic: The Woman Writer and the Nineteenth-Century Literary Imagination.* New Haven: Yale Univ. Press, 1979.

Gilligan, Carol. *In a Different Voice.* Cambridge, Mass.: Harvard Univ. Press, 1982.

Gladstein, Mimi Reisel. *The Indestructible Woman in Faulkner, Hemingway, and Steinbeck.* Studies in Modern Literature 45. Ann Arbor: UMI Research Press, 1986.

Greene, Gayle, and Coppelia Kahn, eds. *Making a Difference: Feminist Literary Criticism.* London: Methuen, 1985.

Gregory, Eileen. "Caddy Compson's World." In *The Merrill Studies in "The Sound and the Fury,"* ed. James B. Meriwether, pp. 89–101. Columbus, Ohio: Charles E. Merrill, 1970.

Gresset, Michel. "Introduction: Faulkner between the Texts." In *Intertextuality in Faulkner.* Ed. Michel Gresset and Noel Polk. Jackson: Univ. Press of Mississippi, 1985.

Gresset, Michel, and Noel Polk, eds. *Intertextuality in Faulkner.* Jackson: Univ. Press of Mississippi, 1985.

Gresset, Michel, and Patrick Samway, S. J., eds. *Faulkner and Idealism: Perspectives from Paris.* Jackson: Univ. Press of Mississippi, 1983.

Gubar, Susan. "'The Blank Page' and the Issues of Female Creativity." In *Writing and Sexual Difference,* ed. Elizabeth Abel, pp. 73–94. Chicago: Univ. of Chicago Press, 1982.

Guerard, Albert J. "Faulkner the Innovator." In *The Maker and the Myth,* ed. Evans Harrington and Ann J. Abadie, pp. 71–88. Jackson: Univ. Press of Mississippi, 1978.

Gutman, Herbert G. *The Black Family in Slavery and Freedom, 1750–1925* New York: Pantheon, 1976.

Gwin, Minrose C. *Black and White Women of the Old South: The Peculiar Sisterhood in American Literature.* Knoxville: Univ. of Tennessee Press, 1985.

Haag, William G. "The Geography and the Cultural Anthropology of The Mississippi River." *Mississippi Quarterly* 16 (Fall 1963): 171–80.

Hagopian, John V. "Black Insight in *Absalom, Absalom!*" *Faulkner Studies* 1 (1980): 29–37.

Harrington, Evans, and Ann J. Abadie, eds. *The Maker and the Myth: Faulkner and Yoknapatawpha, 1977.* Jackson: Univ. Press of Mississippi, 1978.

Harrington, Gary. "Distant Mirrors: The Intertextual Relationship of Quentin Compson and Harry Wilbourne." *Faulkner Journal* 1 (Fall 1985): 41–45.

Heilbrun, Carolyn. *Toward a Recognition of Androgyny.* New York: Knopf, 1964.

Heilbrun, Carolyn, and Catharine Stimpson. "Theories of Feminist Criticism: A Dialogue." In *Feminist Literary Criticism,* ed. Josephine Donovan, pp. 61–73. Lexington: Univ. of Kentucky Press, 1975.

Hill, Douglas B., Jr. "Faulkner's Caddy." *Canadian Review of American Studies* 7 (Spring 1976): 26–38.

Hoffman, Frederick J., and Olga W. Vickery, eds. *William Faulkner: Two Decades of Criticism.* East Lansing: Michigan State Univ. Press, 1954.

Hooks, Bell. *"Ain't I a Woman?": Black Women and Feminism.* Boston: South End Press, 1981.

Howe, Irving. *William Faulkner.* 3d ed. Chicago: Univ. of Chicago Press, 1975.

Irigaray, Luce. *Speculum of the Other Woman.* Trans. Gillian C. Gill. Ithaca: Cornell Univ. Press, 1985.

———. *This Sex Which Is Not One.* Trans. Catherine Porter with Carolyn Burke. Ithaca: Cornell Univ. Press, 1985.

Irwin, John T. *Doubling and Incest/Repetition and Revenge: A Speculative Reading of Faulkner.* Baltimore: Johns Hopkins Univ. Press, 1975.

Jacobus, Mary. *Reading Woman: Essays in Feminist Criticism.* Gender and Culture Series. Ed. Carolyn G. Heilbrun and Nancy K. Miller. New York: Columbia Univ. Press, 1986.

Jardine, Alice A. *Gynesis: Configurations of Woman and Modernity.* Ithaca: Cornell Univ. Press, 1985.

Jehlen, Myra. "Archimedes and the Paradox of Feminist Criticism." *The Signs Reader: Women, Gender, and Scholarship.* Chicago: Univ. of Chicago Press, 1983.

Jelliffe, Robert A., ed. *Faulkner at Nagano.* Tokyo: Kenkyusha, 1956.

Jenkins, Lee. *Faulkner and Black-White Relations: A Psychoanalytic Approach.* New York: Columbia Univ. Press, 1981.

Jewkes, W.T. "Counterpoint in Faulkner's *The Wild Palms.*" *Wisconsin Studies in Contemporary Literature* 2 (Winter 1961): 39–53.

Johnson, Barbara. *The Critical Difference: Essays in the Contemporary Rhetoric of Reading.* Baltimore: Johns Hopkins Univ. Press, 1980.

———. "Teaching Ignorance: *L'École des Femmes.*" *Yale French Studies* 63 (1982): 165–82.

———. *A World of Difference.* Baltimore: Johns Hopkins Univ. Press, 1987.

Jones, Ann Rosalind. "Inscribing Femininity: French Theories of the Feminine." In *Making a Difference,* ed. Gayle Greene and Coppelia Kahn, pp. 80–112. London: Methuen, 1985.

————. "Writing the Body: Toward an Understanding of *L'Écriture Féminine*." In *The New Feminist Criticism,* ed. Elaine Showalter, pp. 361–77. New York: Pantheon, 1985.

Jones, Anne Goodwyn. *Tomorrow is Another Day: The Woman Writer in the South, 1859–1936.* Baton Rouge: Louisiana State Univ. Press, 1981.

Kahane, Claire. "Introduction: Part Two." In *In Dora's Case,* ed. Charles Bernheimer and Claire Kahane, pp. 19–32. New York: Columbia Univ. Press, 1985.

Kartiganer, Donald M. *The Fragile Thread: The Meaning of Form in Faulkner's Novels.* Amherst: Univ. of Massachusetts Press, 1979.

Kent, George. "The Black Woman in Faulkner's Works, with the Exclusion of Dilsey." *Phylon* 35 (Dec. 1974): 430–41; *Phylon* 36 (March 1975): 55–67.

Kermode, Frank. *The Art of Telling: Essays on Fiction.* Cambridge: Harvard Univ. Press, 1983.

Kerr, Elizabeth M. *Yoknapatawpha: Faulkner's "Little Postage Stamp of Native Soil."* New York: Fordham Univ. Press, 1969.

Kolodny, Annette. "Dancing through the Minefield: Some Observations on the Theory, Practice, and Politics of a Feminist Literary Criticism." *Feminist Studies* 6 (Spring 1980): 1–22.

————. "A Map for Rereading; or, Gender and the Interpretation of Literary Texts." In *The (M)Other Tongue,* ed. Shirley Garner, Claire Kahane, and Madelon Sprengnether, pp. 241–59. Ithaca: Cornell Univ. Press, 1985.

Kreiswirth, Martin. "Learning as He Wrote: Re-Used Materials in *The Sound and the Fury*." *Mississippi Quarterly* 34 (Summer 1981): 281–98.

Kristeva, Julia. *Desire in Language: A Semiotic Approach to Literature and Art.* Ed. Leon S. Roudiez. New York: Columbia Univ. Press, 1980.

————. "Oscillation between Power and Denial." In *New French Feminisms,* ed. Elaine Marks and Isabelle de Courtivron, pp. 165–67. Amherst: Univ. of Massachusetts Press, 1980.

————. *Revolution in Poetic Language.* Trans. Margaret Waller. Intro. Leon S. Roudiez. New York: Columbia Univ. Press, 1984.

————. "Women's Time." *Signs.* 7 (1981): 13–35.

Kuhn, Thomas. *The Structure of Scientific Revolution.* Chicago: Univ. of Chicago Press, 1970.

Lacan, Jacques. *Écrits: A Selection.* Trans. Alan Sheridan. London: Tavistock, 1977.

————. *Feminine Sexuality: Jacques Lacan and the École Freudienne.* Ed. Juliet Mitchell and Jacqueline Rose. Trans. Jacqueline Rose. London: McMillan, 1982.

Langford, Gerald. *Faulkner's Revision of "Absalom, Absalom!"* Austin: Univ. of Texas Press, 1971.

Lanser, Susan Sniader. *The Narrative Act: Point of View in Prose Fiction.* Princeton, N.J.: Princeton Univ. Press, 1981.

de Lauretis, Teresa. *Alice Doesn't: Feminism, Semiotics, Cinema.* Bloomington: Indiana Univ. Press, 1984.

————, ed. *Feminist Studies/Critical Studies.* Theories of Contemporary Culture 8. Bloomington: Indiana Univ. Press, 1986.

Lebsock, Suzanne. *The Free Women of Petersburg: Status and Culture in a Southern Town, 1784–1860.* New York: Norton, 1984.

Longley, John L., Jr. "'Who Never Had a Sister': A Reading of *The Sound and the Fury.*" *Mosaic* 7 (1973): 35–53.

Lorch, Thomas. "Thomas Sutpen and the Female Principle." *Mississippi Quarterly* 20 (Winter 1967): 38–42.

Lyotard, Jean François. *The Postmodern Condition: A Report on Knowledge.* Trans. Geoff Bennington and Brian Massumi. Foreword by Fredric Jameson. Theory and History of Literature Series 10. Minneapolis: Univ. of Minnesota Press, 1984.

McGrath, William J. *Freud's Discovery of Psychoanalysis: The Politics of Hysteria.* Ithaca: Cornell Univ. Press, 1986.

McHaney, Thomas L. *William Faulkner's* The Wild Palms: *A Study.* Jackson: Univ. Press of Mississippi, 1975.

McLeod, Anne. "Gender Difference: Relativity in GDR-Writing, or: How to Oppose Without Trying." *Oxford Literary Review* 7 (1985): 41–61.

Malin, Irving. *William Faulkner: An Interpretation.* Stanford, Calif.: Stanford Univ. Press, 1957.

de Man, Paul. *Blindness and Insight: Essays in the Rhetoric of Contemporary Criticism.* 2d ed. Intro. by Wlad Godzich. Theory and History of Literature Series 7. Minneapolis: Univ. of Minnesota Press, 1983.

Marks, Elaine, and Isabelle de Courtivron, eds. *New French Feminisms: An Anthology.* Amherst: Univ. of Massachusetts Press, 1980.

Matthews, John T. *The Play of Faulkner's Language.* Ithaca: Cornell Univ. Press, 1982.

Mehlman, Jeffrey. *Revolution and Repetition: Marx, Hugo, Balzac.* Berkeley: Univ. of California Press, 1977.

Meindl, Dieter. "Romantic Idealism and *The Wild Palms.*" In *Faulkner and Idealism: Perspectives from Paris,* ed. Michel Gresset and Patrick Samway, S.J., pp. 86–96. Jackson: Univ. Press of Mississippi, 1983.

Meriwether, James B., ed. *The Merrill Studies in "The Sound and the Fury."* Columbus, Ohio: Charles E. Merrill, 1970.

Meriwether, James B., and Michael Millgate, eds. *Lion in the Garden: Interviews with William Faulkner, 1926–1962.* New York: Random House, 1968.

Messerli, Douglas. "The Problem of Time in *The Sound and the Fury*: A Critical Reassessment and Reinterpretation." *Southern Literary Journal* 6 (Spring 1974): 19–41.

Miller, David M. "Faulkner's Women." *Modern Fiction Studies* 13 (Spring 1967): 3–17.

Miller, J. Hillis. "Deconstructing the Deconstructors." *Diacritics* 5 (1975): 24–31.

Miller, Nancy K. "Arachnologies: the Woman, the Text, and the Critic." In *The Poetics of Gender,* ed. Nancy K. Miller, pp. 270–95. New York: Columbia Univ. Press, 1986.

———, ed. *The Poetics of Gender.* New York: Columbia Univ. Press, 1986.

Millgate, Michael. *The Achievement of William Faulkner.* New York: Vintage, 1963.

Milliner, Gladys. "The Third Eve: Caddy Compson." *Midwest Quarterly* 16 (April 1975): 268–75.

Minter, David L. *William Faulkner: His Life and Work.* Baltimore: Johns Hopkins Univ. Press, 1980.

Mitchell, Juliet. *Women: The Longest Revolution.* New York: Pantheon, 1966.

Modleski, Tania. "Feminism and the Power of Interpretation: Some Critical Readings." In *Feminist Studies/Critical Studies,* ed. Teresa de Lauretis, pp. 121–38. Bloomington: Indiana Univ. Press, 1986.

———. "Rape versus Mans/laughter: Hitchcock's *Blackmail* and Feminist Interpretation." PMLA 102 (May 1987): 304–15.

Moi, Toril. *Sexual/Textual Politics: Feminist Literary Theory.* New Accents Series. Gen. Ed. Terence Hawkes. London: Methuen, 1985.

Moldenhauer, Joseph J. "Unity of Theme and Structure in *The Wild Palms.*" In *William Faulkner: Three Decades of Criticism,* ed. Frederick J. Hoffman and Olga W. Vickery, pp. 305–22. East Lansing: Michigan State Univ. Press, 1960.

Moore, Robert R. "Desire and Despair: Temple Drake's Self-Victimization." In *Faulkner and Women,* ed. Doreen Fowler and Ann J. Abadie, pp. 112–27. Jackson: Univ. Press of Mississippi, 1986.

Mortimer, Gail. *Faulkner's Rhetoric of Loss.* Austin: Univ. of Texas Press, 1983.

———. "The Ironies of Transcendent Love in Faulkner's *The Wild Palms.*" *Faulkner Journal* 1 (Spring 1986): 30–42.

———. "The Smooth, Suave Shape of Desire: Paradox in Faulknerian Imagery of Women." *Women's Studies* 13 (1986): 149–61.

Moses, W.R. "Water, Water Everywhere: 'Old Man' and *A Farewell to Arms. Modern Fiction Studies* 5 (Summer 1959): 172–74.

Muhlenfeld, Elisabeth. "*Faulkner's Women.*" *Mississippi Quarterly* 26 (Summer 1973): 435–50.

———. *William Faulkner's* Absalom, Absalom!: *A Critical Casebook.* New York: Garland, 1984.

Nilon, Charles. *Faulkner and the Negro.* New York: Citadel, 1965.

Page, Sally. *Faulkner's Women: Characterization and Meaning.* Deland, Fla.: Everett/Edward, 1972.

Parker, Robert Dale. *Faulkner and the Novelistic Imagination*. Urbana: Univ. of Illinois Press, 1985.

Parks, Kae Irene. "Faulkner's Women: Archetype and Metaphor." Ph.D. dissertation, Univ. of Pennsylvania, 1980.

Pearce, Richard. *The Novel in Motion: An Approach to Modern Fiction*. Columbus: Ohio State Univ. Press, 1983.

Pitavy, François. "Forgetting Jerusalem: An Ironical Chart for *The Wild Palms*." In *Intertextuality in Faulkner*, ed. Michel Gresset and Noel Polk, pp. 114–27. Jackson: Univ. Press of Mississippi, 1985.

Poirier, Richard. "'Strange Gods' in Jefferson, Mississippi: Analysis of *Absalom, Absalom!*" In *William Faulkner's* Absalom, Absalom!: *A Critical Casebook*, ed. Elisabeth Muhlenfeld, pp. 1–22. New York: Garland, 1984.

Polk, Noel. "The Dungeon Was Mother Herself." In *New Directions in Faulkner Studies*, ed. Doreen Fowler and Ann J. Abadie, pp. 61–93. Jackson: Univ. Press of Mississippi, 1984.

Ragan, David Paul. "'That Tragedy Is Second-Hand': Quentin, Henry, and the Ending of *Absalom, Absalom!*" *Mississippi Quarterly* 34 (Summer 1986): 337–50.

Rank, Otto. *The Double: A Psychoanalytic Study*. Trans. and ed. Harry Tucker, Jr. Chapel Hill: Univ. of North Carolina Press, 1971.

Reed, Joseph W., Jr. *Faulkner's Narrative*. New Haven: Yale Univ. Press, 1973.

Reeves, Carolyn. "*The Wild Palms*: Faulkner's Chaotic Cosmos." *Mississippi Quarterly* 20 (Summer 1967): 148–57.

Reich, Wilhelm. *Reich Speaks of Freud*. New York: Noonday, 1968.

Rhodes, Pamela, and Richard Godden. "*The Wild Palms*: Degraded Culture, Devalued Texts." In *Intertextuality in Faulkner*, ed. Michel Gresset and Noel Polk, pp. 83–113. Jackson: Univ. Press of Mississippi, 1985.

Rich, Adrienne. *Of Woman Born: Motherhood as Experience and Institution*. New York: Norton, 1977.

———. "When We Dead Awaken: Writing as Re-Vision." *College English* 34 (1972): 18–30.

Richardson, H. Edward. "The 'Hemingwaves' in Faulkner's *The Wild Palms*." *Modern Fiction Studies* 4 (Winter 1958–59): 357–60.

Richardson, Kenneth. *Force and Faith in the Novels of William Faulkner*. The Hague: Mouton, 1967.

Robin, Régine. "*Absalom, Absalom!*": Le Blanc et le noir chez Melville et Faulkner*. Ed. Viola Sachs. The Hague: Mouton, 1974.

Rose, Jacqueline. "Dora: Fragment of an Analysis." In *In Dora's Case*, ed. Charles Bernheimer and Claire Kahane, pp. 128–48. New York: Columbia Univ. Press, 1985.

Ross, Stephen M. "The 'Loud World' of Quentin Compson." In *William Faulkner's "The Sound and the Fury"*: A Critical Casebook*, ed. André Bleikasten, pp. 101–114. New York: Garland, 1982.

————. "Oratory and the Dialogical in *Absalom, Absalom!*" In *Intertextuality in Faulkner,* ed. Michel Gresset and Noel Polk, pp. 73–86. Jackson: Univ. Press of Mississippi, 1985.

————. "Rev. Shegog's Powerful Voice." *Faulkner Journal* 1 (Fall 1985): 8–16.

Salvaggio, Ruth. *Enlightened Absence: Neoclassical Configurations of the Feminine.* Urbana: Univ. of Illinois Press, 1988.

Sartre, Jean-Paul. "Time in Faulkner: *The Sound and the Fury.*" In *William Faulkner: Two Decades of Criticism,* ed. Frederick J. Hoffman and Olga W. Vickery, pp. 180–88. East Lansing: Michigan State Univ. Press, 1954.

Schleifer, Ronald. "The Space and Dialogue of Desire: Lacan, Greimas, and Narrative Temporality." In *Lacan and Narration,* ed. Robert Con Davis, pp. 871–90. Baltimore: Johns Hopkins Univ. Press, 1983.

Schumacher, Dorin. "Subjectivities: A Theory of the Critical Process." In *Feminist Literary Criticism,* ed. Josephine Donovan, pp. 29–37. Lexington: Univ. of Kentucky Press, 1975.

Schweickart, Patrocinio P. "Reading Ourselves: Toward a Feminist Theory of Reading." In *Gender and Reading,* ed. Elizabeth A. Flynn and Patrocinio P. Schweickart, pp. 31–62. Baltimore: Johns Hopkins Univ. Press, 1986.

Scott, Anne Firor. *The Southern Lady: From Pedestal to Politics, 1830–1930.* Chicago: Univ. of Chicago Press, 1970.

Sensibar, Judith L. "'Drowsing Maidenhead Symbol's Self': Faulkner and the Fictions of Love." In *Faulkner and the Craft of Fiction: Faulkner and Yoknapatawpha, 1987,* ed. Doreen Fowler and Ann J. Abadie, pp. 124–46. Jackson: Univ. Press of Mississippi, 1989.

————. "Pop Culture Invades Jefferson: Faulkner's Real and Imaginary Photos of Desire." In *Faulkner and Popular Culture: Faulkner and Yoknapatawpha, 1988,* ed. Doreen Fowler and Ann J. Abadie. Jackson: Univ. Press of Mississippi (in press).

Showalter, Elaine. "Feminist Criticism in the Wilderness." *Critical Inquiry* (Winter 1981): 179–205; rptd. in *Writing and Sexual Difference,* ed. Elizabeth Abel, pp. 9–36. Chicago: Univ. of Chicago Press, 1982.

————, ed. *The New Feminist Criticism: Essays on Women, Literature, and Theory.* New York: Pantheon, 1985.

————. "Women and the Literary Curriculum." *College English* 32 (1971): 855–62.

Siegle, Robert. *The Politics of Reflexivity: Narrative and the Constitutive Poetics of Culture.* Baltimore: Johns Hopkins Univ. Press, 1986.

Simpson, Lewis P. "Sex and History: Origins of Faulkner's Aprocrypha." In *The Maker and the Myth,* ed. Evans Harrington and Ann J. Abadie, pp. 43–70. Jackson: Univ. Press of Mississippi, 1978.

Slatoff, Walter J. *Quest for Failure: A Study of William Faulkner.* Ithaca: Cornell Univ. Press, 1960.

Snead, James A. *Figures of Division: William Faulkner's Major Novels.* New York: Methuen, 1986.

Spivak, Gayatri Chakravorty. "French Feminism in an International Frame." *Yale French Studies* 62 (1981): 154–84.

———. "Love Me, Love My Ombre, Elle." *Diacritics* (Winter 1984): 19–36.

Sprengnether, Madelon. "Enforcing Oedipus: Freud and Dora." *In Dora's Case,* ed. Charles Bernheimer and Claire Kahane, pp. 254–74. New York: Columbia Univ. Press, 1985; rptd. in *The (M)other Tongue,* ed. Shirley Garner, Claire Kahane, and Madelon Sprengnether, pp. 51–71. Ithaca: Cornell Univ. Press, 1985.

Steinberg, Aaron. "*Intruder in the Dust*: Faulkner as Psychologist of the Southern Psyche." *Literature and Psychology* 16 (Spring 1965): 120–24.

Straumann, Heinrich. "Black and White in Faulkner's Fiction." *English Studies* 60 (Aug. 1979): 462–70.

Sundquist, Eric J. *Faulkner: The House Divided.* Baltimore: Johns Hopkins Univ. Press, 1983.

Sweeney, Patricia E. *William Faulkner's Women Characters: An Annotated Bibliography of Criticism, 1930–1983.* Santa Barbara, Calif.: ABC-Clio, 1985.

Taylor, Nancy Dew. "The River of Faulkner and Twain." *Mississippi Quarterly* 16 (Fall 1963): 191–99.

Taylor, Walter. "Faulkner: Nineteenth-Century Notions of Racial Mixture and the Twentieth-Century Imagination." *Southern Carolina Review* 10 (Nov. 1977): 57–68.

———. *Faulkner's Search for a South.* Urbana: Univ. of Illinois Press, 1983.

Theweleit, Klaus. *Male Fantasies, 1. Women, Floods, Bodies, History.* Trans. Stephen Conway. Foreword by Barbara Ehrenreich. Theory and History of Literature Series 22. Minneapolis: Univ. of Minnesota Press, 1987.

Turner, Darwin. "Faulkner and Slavery." In *The South and Faulkner's Yoknapatawpha: The Actual and the Apocryphal,* ed. Evans Harrington and Ann J. Abadie, pp. 62–75. Jackson: Univ. Press of Mississippi, 1977.

Twigg, Carol Ann. "The Social Role of Faulkner's Women: A Materialist Interpretation." Ph.D. dissertation, State Univ. of New York at Buffalo, 1978.

Vickery, Olga. *The Novels of William Faulkner.* 2d ed. Baton Rouge: Louisiana State Univ. Press, 1964.

Volpe, Edmund. *A Reader's Guide to William Faulkner.* New York: Farrar, Straus, & Giroux, 1964.

Wagner, Linda W. "Language and Act: Caddy Compson." *Southern Literary Journal* 14 (1982): 49–61.

Wadlington, Warwick. *Reading Faulknerian Tragedy.* Ithaca and London: Cornell Univ. Press, 1987.

Walker, Margaret. "Faulkner and Race." In *The Maker and the Myth: Faulkner and Yoknapatawpha,* ed. Evans Harrington and Ann J. Abadie, pp. 105–21. Jackson: Univ. Press of Mississippi, 1978.

Warren, Robert Penn, ed. *Faulkner: A Collection of Critical Essays.* Englewood Cliffs, N.J.: Prentice Hall, 1966.

Watson, James G. *William Faulkner: Letters and Fictions.* Austin: Univ. of Texas Press, 1987.

Weinstein, Arnold L. *Vision and Response in Modern Fiction.* Ithaca: Cornell Univ. Press, 1974.

Weinstein, Philip M. "Meditations on the Other: Faulkner's Rendering of Women." In *Faulkner and Women,* ed. Doreen Fowler and Ann J. Abadie, pp. 81–99. Jackson: Univ. Press of Mississippi, 1986.

Werner, Craig. "Tell Old Pharaoh: The Afro-American Response to Faulkner." *Southern Review* 19 (Autumn 1983): 711–35.

Williams, David. *Faulkner's Women: The Myth and the Muse.* Montreal: McGill-Queen's Univ. Press, 1977.

Williams, J. Gary. "Quentin finally sees Miss Rosa." *Criticism* 21 (1979): 331–46.

Wittenberg, Judith Bryant. "A Feminist *Sanctuary* for Temple Drake?" Paper presented at Modern Language Association Conference, New York, Dec. 1985.

———. "William Faulkner: A Feminist Consideration." In *American Novelists Revisited: Essays in Feminist Criticism,* ed. Fritz Fleschmann, pp. 325–39. Boston: G.K. Hall, 1982.

———. *William Faulkner: The Transfiguration of Biography.* Lincoln: Univ. of Nebraska Press, 1979.

Woodward, C. Vann. *The Burden of Southern History.* Baton Rouge: Louisiana State Univ. Press, 1960.

Zender, Karl F. "Money and Matter in *Pylon* and *The Wild Palms.*" *Faulkner Journal* 1 (Spring 1986): 17–29.

Index

The Feminine and Faulkner was designed by Dariel Mayer, composed by Lithocraft, Inc., printed and bound by Braun-Brumfield, Inc. The book is set in Compugraphic Garamond, with Janson used for display, and printed on 60-lb Glatfelter Natural Smooth, B-16.